Ann

With thanks

Hilary

GW00503171

μ
$\frac{1}{7}\frac{26}{12}$

Oct 2009

Priestley's England

MANCHESTER
1824
Manchester University Press

Priestley's England

J. B. Priestley and English culture

John Baxendale

Manchester University Press
Manchester and New York

distributed exclusively in the USA by Palgrave

Copyright © John Baxendale 2007

The right of John Baxendale to be identified as the author of this work has been asserted by him in accordance with the Copyright, Designs and Patents Act 1988.

Published by Manchester University Press
Oxford Road, Manchester M13 9NR, UK
and Room 400, 175 Fifth Avenue, New York, NY 10010, USA
www.manchesteruniversitypress.co.uk

Distributed exclusively in the USA by
Palgrave, 175 Fifth Avenue, New York,
NY 10010, USA

Distributed exclusively in Canada by
UBC Press, University of British Columbia, 2029 West Mall,
Vancouver, BC, Canada V6T 1Z2

British Library Cataloguing-in-Publication Data
A catalogue record for this book is available from the British Library

Library of Congress Cataloging-in-Publication Data applied for

ISBN 978 0 7190 7286 4   *hardback*

First published 2007

16 15 14 13 12 11 10 09 08 07   10 9 8 7 6 5 4 3 2 1

Typeset in Sabon with Gill Sans display
by Action Publishing Technology Ltd, Gloucester
Printed in Great Britain
by Biddles Ltd, King's Lynn

Contents

Acknowledgements   *page* vi

Introduction   1

1 'A serious writer with a message'   5

2 Bruddersford and beyond   35

3 Englands and Englishness   76

4 This new England   105

5 Priestley's war   140

6 'Now we must live up to ourselves': New Jerusalem and beyond   166

Bibliography   194
Index   209

Acknowledgements

Priestley once said that the task of the novelist is 'to write as well as he can the kind of novel he wants to write'. Assuming this applies to historians as well, it still cannot be achieved without the support of others. I am fortunate to work in a department which happily and successfully combines high-quality teaching and research, and I thank all my colleagues at Sheffield Hallam University for creating and maintaining this supportive and scholarly environment, often against the odds – as well as for their friendship, encouragement and intellectual stimulus. There and elsewhere, I owe particular thanks to John and Eva Braidwood, Peter Cain, Gerry Coubro, Roger Fagge, Chris Goldie, Mary Grover, Van Gore, Chris Hopkins, Lisa Hopkins, Chris Pawling, Tom Ryall and John Walton – none of whom, needless to say, is responsible for the no doubt numerous flaws in what I have written. I am also grateful for the support of the Humanities Research Centre at Sheffield Hallam University in the research and writing of this book.

Thanks are also due to the staff of the Heinemann Archive at Rushden, the Bodleian Library, the British Library, the National Newspaper Library at Colindale (that unique and invaluable resource) and Sheffield Hallam University Library. I would like also to make particular mention of Alan Day's comprehensive Priestley bibliography, without which serious research on Priestley's voluminous and widespread output would be difficult to contemplate.

All material from the works of J. B. Priestley is reproduced by permission of PDF (www.pdf.co.uk) on behalf of the Estate of J. B. Priestley, the proprietor of copyright in the works. I am most grateful to Tom Priestley for his help and encouragement, and for his positive engagement with Priestley scholars and enthusiasts in general.

This book incorporates in revised form sections of two articles: '"I had seen a lot of Englands": J. B. Priestley, Englishness and the people', from *History Workshop Journal* 51 (2001), pp. 87–111; and 'Re-narrating the Thirties: *English Journey* revisited', from *Working Papers on the Web 6*

(June 2003) (www.shu.ac.uk/wpw/thirties). Thanks to both journals for permission to make use of this material. In recent years I have given papers based on parts of this book to conferences and other events at Kingston, Presov (Slovakia), Miskolc (Hungary), London, York, Lancaster, Reading, Boston and Sheffield. I am most grateful to all the organisers and participants concerned.

Priestley, who both played and watched football, predicted that the English Revolution would probably be sparked off by Sheffield United having a penalty awarded against them. Happily, no such uprising proved necessary during the inspiring promotion season at Bramall Lane which buoyed up the final stages of writing this book, and for this much thanks to Neil Warnock and the lads.

Finally, last but not least, Sally has not only provided affectionate support and encouragement in good times and bad, but has read all of what follows without suffering any obvious ill-effects. For this, and because a Lancastrian writing about a Yorkshireman needs somebody on the inside, this book is dedicated to her.

Introduction

Although this is a book about a writer, it is neither biography nor literary criticism: it is probably best described as cultural history. It deals with a man who, while pre-eminently an imaginative writer, one of the best known and most widely read in twentieth-century Britain, was several other things as well, often simultaneously: journalist, broadcaster, social commentator, political activist and all-round public figure. The purpose of this book is to ask what this prolific body of work and activity meant, where it came from and how it both shaped and commentated on twentieth-century society, politics and culture, and in the process to gain a better understanding both of Priestley himself and of the time and the place in which he lived.

Priestley was born in 1894, and flourished as a writer from the 1920s, when he came to London from Bradford, through to the 1970s, when his last novels were produced. Despite this long career and considerable popularity, he is, in many ways, an underappreciated figure. This may seem an odd thing to say: after all, his work is still widely known, his plays regularly performed and his public role, especially in the Second World War, frequently acknowledged. A thriving and energetic J. B. Priestley Society testifies to the continuing interest in him. Historians recognise in him a social commentator with a gift for acute observation and a telling phrase, and regularly turn to *English Journey* and other works for illustrative material. But he is not given the serious attention accorded to the modernist writers of the 1920s, the 'Auden Group' of the 1930s, or the ever-present (and almost untouchable) George Orwell. Often when his phrases and observations are quoted, the analysis that underpinned them is overlooked – or, worse, reinvented to fit present-day preconceptions, so that in recent discussions of 'Englishness' he has been reimagined as some kind of conservative ruralist, when his actual views are far more interesting. Priestley deserves better, and so do we.

One reason for this is to do with his cultural status. Priestley was a serious writer, but a popular one. He wrote narrative fiction of a kind liked by many people; his books sold well, and he made a lot of money out of them. But rejecting the modernism which, received opinion has it, was at the cutting edge of literary progress in his time, he wrote in a style regarded as obsolete and 'middlebrow', and so in the narrative of literary history he does not count. It is not for the historian to query these judgements of literary value, but to understand their origins and context, which Chapter 1 seeks to do. But however valid they are, it does seem odd to virtually exclude such a widely read writer from literary history. His prose style and use of literary form, while distinctive and highly readable, were by no means innovative; but formal innovation is not the only thing that makes a writer important. A preoccupation with purely literary values can obscure our understanding of how the public sphere of debate in twentieth-century Britain operated. It can be argued that it was the 'middlebrow' best-sellers who were providing the most consistent and widely read commentary on, as Priestley put it, 'man in the society he has created', just as their Victorian forebears had done. This raises important issues, still current in our own time, about the relationship between commerce and the public sphere, entertainment and information, pleasure and politics.

Another aim of this book is to disentangle the various threads of Priestley's world-view, which can at times seem contradictory, often only because they defy conventional expectations. Priestley was no great theorist, but he was an acute and sensitive observer, and a more complex thinker than he has been given credit for, his ideas lucidly expressed and firmly rooted. Their roots lay in English radicalism, a popular tradition which is now all but forgotten, but which he imbibed along with ethical socialism in the Bradford of his youth. Priestley was a populist rather than a class warrior. For him the nation was the People, who in his radical historical narrative had been deceived and dispossessed by their rulers, but from whom any national renewal must spring. He was therefore suspicious of top-down political reform, trade unions or indeed any organised power-base. His social ideal came from Edwardian Bradford, conjured up in memory and imagination as a culturally classless community, whatever its material inequalities. Chapter 2 investigates the Bradford roots of Priestley's social and political world-view, and how he applied it to the devastated industrial England of the 1930s.

Priestley was a patriot, but of a very particular variety. He had no time for national traditions and ceremonies, recognising them as inventions designed to conceal the operation of power; and the Empire was for him the same bullying 'big England' that had dispossessed the ordinary English people, now trying the same trick abroad. While he loved the English countryside, he did not regard it as the essence of Englishness: the English were now townsfolk, and should try to be properly urban instead of cherishing rural fantasies. If there was an essential Englishness it dwelt in the spirit of the people, in their romantic imagination, their mistrust of reason and reliance on instinct and intuition, their hazy boundary between the conscious and the unconscious minds. Chapter 3 explores these versions of England in the context of interwar discourses of the nation and national character, and argues that Priestley's view of both was more complex and sophisticated than any of the conservative commentators with whom careless observers have sought to align him.

It has been strongly argued in recent years that there is a marked dissonance between modernity and prevailing ideas of English identity. In chapter 4, we explore Priestley's attitude towards the modern world – the 'new England' of *English Journey* – and find him suprisingly positive, fascinated by new industrial processes and gigantic collective artefacts like ocean liners and dams. He is less enthusiastic about the culture of modernity, and here we return to the question of the People. The old popular culture came from below, he argued, and expressed the innate energy and gusto (a favourite word) of the common people. The new, globalising mass culture seemed to come from above, representing a new overweening power exercised over its increasingly passive audiences. But the 'new England' was at least a more democratic England – more like the 'Walt Whitmanish' side of America he so admired, in his complex love–hate relationship with the only other country apart from England in which he showed any real interest.

Chapter 5 moves us on chronologically into what most would consider Priestley's finest hour: the Second World War. Writing and broadcasting with apparently boundless energy to Britain and the world, in a discourse of the nation which both contradicted and complemented Churchill's, he strained every rhetorical sinew to call into being that radicalised People, energised by a common purpose, which alone could transform England after the war was won. In the extraordinary BBC *Postscripts* he presented a sustained hymn of praise to ordinary Englishness, but it was his own ordinariness – his vernacular language and Yorkshire tones – which carried much of the message. But the idealistic spirit of 1940 was difficult to sustain, and, though he energetically supported Labour in the 1945 election, Priestley ended the war with misgivings about the future.

It would be easy, but misleading, to portray Priestley after the war as a disillusioned figure. He regretted, and tried to avert, the onset of the Cold War and the loss of wartime common purpose, and became one of the founders of the Campaign for Nuclear Disarmament, which he saw as an opportunity for national moral renewal, as well as a means of saving the planet. He had profound doubts about the top-down nature of Labour's reforms, and began to put his trust more and more in the 'gentle anarchists', unconventional individuals of flair and imagination, renewing his attack on 'Topside', the British Establishment. Visiting America again, he coined the notion of 'Admass' to describe the culture and power structure of global consumerism and mass culture. But, as we see in Chapter 6, alongside his negative readings of postwar modernity we find an unquenchable, though often well-hidden, optimism: a conviction that, eventually, things can be put right: though, as he said, 'we must wait'. Through the 1950s he kept alive a strong, though idiosyncratic flame of dissent which both conflicted and made common cause with other dissenting movements from the 'angry young men' to the hippies. Later in life, he came to feel that both the underlying problem and its solution were spiritual: a dissociation of inner and outer worlds, which could be healed only at the symbolic, unconscious level from which orthodox religion had withdrawn. Thus, towards the end of his life, his long-standing interest in Jungian psychology converged with his social and political critique of the modern world.

This book is called *Priestley's England* because no one did more to think through England's twentieth-century experience, or strove harder to shape its national imaginary. By 'England', he really did mean England, showing little if any interest in Scotland or Wales, although for the duration of the war he temporarily adjusted his focus to 'Britain'. Priestley's vision of what England was and could be arose not out of any theoretically informed academic analysis but out of a deep and instinctive, but very particular, understanding of English life and culture – one fundamentally different from, say, Churchill's equally deep and instinctive version. Its origins lie in the radical culture which grew up in industrial England in the nineteenth century, and whose roots lie even further back in time: a 'Deep England' at least as deep as the gentlemanly rural fantasies of conventional 'Englishness', but one that has almost disappeared from the cultural map. From Priestley we learn that there are many Englands, not just one, but that it is only out of the English people – that is, as he said in wartime, everybody who is willing to consider themselves the people – that England's best self can be born.

1

'A serious writer with a message'

> Others are proud of reading J. B. Priestley and writers such as him, because they are 'serious writers with a message'. Others have learned that Mr Priestley is a 'middlebrow', and only mention him in terms of deprecation. They tend to read bitterly ironic or anguished literature – Waugh, Huxley, Kafka and Greene.[1]

Thus Richard Hoggart in *The Uses of Literacy* (1957) describes the predicament of a serious working-class reader, seeking the pathway to 'the cultured life', and finding it set about with unexpected dangers. It also encapsulates Priestley's problematic reputation within twentieth-century literary culture. We can easily see why Hoggart's reader takes Priestley for a 'serious' writer. He wrote properly crafted novels, not sensational adventure stories like Edgar Wallace or Mickey Spillane. Though his novels were not afraid to entertain, they were set in the real contemporary world, and they made you think about important issues. His books were reviewed in serious newspapers and magazines, where Priestley himself also wrote. He served his time alongside other famous writers in organisations such as PEN, and in due course was honoured by the state for his literary achievements. When he wrote in the newspaper, or appeared on the radio or the public platform, his authority to be there rested on his reputation as a writer worthy of respect: a serious writer, with a message, to whom serious people should listen.

Such, however, is not the received narrative of twentieth-century literary history – a narrative which Hoggart's working-class reader in due course 'learns'. According to this story, Priestley was out of date before he started, writing novels in an obsolete style which appealed only to readers who knew no better and who craved only the simple emotional comforts that an old-fashioned tale would provide. As there were rather a lot of these readers Priestley made plenty of money, but that should not blind us to the fact that the modernism which he and his readers spurned – Virginia Woolf, D. H. Lawrence, James Joyce, T. S. Eliot et al. – was the only contemporary literature worth considering. Mr Priestley, on the other hand, was a 'middlebrow'.

The purpose of this chapter is to put forward a different view of things. Situating Priestley in the literary culture of his time, it will argue that far from being an old-fashioned writer he was in many ways a very modern one, and it was in his fame and popularity, and his omnipresence in the developing mass media, that much of this modernity lay. It will also investigate the idea of the 'middlebrow', its origins in the cultural warfare of the 1920s and 1930s, and its implications for literary and cultural values. It will argue that Priestley, like other so-called 'middlebrows', was pursuing one of the writer's time-honoured duties: to provide a critical commentary on contemporary society for a wide audience. This multifaceted democratic debate is the underlying theme of Priestley's long writing career, and therefore of this book.

The changing literary field

Hoggart's autodidact had stumbled over what Pierre Bourdieu described as a contest for cultural legitimacy – the 'power to consecrate', to determine what counts as 'proper' culture. According to Bourdieu, such contests are structured around the opposition within literary culture between two conflicting principles: on the one hand restricted production, 'art for art's sake'; and on the other large-scale production: the desire not just for commercial success but to communicate with the largest number of people. Bourdieu also argued that there is continual conflict between generations, orthodoxy versus heresy, establishment versus newcomers.[2] Both these levels of conflict were hard at work in the literary world which Priestley entered in the 1920s. It was a world shaped by two concurrent, and related, developments in cultural history: the expansion of the cultural marketplace, and the rise of literary modernism.

Print culture is always, irretrievably, embroiled in commerce, and there have always been writers who find this troubling. In 1761 Oliver Goldsmith was railing against 'that fatal revolution whereby writing is converted to a mechanic trade'.[3] The new literary forms suited to mass reproduction and commercial sale – newspapers, magazines, novels – that came into their own in the eighteenth and nineteenth centuries, dependent on new technologies, economic expansion and a growing reading public, heralded the Victorian golden age of print. In the late nineteenth and early twentieth centuries commercialised culture entered a new phase. The grip of the circulating libraries on novel production was broken; book sales and titles published more than doubled between 1850 and 1901, and again by 1913; popular halfpenny newspapers, the *Daily Mail* and the *Daily Express*, arrived on the scene, along with new popular magazines such as the *Strand* (1891) and *John Bull* (1906), and cheap periodicals such as *Tit-Bits* (1881) and *Answers* (1888), bringing with them new popular styles of journalism, and often carrying syndicated fiction supplied by agencies – all this happening, it should be noted, before the arrival of broadcasting, and before cinema and recorded music had made their biggest impact.[4]

Out of this expansion came the new world of letters described (and deplored) by George Gissing in *New Grub Street* (1891). Publishers and writers experienced, says Peter Keating, 'a new kind of individual freedom that would release authors from the compromises and concessions that had inhibited the mid-Victorians', while a whole new set of economic relationships emerged, including payment by royalties dependent on sales rather than a lump sum, literary agents, the Society of Authors and new publishers geared up to the expanded fiction market – such as Heinemann, who were to publish almost all of Priestley's books. Publicity and celebrity became central to the promotion of new books, supported by secondary discourses such as reviews and magazine interviews. The world of the best-seller was born.

Writers' reactions to this process varied. While some, like Edmund Gosse, feared for cultural standards, and saw the prospect of 'a revolt of the mob against our literary masters', others, like Willkie Collins, Arnold Bennett and H. G. Wells, were exhilarated by the possibilities of a wider readership – not just for making money but for influencing the thinking of the new democracy.[5] But even Priestley, who certainly liked to do both of these things, would later complain of the 'bargain basement atmosphere about publishing ... snap successes, the Book of the Month, the Smash Hit of the Season'.[6] By 1927 J. M. Keynes was describing publishing as 'a *gambling* business kept alive by occasional windfalls' – a pattern also followed by the film and music industries. 'Literature now is a trade', Jasper Milvain in *New Grub Street* bluntly declares, echoing Goldsmith's lament of 130 years earlier.[7] The fact of the matter is, though, that since writers have to eat, literature has always been a trade, one way or another. What was changing was the way in which that trade was conducted.

Portrait of the artist as a young Bruddersfordian

Meanwhile, in Bradford, young Jack Priestley, a voracious reader, and as such a beneficiary of the expansion of literary production, but dimly aware if at all of the alarms and excursions of the London literary scene, was deciding to become a writer. In his memoir *Margin Released* (1962), he would construct a vivid and affectionate account of this crucial phase of his life, from leaving school at sixteen in 1910 to work in a Bradford wool-merchant's office to joining the army in 1914. The older Priestley evokes for us a young Priestley firmly situated 'outside the fashionable literary movement' by virtue of geography, class and a secure upbringing, but determined to be something – an actor, a musician, a writer.[8] A bright pupil, but bored with school (and perhaps reacting against his school-master father), he saw no connection between 'certificates and degrees' and a future artistic career; none of the authors he admired had been to Oxford or Cambridge, and it certainly never occurred to him that he would need higher education to become a more accomplished writer, let alone reader.[9] Edwardian Bradford, as Priestley was to frequently remind his readers, provided not only the material for writerly observation and speculation but a thriving cultural life: musical, theatrical, artistic and literary.[10] Most crucially, it was independent of London: London, says Priestley, never crossed his mind in those days except as a collection of editors' addresses for the reception of manuscripts and the dispatch of rejection slips. His idea of a literary career was to sell enough pieces to those editors to raise a pound a week, on which he could easily keep himself in a cottage on the edge of the moors, a tuppenny tram-ride and a sharp walk from the centre of town: 'writing for money', if you like, but in a very modest way.[11]

To this end, after work in the wool-office, the teenaged Priestley lived the literary life in the attic of his parents' terraced house, scribbling profusely in pencil in his notebooks in front of the gas fire, turning out prose sketches, short stories and blank-verse narratives about Sir Lancelot and Atlantis, one of which, a short piece of doom-laden free verse entitled 'The song of a mood', he sent to the Irish poet George Russell, receiving a detailed and encouraging response.[12] At sixteen, having already accu-mulated many rejections, he finally sold a short piece – a mock interview entitled 'Secrets of the rag-time king' – to the weekly magazine *London Opinion*, for a guinea.[13] Shortly afterwards he began a weekly (unpaid) column for the local socialist paper, the *Bradford Pioneer*, in which he wrote, as he later put it, 'on everything – books, plays, music, this world and the next – with all the gusto and dogmatism of a precocious boy of 17 or 18'.[14]

Bradford was no Bloomsbury, but it provided ample sustenance for the budding author. Although there were few writers in the town worthy of the name, there were plenty of 'people who read a great deal'. There were three local daily papers, including the estimable *Yorkshire Observer*, for which Priestley was to write a weekly column in 1919–21, and so there were sophisticated young journalists around (including, though Priestley never mentions him, the young Howard Spring), who 'could take the city to pieces over a coffee and a roll-and-butter at Lyons's'; but that cynical newspaper world was not for him.[15] There were even one or two proper, published writers. Cutliffe Hyne, creator of the imperial hero Captain Kettle, lived in Bradford – but, despite some very early attempts at public-school stories ('"Hurrah! Grey Towers at last!" cried Dick, the new boy, as the train steamed into the station'), juvenile genre fiction was not what young Jack had in mind either.[16] More to his taste as a local role-model was the poet James A. Mackereth, who had thrown up his bank clerk's job on inheriting some money, and published a series of poetry books in the 1910s and 1920s, including some truly dreadful Great War patriotic verse. Mackereth had achieved the dreamed-of cottage on the moors, and there on summer evenings he would read young Jack his latest work in the 'deep chanting tone' which even in later life Priestley thought most appropriate for lyric poetry. Mackereth was his first literary friend – a man with published works, press cuttings, letters to and from editors and reviewers – and it is not difficult to see his influence on Priestley's juvenile poetry (was Mackereth working on his dramatic poem *The Death of Cleopatra* while Priestley was trying to write his *Evensong to Atlantis*?) But most of all, he looked the part, '*more like a poet* than any other I have seen and heard': rough tweeds, thick boots, a high-crowned soft hat, 'shaggy and leonine, with formidable brows above deep-set eyes and hollow-cheeks', reading his work 'in the grand manner, with eyes flashing away and one hand beating the measure'.[17]

Young Priestley too began to look the part: floppy bow-tie, light chrome green sports jacket, light grey pegtop trousers, 'as if I were about the join the chorus in the second act of *La Bohème*'. This innocent bohemian dandyism drew the disapproval of straitlaced colleagues in the wool-office and ribald comments from millgirls on the way home, and alarmed and disgusted his father, who despite his radical views and generally tolerant stance towards his son had a position in the community and was anxious not to startle the neighbours.[18] And Jack began to lead a café life, in 'a brief imitation of a Central European character', on the upper floor of Lyons in Market Street, in the company of art students and fellow would-be literati, who lingered for hours over coffee, chatted up the waitresses and later 'walked the moors and dropped in here and there for a manly half-pint of bitter, and argued about life and literature until the moon fell out of the sky'.[19] He was thinking himself into a role, adopting the bohemian visual style and the idea of a way of life which announced him as a writer. But there was more to it than that: he wrote. His café friends all 'wrote bits of things', but he was the only one who became an author. 'The difference between us', he wrote later, 'was not in ability, but in the fact that while at heart they did not really much care about authorship but merely toyed with the fascinating idea of it, I cared like blazes.'[20]

Bohemian style amongst writers, artists and musicians in London was usually associated with the avant-garde.[21] In Bradford it was avant-garde enough to be a writer at all. Young Priestley's demeanour may have shocked the neighbours, but he felt no compelling urge to forge new literary forms for the new age: he was no James Joyce, no Virginia Woolf, no D. H. Lawrence – all a decade his senior. While Joyce at seventeen was announcing to his parents that they had a genius on their hands, Priestley's loving stepmother was using the same epithet ('gee-nius') in gentle and tolerant mockery of the young bohemian scribbler.[22] He eagerly read Shaw, Wells and Bennett – larger than life Edwardian figures, whom he could also read about in the gossip columns of the popular press, a foretaste of the literary celebrity that awaited him.[23] In magazines and newspapers he enjoyed 'the intellectual high spirits of Chesterton, the superb descriptive prose of H. M. Tomlinson', which no doubt inspired his sketches of 'Moorton' life (all unpublished), and he surrounded himself with Nelson's sevenpenny paperback classics.[24] The poetry represented a higher ideal, but the essays and sketches he wrote were a well-tried formula, for which there was a healthy market in the magazines and newspapers. Not driven by a sense of his own genius, or the search for fame and fortune, or even the avoidance of boredom, he wanted only to be a writer, and not have to do anything else to make a living.[25]

His early twenties, when literary interests might have been expected to forge ahead – or die out completely – were consumed by the war: demobbed, across the 'smoking canyon' of the Great War, he was, by his own account, a different man.[26] Back in Bradford, in April 1919 a formidable journalistic career began in earnest with an essay in the *Yorkshire Observer* – then another, then eventually a weekly series which ran up to January 1921, ninety pieces in all which ranged from walking in the Dales to book reviews, to ruminations on such topics as 'The Yorkshirewomen' and 'Bad pianists', and earned him a guinea a time.[27] All that scribbling in front of the gas fire had paid off: he could make his pound a week, and from this point onwards hardly a week was to pass for half a century without something of Priestley's appearing in a newspaper or a magazine. In the meantime, he had gone to Cambridge, on an ex-serviceman's scholarship, where his writing continued, and 'a little book of undergraduate odds and ends' entitled *Brief Diversions* attracted the attention of the London reviewers: but as yet 'no fame ... no sudden big sales, no hasty reprintings'.[28] Then, in September 1922, now married and with a baby on the way, he left Cambridge, turned down offers of teaching posts and the advice of friends and family, and came to London to seek his fortune as a writer.

Literary London in the 1920s was a small but intense world of overlapping and sometimes contending circles based partly on aesthetic affinities, partly on personal acquaintance, partly on self-interest, and sustained by magazines, newspapers and publishing houses, and an invisible hinterland of bookshops, libraries and readers. This social and economic sub-system shaped the development of early twentieth-century literature, fostered its talents and hosted its bitter conflicts. It was, Priestley later argued, already on the road to disintegration in the early 1920s, but it offered him employment and a social life: the two being, of course, closely related.[29] The life of a freelance writer in the early 1920s was hard, but it was viable: arguably, more so than at any time since. The system provided work for writers, provided they could negotiate its social and cultural networks. Most newspapers carried substantial book review pages at least once a week; the public still bought literary magazines such as *John O'London's* and the *London Mercury* which Priestley had read in Bradford; there was still a readership for essays in the Victorian and Edwardian style, which sold respectable numbers when collected into books; and there were the ancillary tasks of literary production to be carried out such as editorial work and reading manuscripts for publishers. It was a world of people who knew each other, and the way into it, and into the work it offered, was through personal contact. The memoirs of writers who began their careers in the 1920s and 1930s all describe the process of making these precious contacts, and the same names crop up, and the same locations: the newspaper and magazine offices, the literary pubs, the dinners and parties.[30] Priestley was a good networker. He had already met a key figure in this world, J. C. Squire, editor and proprietor of the *London Mercury*, who had offered encouragement to the young Cambridge writer, and now introduced him to his circle of literary editors and publishers: men like Robert Lynd of the *Daily News*, Gerald Barry of the *Saturday Review* and later the *Week-End Review*, who gave him work. As the social circles expanded, at the literary parties whose disappearance he later regretted the young writer was able to meet the Edwardian giants he had read as a boy: 'fabulous beings' like Wells, Shaw, Arnold Bennett, J. M. Barrie, Walter de la Mare, and in particular Hugh Walpole, who became a close friend. At lunchtimes in the pub beneath the *London Mercury* offices off Fleet Street he heard 'the liveliest talk I ever remember hearing', from luminaries like Squire, Lynd, Belloc, J. B. Morton, Gerald Gould and others now long forgotten.[31]

So from his new family home in Walham Green, Priestley would catch the number 11 bus to Fleet Street in search of books to review: and with some success. In his first four months in London he published seventeen essays and twelve reviews, in the *Spectator*, *The Challenge* (a Church magazine edited by his friend Edward Davison) and in Squire's *London Mercury*. He soon landed a job, at £6 a week, reading manuscripts for the publisher John Lane, founder and proprietor of the Bodley Head – in which capacity he recommended the first books of, among others, Graham Greene and C. S. Forester. Characteristically attributing his success to hard work rather than innate talent, Priestley describes how he brought to the job of reviewing 'a solid North-country conscientiousness', delivering on time, to the specified length, not using reviews to settle literary scores, and not leaving his review copies behind at parties where too much wine (and too many writers) had been drunk.[32] After all that scribbling in the Bradford attic, he had become a clever, fluent and reliable writer, which editors liked. By January 1923 Lynd had taken him on as a regular reviewer for the *Daily News*, and he was also writing a weekly essay for the *Saturday Review* at six guineas a time, and occasional 'very well paid' pieces for the *Spectator*. In 1928 he moved to the *Evening News*, to write their weekly book review column at £20 a time: an influential platform, as well as a comfortable regular income.[33] During the same period, in addition to regular collections of essays, he wrote five substantial works of literary criticism, and two and a half novels.[34] This world suited a writer like Priestley, who, despite his juvenile attempts at epic poetry, regarded himself as a journeyman rather than an aesthete. 'I belong to the eighteenth century,' he later declared, 'when professional authors were expected to write anything from sermons to farces. Neither Fleet Street nor Bond Street can claim me: I come from Grub Street.'[35] By 1929, aged thirty-five, without being in any way a cultural celebrity, he was a firmly established, well-known and reasonably well-rewarded author. These were not easy years: Priestley was reviewing four or five books every week, writing books of his own (five of them published in 1927) and turning out the light-hearted weekly essays, while 'half out of my mind with overwork and worry' during the long illness and death of his wife.[36] But he had made a success in the Grub Street of the 1920s.

Modern(ist) times

But literary London was changing. As Priestley later admitted, his essays in the *Saturday Review*, though they earned him a worthwhile income – the collection *Open House* (1927) sold a healthy enough six thousand copies – were 'already almost an anachronism'.[37] George Orwell, who came in at the tail-end of it, describes a fogeyish world of 'cheeriness and manliness, beer and cricket, briar pipes and monogamy ... busy pretending that the age-before-last had not come to an end', a picture confirmed in Priestley's various memoirs.[38] But while the *London Mercury*, in its bright orange covers, retained its influence with the general reading public, to whom it sold between ten and twenty thousand copies, to some the future belonged to the *Criterion*, established by T. S. Eliot in 1922, which sold only eight hundred, but placed its editor 'at the centre of first the London and then the continental literary scene'.[39]

Most people in the 1920s would have called the *Criterion*'s kind of writing 'highbrow', and the epitome of highbrow was 'Bloomsbury'. 'Bloomsbury' meant, in literary terms, the novels of Woolf and E. M. Forster and the publications of Virginia and Leonard Woolf's Hogarth Press; in art, the painting and criticism of Roger Fry and Clive Bell; culturally and politically a new critical frankness, a rejection of Victorian values, morality and behaviour patterns, expressed in the philosophy of

G. E. Moore and the essays of Lytton Strachey, and a sincere though rather paternalistic social conscience.[40] Personal connections were important here as in Grub Street, but they were of a different kind. Socially, 'Bloomsbury' consisted of an interlocking and often intermarried set of friends and families, almost all educated at public school and Oxbridge, and with strong personal and institutional connections to the 'gentlemanly capitalist' establishment, in particular its more elevated public service branch. It was these connections which brought them together to develop their roughly homologous world-view.[41] Money also counted. A 'highbrow' novel, Queenie Leavis observed, would do well to sell three thousand copies overall, and the eight hundred readers of the *Criterion* would hardly keep anyone's body and soul together.[42] Those able to support themselves in other ways – whether through private income or T. S. Eliot's bank job, were clearly better able to survive on small sales. By contrast, Priestley and his circle – including the older members – were almost all of humbler, lower middle- or working-class origins, lacking private means and, in most cases, an elite education. It is not surprising that they viewed writing as a means of earning a living. The teenaged Priestley, while regarding poetry as the 'real thing' nevertheless planned to support himself by writing essays: he was not proposing to starve in a garret for his art. With a Cambridge degree but no money, he cashed in his cultural capital in Grub Street, where he could make enough to live on.

But it was not just a matter of money: the two groups were differently situated historically as well as materially. Moderns they may have been, but the Bloomsburyites came from the heart of the Victorian governing class which they so acerbically spurned, and in the 1920s, partly because of their efforts, the future of this class seemed in doubt. Priestley, the son of a Bradford schoolteacher, came, like Wells and Bennett, from the rising class of the late Victorian and Edwardian era – the lower middle class of small business, minor professionals, state functionaries, clerks and the like, a class expanding in numbers, whose next generation became the suburbanites and, as Humble argues, the 'middlebrow' readers of the 1930s.[43] Arguably, this social group had a better grasp of social reality: at any rate, they were unlikely to measure historical change, as Virginia Woolf did, by reference to 'the character of one's cook'.[44]

'Social reality' lay at the heart of the aesthetic conflict between these two groups. The conventions of the Victorian novel were characteristically realist. Realism can mean a number of things. At the most obvious level, it means novels which make social and physical reality their subject matter, dealing with real events and offering a recognisable account of the social world. Such novels, though they do not neglect the inner lives of their characters, tend to focus on externals, on actions and settings, on social, political and moral issues, on social relationships. This focus was linked to a series of artistic techniques and conventions: a broadly linear

narrative structure with the plot resolved at the end; characters seen as
stable and objectively knowable; a reliable, omniscient narrator, and
language accessible to the general public. This was the kind of novel
Priestley wrote, and would continue to write. Many or most of these
features modernism rejected.

There were a number of reasons for this rejection. One was the belief
that modernist techniques set art and the artist free to be 'more intuitive,
more poetic' and grasp a deeper reality. No longer tied to representing the
'real', 'art turns from realism and humanistic representation towards
style, technique and spatial form in pursuit of a deeper penetration of
life'.[45] A second claim of modernists was that the conditions that gave rise
to the realist novel in the previous century no longer prevailed. Modern
thought had overturned conventional notions of causation and objective
truth, and questioned the unitary nature of individual character; modern
civilisation had brought chaos and the destruction of a common sense of
reality. Modernism was an expressive response to this chaos. Famously,
Virginia Woolf declared, in her piece 'Mr Bennett and Mrs Brown'
(1924), that 'on or about December 1910' human nature had changed,
and now required a different kind of writing. Novelists should no longer
focus on the material externals of life, as 'Georgian' writers like H. G.
Wells, Arnold Bennett or John Galsworthy had done, or 'preach
doctrines, sing songs, or celebrate the glories of the British Empire ...
otherwise, they would not be novelists; but poets, historians or pamphlet-
eers'. Rather, their focus should be on character, and on the inner lives of
characters.[46] It was necessary to recognise, as Woolf had argued in
Modern Fiction (1919), that 'Life is not a series of gig lamps symmetri-
cally arranged; life is a luminous halo, a semi-transparent envelope
surrounding us from the beginning of consciousness to the end', and
consequently 'much of the enormous labour of proving the solidity, the
likeness to life, of the story' – in other words, its realism - 'is not merely
labour thrown away but labour misplaced'.

Clearly, this is a critique not just of literary method but also of the
purpose of literature as those Victorian and Edwardian novelists – and
Priestley – saw it, and the relationship it assumed between art and life.
Woolf criticised them for being mainly interested in externals such as
social conditions, class, the furnishing of rooms, the outward facts of the
characters' lives, leaving the reader with 'a feeling of incompleteness and
dissatisfaction' which could be dealt with only by doing something:
joining a society, or writing a cheque. But for some writers this was
exactly what novels were for. In an acrimonious dispute with Henry
James in 1914–15 H. G. Wells asserted the exactly opposite view from
Woolf's: that literature was not an end in itself but a means to an end, and
declared that he himself would rather be called a journalist than an
artist.[47] Wells recognised just as much as Woolf did that the world had

changed, and considered his writing a response to those changes. The issue was not whether to acknowledge modernity but how best to do so.

'Battle of the brows'

'When I was growing up,' said Priestley, looking back more than half a century to the 1910s, 'there wasn't any consciousness of brows. The major writers weren't writing for an elite but for everybody.'[48] But in or around the early 1920s, for the first time 'the reading public was fatally divided into high, low and middle brows, [and] writing began to be assessed not in terms of its own qualities ... but in terms of its possible audience, that writers whose books began to sell (and I have yet to meet one who did not want his books to sell) were denounced at once as charlatans'.[49] The *Oxford English Dictionary* broadly supports his chronology. 'Highbrow' and 'lowbrow' were current in the Edwardian years, but 'middlebrow' is not found before the mid-1920s: the *OED*'s first example is from *Punch* in 1925, and refers, interestingly enough, to the BBC. Thereafter, the tripartite language of 'high/middle/low' rapidly became common currency, and within a short time the 'battle of the brows' was attracting public and media attention.

Recent scholars, influenced by feminism, the questioning of the canon and the 'cultural turn', have begun to rescue 'middlebrow' writing from what E. P. Thompson called the 'immense condescension of posterity', exploring its role in the development of gender, class and national identities, and in the lives of its readers.[50] This excellent and necessary work has taught us a great deal about popular reading and 'mainstream' culture in the interwar period. However, what it has not produced is a clear definition of what the 'middlebrow' actually is. Rosa Maria Bracco is sure that it is a 'well-delimited class of fiction', and Nicola Humble argues that it has 'a generic identity of its own', but Alison Light's case studies range from Ivy Compton-Burnett to Agatha Christie, and Humble admits that it embraces a wide range of genres, including romance, country-house saga, detective stories, children's fiction and comedy. Ultimately, as the term implies – as well as the title of Bracco's study, *Betwixt and Between* – 'middlebrow' usually ends up being defined in terms of what it is not: it is neither popular genre fiction nor 'highbrow' modernism; it embraces everything that falls between the 'original and artistic aims of great works of literature', and the 'standardized techniques of writing' of pulp fiction.[51]

The problem is not just that these are very broad categories but that they leave unexamined the ideological baggage which the term carries, and the way it works within the cultural field. In Bourdieu's view 'art and cultural consumption are predisposed, consciously and deliberately or not, to fulfil a social function of legitimating social differences', as patterns of taste become consecrated as cultural distinctions. 'Taste classifies, and it classifies the classifier.'[52] The ability to appropriate particular forms of culture depends on, and signals, the individual's cultural competence, 'cultural capital' which may be acquired, for example, by family background, or through education, and those like Hoggart's autodidact who lack cultural capital run the risk of being humiliated. 'Tastes are perhaps first and foremost distastes', and it is supremely important not to like the wrong thing.[53] The key to an object's cultural status is the social position of those who admire it: and vice versa: the petty-bourgeois can 'make "middle-brow" whatever it touches', for 'legitimate culture is not made for him (and is often made against him)'; while 'the legitimate gaze "saves" whatever it lights upon', and may rescue things hitherto regarded as middlebrow 'by one of those tastemaker's coups which are capable of rehabilitating the most discredited object'.[54]

For its first users, 'middlebrow' was not a neutral descriptive category but highly tendentious, part of a hierarchical model of culture and a narrative of cultural decline, which offered a defence against the threat to cultural authority presented by commercialisation and democratisation. As the postwar modernist critic Clement Greenberg put it, 'the demands of a new and open cultural market, middlebrow demands' forced artists to withdraw into the ivory tower of modernism, with its less accessible artistic forms. 'Without these threats, which came mostly from a new middle-class public, there would have been no such thing as Modernism.'[55] The narrative of decline was also one of fragmentation. Q. D. Leavis imagined a time, less than two centuries ago, when 'any one who could read would be equally likely to read any novel, or every novel, published' – while in the present the common reader was 'shut off from the best works of his contemporaries'. Leavis blamed this supposed decline on the conditions of modern urban industrial life, which obliged people to use middlebrow literature as 'a means of easing a desolating sense of isolation and compensat[ing] for the poverty of their emotional lives'. [56] This literature tends to use forms, such as realism, which look legitimate, and indeed used to be so, but have now become outworn conventions. Hence, the OED defines the middlebrow as 'of limited intellectual or cultural value; demanding or involving only a moderate degree of intellectual application, typically as a result of not deviating from convention'.[57] This resemblance to the real thing – in Leavis's terms, the faux bon – makes the middlebrow particularly treacherous for unwary readers, like Hoggart's autodidact. 'Their style is easily recognised by the uncritical as "literature" ... their readers are left with the agreeable sensation of having improved themselves without incurring fatigue.'[58]

But Priestley too had a narrative of cultural decline. In his story,

Greenberg's strategic withdrawal into the ivory tower is read as a *trahison des clercs*, a case of cultural betrayal. The nineteenth-century narrative of social progress had promised a steadily more inclusive political and cultural community, an ideal which, according to Priestley, had still seemed attainable in Edwardian times. But the avant-garde of the 1920s and 1930s had deliberately reneged on this promise, for purely selfish reasons. '[T]hey wanted literature to be difficult. They grew up in revolt against the mass communication antics of their age. They did not want to share anything with the crowd.'[59] 'The development of mass communications and mass standards which had to be kept at bay encouraged a haughty aloofness, an inner ring attitude, a sensitivity-on-a-private-income view of life and letters.' Lost was the 'unselfconscious breadth of appeal' of pre-1914 writers, along with 'the idea that serious authors should concern themselves with man in society'. Consequently, 'the general reader ... having been warned off, began to feel that contemporary literature was not for him'.[60] A leading part in the betrayal was played by the new literary critics, who rejected the task of helping general readers and instead set out to exclude them:

> intolerant in manner, arrogant in tone ... theological and absolutist: severe high priests moved in. Only a small amount of writing, written by and for an elite, was Literature, all else was rubbish. Few would be saved. It coldly rejected the idea, which my Twenties friends held and I still hold, that criticism should address itself to intelligent men and women of the world, asking for many different kinds of pleasure from many different kinds of books and authors. These new critics were like members of grim little secret society, making out lists of the few who would be allowed to survive, the many who must be assassinated. [61]

The villain of the piece here, of course, is F. R. Leavis – no friend to Bloomsbury, it must be said – who in *The Great Tradition* (1948) opined that 'life isn't long enough to permit of one's giving much time to Fielding or any to Mr Priestley'.[62] But if Fielding is not worth much of our time, why, responded Priestley, was Dr Leavis worth any of it?[63] And in his comic novel *Festival at Farbridge* (1951) he took his revenge. Here we meet the Cambridge critic Leonard Mortory, author of major critical works entitled *Disavowals*, *Rejections*, *Exclusions*, and *Refusals*, who 'hardly likes anything', and takes the view that 'life is too short for any intelligent reader to waste his time reading most so-called great novelists ... Fielding, Sterne, Dickens, Thackeray'.[64] For Priestley, there had been a deliberate narrowing of the field of legitimate culture to exclude not simply the 'popular' but the taste of much of the reading public, including, needless to say, Priestley himself. 'As their influence grew, I was out-of-date before I even began.'[65]

In a *Saturday Review* essay in 1926 – more light-hearted in mood, perhaps because the 'high priests' had not yet made their appearance –

Priestley appealed against the tendency to cultural fragmentation, mocking 'highbrows' and 'lowbrows' alike.[66] 'Some people may want to cry out against this "brow" business altogether ... but protest now is useless', so the only thing to do was to claim the best label for oneself. 'I and my friends', he announced, were neither highbrows nor lowbrows, but 'Broadbrows'. Highbrows and Lowbrows, 'moving in herds to decry this and praise that', are just different breeds of sheep: 'Just as Low, you might say, is the fat sheep with the cigar from the City or Surbiton, so High is the thin sheep with the spectacles and the squeak from Oxford or Bloomsbury.'[67] Highbrows love foreigners, Lowbrows loathe them; if 'Low will have nothing but happy endings in his fiction ... High will have nothing but unhappy ones'. Lowbrows may be manipulated by mass culture, but Highbrows are just as much slaves to the latest artistic fashion – '[a] few years ago they sneered your head off if you mentioned the films, but now they visit the pictures in a solemn body and you cannot see the feet of Mr Chaplin for their prostrate forms'. Far better to be one of the Broadbrows, who carry with them their own set of values and snap their fingers at fashion: 'who only ask that a thing should have character and art, should be enthralling, and do not give a fig whether it is popular or unpopular, born in Blackburn or Baku'.[68] In a splendid peroration he called on his readers to bring their values, critical faculties and capacity for enjoyment to bear on every cultural form under the sun:

> Russian dramas, variety shows, football matches, epic poems, grand opera, race meetings, old churches, new town halls, musical comedies, picture galleries, boxing booths, portfolios of etchings, bar parlours, film shows, symphony concerts, billiard matches, dance halls, detective stories, tragedies in blank verse, farces, and even studio teas and literary parties ... [69]

Beneath the wit and ebullience of the essay, and a characteristically robust appeal to popular common sense, Priestley is making a serious plea for the healing of a fragmented culture – and this, as we shall see, was to be a running theme throughout his writing.

A middlebrow culture?

But if the highbrows were as powerful as Priestley implied, it certainly didn't seem that way to them. Popular media interest in the 'battle of the brows' focused on the alleged snobbism of Bloomsbury, and took a robustly populist line. Mockery of highbrows and modernists became, and remained, an endemic feature of public discourse. [70] 'Highbrows' bemoaned the stubborn refusal of the reading public to take the advice of the 'select, cultured element of the community', turning instead to their own, 'middlebrow' guides.[71] F. R. Leavis's pamphlet *Mass Civilisation and Minority Culture* (1930) is largely directed against the likes of Arnold Bennett, chief reviewer on the *Evening Standard*, labelled by Leavis as 'the most powerful maker of literary reputations in England' – later succeeded by Priestley, and in turn by another best-selling novelist, Howard Spring.[72] Here, and in the novelist Ethel Mannin's blurb for the Book Guild, also quoted by Leavis, we can see the spectre of an alternative cultural power structure which paid no lip-service to the 'legitimate', and which promised, in a neat reversal of Bourdieu's process of 'distinction', 'to sift really good stuff out of the mass of the affected and pretentious':

> [H]ow on earth is the ordinary person to sift the sheep from the goats? Distinguished critics attempt to guide the public, but they are often so hopelessly 'high brow' and 'precious,' and simply add to the general confusion and bewilderment.

The Book Guild, Mannin went on, will 'cater for the ordinary intelligent reader, not for the highbrows'.[73] Perhaps Q. D. Leavis was right, and only a 'armed and conscious' guerrilla movement working stealthily through schools and universities could rescue the situation.[74]

In the 1920s and 1930s popular novels rode a wave of market expansion. In the words of one of its historians, 'the "fiction trade" ... emerged as a prominent commercial and cultural institution more obviously than ever before'.[75] The process began with the demolition of the restrictive Victorian publishing system in 1894, partly at the hands of Priestley's publishers, Heinemann, whose single-volume six-shilling edition of Hall Caine's *The Manxman*, which sold four hundred thousand copies, was credited with killing off the Victorian three-decker novel.[76] Under the guidance of A. F. Frere and C. S. Evans, Heinemann built up an unrivalled list of respectable but popular authors, including Galsworthy, Richard Aldington, Somerset Maugham and Daphne du Maurier, while also publishing D. H. Lawrence's first novel, *The White Peacock* (1911). The following year they turned down *Sons and Lovers*, reckoning that its 'want of reticence' would make it unsaleable to the lending libraries.[77] These reservations are also an indication of Heinemann's target market. According to the firm's historian, Evans had an unrivalled nose for 'potentially successful "broadbrow" fiction, stories which promised a good long read, and which probably reflected his personal taste as well as that of a large middle-class public'.[78] The enthusiastic welcome he gave to Priestley's *The Good Companions* confirms his talent in tapping the new mass market for fiction.

After the hiatus of wartime, the number of new novels published and sold continued to rise steadily, as did the numbers of people buying and reading them. Competition was intense, and more and more was spent on promotional activities, exploiting all the rapidly developing techniques of the advertising and PR industries – blanket newspaper adverts, posters, bookshop and library displays, magazine and newspaper interviews with celebrity authors, even cinema newsreels – in search of the elusive best-seller which would balance the books, or better.

Lending libraries were booming – not the elite circulating libraries like Mudie's, which finally gave up the ghost in 1937, but local authority libraries, and popular commercial libraries such as W. H. Smith's and Boots Booklovers, based in the high-street retail chains. Both public and private sector libraries steadily grew in numbers, subscribers and book issues through the 1920s and 1930s, while smaller-scale 'tuppenny libraries', run as adjuncts to newsagents, corner shops or department stores, and supplied by wholesalers such as Foyles, offered formidable competition which kept subscription rates down; while, for those who wished to buy their books, Penguin initiated in 1935 the cheap, high-quality paperback.[79] The reviews pages of large-circulation newspapers and magazines offered readers advice on what to buy or borrow, and the Book Clubs offered help to the reader in the form of monthly selections recommended by a panel of experts, and eventually, when their purchasing power had grown, cheap editions of successful books. The Book Society, modelled on the American Book of the Month Club, was founded in 1927, its Selection Committee including Priestley and Walpole. By 1930 it had ten thousand subscribers, and was imitated by others such as the Book Guild (1930), and the Readers Union (1937).[80] This combination of libraries, newspaper and magazine reviews, book clubs and best-sellers was the foundation of what came to be labelled a 'middlebrow culture': a mass middle-class, suburban, perhaps predominantly female readership, receiving their monthly choice from the Book Club, changing their books every week at Boots, like the Celia Johnson character in Noel Coward's *Brief Encounter*, their taste formed by the advice of librarians, book club selection panels and reviewers in the *Daily Mail* or the *Evening Standard*.[81] Gosse's nightmare has come true, said Leavis: 'authority – the authority vested in tradition – has disappeared', no doubt to be replaced by that of the librarian at Boots.[82]

The rise of the literary marketplace in the late eighteenth century has been attributed to the rise of a middle-class readership, and it is no surprise to find the same process under way in the interwar years. Not only were there more middle-class people, but more of them were in salaried jobs such as the scientific and technical professions, teaching, management and administration, which required more than a basic level of education, though hardly to the standard of the London literati.[83] Their typical habitat, suburbia, was undergoing its classic period of growth, much to the alarm of those (including Priestley) who saw the countryside being eaten up by speculative jerry-built semis, whose occupants' lives were regularly depicted as narrow and culturally deprived. 'We have allowed the slum which stunted the body to be replaced by a slum which stunts the mind', declared one medical observer.[84] What else were the inhabitants of this intellectual slum to do but indulge in the 'substitute living' which only second-rate fiction could provide – and what else can the novelist do except provide this kind of thing, or else write books which only highbrows would read?[85] All these cultural changes and more Priestley would comment on.[86] But he was also part of them, as novelist, reviewer, journalist, broadcaster and Book Society panellist, making him a favourite target of the anti-middlebrows.

The Good Companions

But the chief problem, of course, was the kind of books he wrote: and in particular, his first best-seller, *The Good Companions*. By the mid-1920s his *Saturday Review* and *Week-End Review* essays, 'personal in tone but elaborately composed', were bringing in a worthwhile income. But to move on, he had to write novels, a task which he did not feel came naturally to him.[87] His first two novels, *Adam in Moonshine* and *Benighted*, both came out in 1927, and represent Priestley's attempt to 'keep company with the most advanced "modernists"' – up to a point. It was natural, he argued, that fiction should reflect the 'self-conscious, introspective, Hamlet-ish age', but it still needed to tell a story. He therefore tried to combine a 'subjective' focus on the interior life of the characters with 'some sort of objective narrative'.[88] *Adam*, which tells of the strange adventures of a young man during a period of four days, was received as a 'light fantastic farcical tale', but what Priestley was trying to do was to explore the young man's subjective state of mind, not in the style of Virginia Woolf in, for example, *Mrs Dalloway* but by 'objectifying the whole thing', and making all the characters apart from Adam himself 'creatures of symbolism, shadows of a dream'. Interestingly, *Adam* was greeted by the *Daily News* as likely to 'appeal to "highbrow" and "lowbrow" alike'.[89] *Benighted*, a story of travellers seeking refuge in an old dark house, showed more than a touch of the Gothic, and attempted to 'transmute the thriller into symbolical fiction with some psychological depth'. The inmates of the house, Priestley said, were 'only various forms of postwar pessimism pretending to be people'.[90] But Priestley concluded that these experimental flirtations with modernism had not been successful. Now he would go for 'really big novels, with a broad sweep of narrative and a wide canvas'.[91] In other words, *The Good Companions*, which came to be regarded as the ultimate middlebrow novel.

Published in the summer of 1929, *The Good Companions* was an unfashionably long book at 250,000 words, selling at the 'stiff price' of 10s 6d. Heinemann were wary, but hoped to sell seven or eight thousand copies. Despite some good reviews, the book started slowly, but then, 'in autumn the balloon went up'. By Christmas it had sold thirty thousand copies, Heinemann could hardly get enough into the bookshops to meet the demand, and Priestley became famous overnight.[92] Reprinted eight times in 1929, nine times in 1930 and repeatedly thereafter, *The Good Companions* was reckoned by 1978 to have sold over four million copies in various editions.[93] Priestley never looked back. A year later came *Angel Pavement*, almost equally successful, and then a sequence of mostly solid best-sellers through to the 1960s, successful plays starting with *Dangerous Corner* in 1932, and throughout this time more – and presumably better-paid – journalistic work, radio broadcasts, film scriptwriting. Priestley had become rich and famous, part of the new culture of celebrity and mass communication in which some heard the death-knell of high culture – and he had become more prolific than ever.

The Good Companions, in contrast to its predecessors, was a 'novel of escape, conceived in the spirit of comedy', optimistic in tone, and realist in style – a 'fairy tale', as he several times described it.[94] It concerned three characters, varying in class, gender and age, who for various reasons take to the road, and end up involved with the eponymous travelling concert-party, whose ups and downs and general adventures form the subject matter of the novel. It features a huge cast of well-drawn subsidiary characters, and an incident-packed, often comic narrative, taking England as a whole as its backdrop: 'but an England discovered chiefly in a holiday mood'; and it has a happy ending, more or less, for everyone.[95] Its England, as Holger Klein has suggested, is 'a small, surveyable and unified world ... an imaginary place very like it, but not quite': a heightened version of the real thing.[96] By any standard *The Good Companions* is a tour-de-force of writing.[97]

The spirit in which the novel was written was not calculated to win friends amongst the intelligentsia. Its author saw it as a deliberate riposte to the gloomy and pessimistic tone of much 1920s writing. He told his publisher, Charles Evans, 'I am of course deliberately breaking with everything that is characteristic of highbrow fiction of the moment, the vague crowds of clever idlers, the dreary futility, and all the rest of it. Let's have some Real People, says I.'[98] And many critics welcomed it in the same vein. Priestley's friend J. C. Squire hailed it in the *Observer* as a corrective to the 'dyspeptic gloom, solemn obscenity, perversion, lovelessness and cruelty' of much contemporary fiction.[99] Conversely, that scourge of the middle-brow, Q. D. Leavis, found in the book 'a faked sensibility ... a lack of discrimination ... the functioning of a second-rate mind ... complacent, hearty knowingness'.[100] This reputation has followed the book ever after. Consider the blurb on the back cover of *The Good Companions* when it was reissued as a Penguin Modern Classic in 1962:

> Since *The Good Companions* was published over thirty years ago it has defied the cheap sneers of some highbrows with more than forty English

editions and impressions alone. The reason is not difficult to find. Into this grand and positive pageant of English life Priestley packed as enchanting a cast of characters as can be found in any work of Fielding or Dickens. The adventures in the theatrical world of Jess Oakroyd, probably the most lovable Yorkshireman in all literature ... plaited together into a story which is unforgettable ... [101]

It is almost impossible to defend the book against praise like this. Small wonder that Priestley in later years often complained at being forever tied down to *The Good Companions* and its reputation. He had written other, and better novels, he insisted, rightly, and never tried to repeat his first success, however much readers implored him to do so. The book's optimism was a one-off, a holiday from the gloom caused by war and family tragedy. 'And because a lot of other people then must have felt in need of such a holiday', the balloon went up.[102] October 1929, of course, saw the Wall Street Crash, and the start of the Slump. But not everybody seems to have felt in need of the 'holiday' which *The Good Companions* offered.

Mrs Woolf and Mr Priestley

In August 1929 Virginia Woolf asked her, and Priestley's, good friend Hugh Walpole for some advice about *The Good Companions*: 'Ought I to read Mr Priestley's book? ... From the reviews, chiefly by Jack Squire, I am sure that I should hate it – but I suspect that I may be wrong.' Squire's review is quoted above, and we can see why it would have put Woolf off: but she knew Walpole was fond of Priestley, and seemed prepared to give him a chance.

A year later, she still had not read the book, but Priestley was still in her thoughts. By this time they were not kindly thoughts. She speculates in her diary that

> At the age of 50 Priestley will be saying 'why don't the highbrows admire me? It isn't true that I write only for money'. He will be enormously rich; but there will be that thorn in his shoe – or so I hope.

She goes on: 'Yet I have not read, & I daresay shall never read, a book by Priestley.'[103] Unlike Hoggart's autodidact, then, Virginia has 'learned' all she needs to know about Priestley, without making the mistake of reading his books, which just shows what a little cultural capital will do for you. And, getting at last to the heart of the matter, Woolf concludes her diary entry with the words: 'I invent this phrase for Bennett & Priestley "the tradesmen of letters".'

In 1932, the 'battle of the brows' was hotting up, and Priestley, now famous, occupied the influential (and distinctly middlebrow) position of lead *Evening Standard* book critic. In this capacity, on 13th October he reviewed Woolf's *The Second Common Reader*, along with books by her friends Vita Sackville-West and Harold Nicolson, and Winifred Holtby's *Virginia Woolf*. The review criticised Nicolson, praised Sackville-West and, with reference to the Holtby book, described Woolf's *To the Lighthouse* as 'one of the most moving and beautiful pieces of fiction of our time'.[104] Even so, the review caused offence, and Woolf wrote to Sackville-West expressing her 'unadulterated disgust'.[105] The problem was that Priestley had not only repeated Arnold Bennett's loathsome epithet 'the High Priestess of Bloomsbury' but referred, rather hurtfully, to 'terrifically sensitive, cultured, invalidish ladies with private means'.[106]

The 'battle of the brows' had attracted the attention of the BBC. Just four days after this review appeared, Priestley delivered a radio talk entitled 'To a highbrow', in which he repeated the gist of the 1926 essay, though rather more bitterly, mocked the pretensions of the camp-followers of modernism and again declared himself an unrepentant 'broadbrow'.[107] The talk, a version of which was later published in the distinctly middlebrow magazine *John O'London's*, made it clear that the target of his derision was not the genuine intellectual – nobody would call Einstein a 'highbrow' – but those who go to absurd lengths to distance themselves from ordinary humanity by rejecting anything popular – 'So-and-so suddenly writes a book that sells more than two or three thousand copies, and what is the result? So-and-so immediately begins to lose prestige with you ... Poor old so-and-so is finished now that he's *popular*' – even rejecting England itself and going abroad as much as they can – and talking and behaving in a ludicrously affected manner: 'you decide – and God knows why – to over-emphasise all your sibilants, so that you sound like a hissing serpent'. This caricature of the affected highbrow was to recur in Priestley's fiction over the years. It had been gently mocked in *The Good Companions*, in the shape of Miss Trant's nephew Hilary, who believes that 'art has got to be beyond emotion', and runs a review called *The Oxford Static*.[108] Highbrows were to be discovered, 'hissing amiably at one another and smiling and swaying and waving their delicate little paws', at a London cocktail party in *Wonder Hero* (1933); while in *Let the People Sing* (1939) we encounter 'Mr Churton Talley, the great art critic and expert', who proves to be 'a slender, wavy-haired youth of about fifty-five, with enamelled pink cheeks, a cherry lip, and the eyes of a dead codfish', who minces and hisses 'with those long drawn-out sibilants'.[109] Well might the radio talk conclude with the stirring, if jarringly masculinist, rallying-cry, 'Don't be either a highbrow or a lowbrow. Be a man. Be a broadbrow.'

A week after Priestley's broadcast, Harold Nicolson was called in to deliver a rebuttal, 'To a lowbrow', the text of which unfortunately does not survive. The following week's *New Statesman* carried a discussion of the debate, which unsurprisingly gave the verdict to Nicolson, and this prompted Woolf to write a long letter to the magazine, which was not sent but was posthumously published under the title 'Middlebrow'.[110] This letter was clearly a response both to Priestley's *Evening Standard* review and to his BBC talk, and there is ample textual evidence that its main (if not sole) target is Priestley himself: phrases from his review crop up, there is a sarcastic reference to his latest novel, *Faraway*, and a veiled account of a visit to his house. This is a far less reasoned, more rhetorical and more vituperative piece than 'Mr Bennett'. It is also, as Melba Cuddy-Keane has shown, quite a complex piece of writing, whose meaning requires close unpicking: so much so that despite its literary merits it cannot be said to advance much of an argument, more to state a position.[111]

Highbrows, Woolf tells us, pursue ideas; lowbrows pursue life; however, 'the middlebrow is the man, or woman, of middlebred intelligence ... in pursuit of no single object, neither art itself nor life itself, but both mixed indistinguishably, and rather nastily, with money, fame, power or prestige'. Highbrows make enough money to live on, and then live with taste: the middlebrow carries on earning so as to accumulate worthless goods, such as 'Georgian style' houses stocked with fake Queen Anne furniture, first editions and pictures by dead artists ('for to buy living art requires living taste'). This is unmistakably a personal attack on Priestley, who had recently moved to a Georgian (not, as Woolf surely knew, merely 'Georgian style') house in Highgate, and this may be one reason why Leonard Woolf dissuaded her from sending the letter. Priestley is being criticised, not for what he writes (which is not discussed) but for writing it for money, and for the way he spends that money. As for middlebrow writing, it is merely a 'mixture of geniality and sentiment stuck together with a sticky slime of calves-foot jelly'. In a trope drawn straight from the repertoire of English Toryism, she invokes the lowbrow as the natural ally of the highbrow: both should unite to drive out the middlebrow. Although she is careful to deny the association of 'brows' with classes, an undeniable tone of class condescension runs through her conception of the lowbrow. Lowbrows pursue life with 'thoroughbred vitality', they write beautifully because they write 'naturally'. In other words, highbrow is authentic because it is Art, lowbrow because it is 'natural'; middlebrow is not authentic at all.

Though this piece was never published in her lifetime, Woolf's hostility towards Priestley remained implacable. By the end of 1933 she was consigning him along with the other denizens of Grub Street to the 'the stinking underworld of hack writers – people like Priestley, Lynd, Squire, and others so covered in mud one cant name them even', and habitually referring to Priestley, with heavy-handed sarcasm, as 'the great novelist' – something he never claimed to be.[112] Late in 1936 they met at her brother Adrian's house, in support of Republican Spain: 'how we glared at each other'.[113] Well they might.

This exchange continues to ruffle feathers to this day. Present-day Virginia Woolf scholars are as vituperative towards Priestley as Virginia herself was. Melba Cuddy-Keane takes no prisoners in dealing with the exchanges of autumn 1932: Priestley's broadcast is 'aggressive' and 'nasty'; his implicit message, she says, is that 'nothing is worth the trouble of thinking about' – although in fact, he could equally be saying that *everything* is worth thinking about – while the aggression and nastiness in Woolf's unpublished response is overlooked.[114] 'Behind Priestley's "don't be a highbrow, be a man"', Cuddy-Keane suggests, 'lies an entire cultural discourse intimately connected with war': a little simplistic, and unconvincing in view of Priestley's record as an anti-war campaigner.[115] Another Woolfite, Mark Hussey, extraordinarily unmasks Priestley as a progenitor of Thatcherism.[116] This is because he spoke for 'a middlebrow culture that appealed to plain folk such as Alfred Roberts, Margaret Thatcher's father', at whose knee, of course, Margaret learned all her political principles. Moreover, damningly, the Roberts family heard Priestley's wartime *Postscripts* on the family wireless. No one who knows what the *Postscripts* actually said is likely to be convinced by this tenuous link: indeed, Hussey's main source, Thatcher herself, accuses Priestley of 'cloaking left-wing views as solid, down to earth, Northern homespun philosophy' – not surprisingly, as he was regarded as one of the architects of the 'postwar consensus' which she devoted her political life to demolishing.[117]

The point here is not to deny that the Robertses were 'middlebrow' – they subscribed to *John O'London's Weekly*, a damning piece of evidence that Hussey somehow overlooks – but that within the 'middlebrow' there were different political positions available, left as well as right. The attempt to squeeze Priestley into a mould of complacent suburban Toryism cannot long survive any acquaintance with what he actually wrote, but it is symptomatic of the threat which the so-called middlebrow still represents in the eyes of the apostles of modernism.

'Men in a particular society'

Priestley once said of himself that 'though fiercely radical politically and socially, culturally I am conservative, like many a better man before me'.[118] His taste ran in art to representational works and the English watercolour landscape, and in music to the standard classical concert repertoire, although he was also a keen appreciator of popular performance, particularly comedy.[119] Nevertheless, whatever he may have said about 'highbrows' in the heat of the 'battle of the brows', in his capacity as literary critic Priestley was not particularly hostile towards modernism. In *Literature and Western Man* (1960), his major critical work, he has praise (though not unqualified) for Proust, Joyce, Lawrence, Woolf herself, amongst other moderns. However, his own inclination is clearly for a different kind of novel, and he generally finds modernist writers more agreeable the closer they get to realism: Proust, for example, is most successful in showing us 'a host of characters, indeed a whole society, moving with Time'.[120] And Virginia Woolf's best work, *To the Lighthouse*, while experimental, is still 'closer to a more or less traditional method than her initial theory would allow'.[121]

Commenting on Woolf's rejection of the Wells/Bennett approach, and her notion of life as 'a luminous halo', Priestley presented a reasoned defence of his own novelistic practice:

> But the novel is a very lose, wide form; and the task of the novelist is to write as well as he can the kind of novel he wants to write. If his fiction is concerned with men in a particular society, and with the character of that society, then this highly subjective, interior-monologue, halo-and-envelope method will not serve his purpose at all. In the unending dazzle of thoughts and impressions society disappears, and even persons begin to disintegrate. Indeed, it might be argued that a writer who feels that life can only be described and recorded in this fashion should not be writing novels at all but poetry.[122]

The central task of the novel, he declared, is to 'show us Man in the society he has created – and with a major novelist, society itself will be an all-important character'.[123] The Victorian novelists, feeling near the cultural centre of their society, had assumed that literature had the power to intervene in that society, describe it, criticise it, influence its thinking.[124] Some writers had abandoned that task: others, including Priestley, had not.

Priestley was one of many writers who, in a supposedly modernist age, continued to write about 'people in society', and to employ the conventions of realism in so doing. This choice was also influenced by their preference for a wide readership, rather than just the appreciation of a small minority. Woolf may dismiss this as 'writing for money', but it is also follows from the view that literature should play a social role. Thus, while some writers moved aside into a special world of literary values, Priestley and those like him reoccupied the centre ground of the culture. He flung himself into the new media, the popular press, broadcasting and cinema, as additional means not just of making a living but of continuing the social engagement which he considered central to the writer's role. Writing in the *Evening Standard* in 1932 about George Moore ('the detached, pure artist') and H. G. Wells ('the man of creative gusto'), he explains his choice:

> I respect the man who, following Mr Moore, says: 'This is a mad age, and because it is a mad age I will serve at my secret altar of art,' but I cannot

agree with him. I believe this to be a time when literature must be an impure art, a rough compromise between perfect statements, fine forms, and the hasty improvisations of the man who is charging into the middle of life. More perfect artists in words may possibly return when security and tranquillity return to the world.[125]

We are reminded of Wells's declaration in 1915 that 'I had rather be called a journalist than an artist, and that is the essence of it', and Winifred Holtby's modest self-deprecation:

> I have no illusions about my work. I am primarily a useful, versatile, sensible and fairly careful artisan. I have trained myself to write quickly, punctually and readably to order over a wide range of subjects. That has nothing to do with art. It has quite a lot to do with politics.[126]

From the left it has sometimes been argued that the conventions of realism are irredeemably tainted with bourgeois ideology and thus incapable of delivering a truly radical view of society or politics.[127] Against this we can argue that – embracing modernity, if not modernism – they helped to constitute readers as social subjects, engaged in collective self-scrutiny across a broad front of social issues, and to some degree rescued the narrative of social progress from the pessimism into which it had fallen since 1914. As we shall see in the next chapter, the books Priestley wrote in the 1930s, including *Angel Pavement* (1930), *Wonder Hero* (1933), *English Journey* (1934) and *They Walk in the City* (1936), all sought to explore British society in a serious and searching vein. In this, Priestley was not alone. A. J. Cronin's *The Stars Look Down* (1935) explored social and political conflict in a mining community, while *The Citadel* (1937) critically analysed the failings of the pre-NHS medical system across a broad canvas from pit-village to Harley Street. Winifred Holtby's *South Riding* (1934) set out the political and ideological battle-lines of the time in a rural Yorkshire landscape.[128] Howard Spring's *Fame Is the Spur* (1940) explored the recent history and problems of the Labour party through the rise and fall of a Ramsay MacDonald figure. I could go on.

All these novels sold well, most were turned into films and all offer the usual popular narrative pleasures, but it is difficult to see how anyone could engage with them without also engaging with broader narratives of social improvement. Some of these writers were journalists by trade; others, like Priestley, took up journalism, and in novels and journalism they kept alive the idea of a common culture in a time of cultural fragmentation, and of social improvement in an age of widespread despair. They were in many ways the successors, in a democratic age, to the Victorian 'public moralists'.[129] In *Enemies of Promise* (1938), that highbrow's highbrow Cyril Connolly warned of the 'penalty of writing for the masses. As the writer goes out to meet them half-way he is joined by other writers going out to meet them half-way and they merge into the same creature – the talkie journalist, the advertising, lecturing, popular novelist.'[130] This was a fate Priestley and many of his so-called 'middlebrow' contemporaries were only too happy to embrace, as they played their full part in this new, democratic – and sometimes lucrative – public sphere.

Notes

1 Richard Hoggart, *The Uses of Literacy* (Harmondsworth: Penguin, [1957] 1958), p. 309.
2 Pierre Bourdieu, *The Field of Cultural Production*, ed. Randal Johnson (Cambridge: Cambridge University Press, 1993); Peter D. MacDonald, *British Literary Culture and Publishing Practice, 1880–1914* (Cambridge: Cambridge University Press, 1997), pp. 10–11.
3 Ian Watt, *The Rise of the Novel* (Harmondsworth: Penguin, 1963) p. 59.
4 Malcolm Bradbury, *The Social Context of Modern English Literature* (Oxford: Oxford University Press, 1971), pp. 203–6; Peter Keating, *The Haunted Study: A Social History of the English Novel 1875–1914* (London: Fontana, 1991), pp. 22–36.
5 Gosse's statement of 1891, quoted in Q. D. Leavis, *Fiction and the Reading Public* (London: Chatto and Windus, [1932] 1965), p. 190. See also MacDonald, *Literary Culture*, pp. 1–9.
6 Rosa Maria Bracco, *'Betwixt and Between': Middlebrow Fiction and English Society in the Twenties and Thirties* (Melbourne: University of Melbourne, 1990), pp. 9–14; Joseph McAleer, *Popular Reading and Publishing in Britain, 1914–1950* (Oxford: Oxford University Press, 1992), pp. 42–59; J. B. Priestley, *Midnight on the Desert* (London: Heinemann, 1937), p. 12.
7 Keating, *Haunted Study*, pp. 15–22; 31.
8 J. B. Priestley, *Margin Released: A Writer's Reminiscences and Reflections* (London: Heinemann, 1962), p. 10.
9 Ibid., p. 7.
10 J. B. Priestley, 'On education', *Thoughts in the Wilderness* (London: Heinemann, 1957), pp. 49–50. Originally published *New Statesman* (13 March 1954).
11 Priestley, *Margin*, p. 30.
12 Ibid., pp. 38–9, 47–9.
13 Ibid., pp. 67–8.
14 J. B. Priestley, 'How I began', *Daily News* (18 June 1927), p. 4.
15 Howard Spring, *In the Meantime* (London: Constable, 1942), pp. 32–46; 86–8. Priestley, *Margin*, pp. 30, 13. M. H. Spring, 'Spring, (Robert) Howard (1889–1965)', rev. Katherine Mullin, *Oxford Dictionary of National Biography* (Oxford: Oxford University Press, 2004) (http://www.oxforddnb.com/view/article/36223, accessed 21 October 2004).
16 Priestley, 'How I began'.
17 Priestley, *Margin*, pp. 33–6; J. B. Priestley, *Delight* (London: Heinemann, 1949), p. 146.

18 Priestley, *Margin*, pp. 18, 20; J. B. Priestley, *Outcries and Asides* (London: Heinemann, 1974), pp. 109, 148; J. B. Priestley, 'The Bradford schoolmaster', *Listener* (23 July 1959), p. 129.

19 Priestley, *Margin*, pp. 75–6; J. B. Priestley, *Rain Upon Godshill* (London: Heinemann, 1939), p. 176.

20 Priestley, *Rain*, p. 176.

21 Bradbury, *Social Context*, pp. 82–3.

22 Richard Ellman, *James Joyce* (Oxford: Oxford University Press, 1959), p. 54; Priestley, *Margin*, p. 10.

23 Ibid., pp. 163–4.

24 J. B. Priestley, 'The writer in a changing society' (1955), in Priestley, *Wilderness*, p. 222.

25 Priestley, *Margin*, p. 39.

26 Ibid., p. 79.

27 J. B. Priestley, *The Balconinny* (London: Methuen, 1929), p. 8.

28 Ibid., p. 142.

29 Ibid., pp. 153–5.

30 See John Lehmann (ed.), *Coming to London* (London: Phoenix House, 1957), passim.

31 J. B. Priestley in Lehmann, *Coming to London*, pp. 66, 68.

32 Ibid., p. 60.

33 Vincent Brome, *J. B. Priestley* (London: Hamish Hamilton, 1988), pp. 79, 96; Alan Day, *J. B. Priestley: An Annotated Bibliography* (London: Garland, 1980), pp. 93–128. Most of the *Saturday Review* essays are reprinted in Priestley, *Open House* (London: Heinemann, 1927), *Apes and Angels* (London: Methuen, 1928) and *The Balconinny* (London: Methuen, 1929).

34 J. B. Priestley, *The English Comic Characters* (London: John Lane The Bodley Head, 1925), *George Meredith* (London: Macmillan and Co., 1926), *Adam in Moonshine* (London: Heinemann, 1927), *Thomas Love Peacock* (London: Macmillan, 1927), *Benighted* (London: Heinemann, 1927), *The English Novel* (London: Ernest Benn, 1927), *Farthing Hall* (with Hugh Walpole) (London: Macmillan, 1929), *English Humour* (London: Longman, 1929).

35 Priestley, *Margin*, p. 180.

36 Judith Cook, *Priestley* (London: Bloomsbury, 1997), p. 63.

37 Priestley, *Margin*, pp. 154–6; 'Complete analysis of the works of J. B. Priestley', dated 31 May 1956, in Heinemann Archive, Rushden.

38 George Orwell, 'Inside the whale', in Sonia Orwell and Ian Angus (eds), *The Collected Essays, Journalism and Letters of George Orwell*, vol. 1 (London: Penguin Books, 1970), p. 555.

39 Bradbury, *Social Context*, pp. 187–91; Ronald Bush, 'Eliot, Thomas Stearns (1888–1965)', *Oxford Dictionary of National Biography* (Oxford: Oxford University Press, 2004) (www.oxforddnb.com/view/article/32993, accessed 13 April 2005).

40 Raymond Williams, 'The Bloomsbury fraction', in *Problems in Materialism and Culture* (London: Verso, 1980).

41 Ibid.

42 Leavis, *Fiction*, p. 79.

43 Nicola Humble, *The Feminine Middlebrow Novel* (Oxford: Oxford

University Press, 2001), p. 3; Ross McKibbin, *Classes and Cultures in England 1918–1951* (Oxford: Oxford University Press, 1998), pp. 46–7; Geoffrey Crossick (ed.), *The Lower Middle Class in Britain* (London: Croom Helm, 1977).

44 Virginia Woolf, 'Mr Bennett and Mrs Brown', *Collected Essays*, vol. 1 (London: Hogarth Press, [1924] 1966), p. 321.

45 Malcolm Bradbury and James McFarlane (eds), *Modernism: A Guide to European Literature 1890–1930* (London; Penguin 1976), p. 24.

46 Woolf, 'Mr Bennett and Mrs Brown'.

47 Keating, *Haunted*, pp. 289–93.

48 Susan Cooper, 'That's J. B. Priestley for you', *Sunday Times Magazine* (7 September 1969), p. 11.

49 Priestley in Lehmann (ed.), *Coming to London*, p. 68.

50 Alison Light, *Forever England: Femininity, Conservatism and Literature Between the Wars* (London: Routledge, 1981); Bracco, *'Betwixt and Between'*; Humble, *Middlebrow*; Joan Shelley Rubin, *The Making of Middlebrow Culture*, (Chapel Hill: University of North Carolina Press, 1992); Janice A. Radway, *A Feeling for Books. The Book-of-the-Month Club, Literary Taste and Middle-Class Desire* (Chapel Hill, University of North Carolina Press, 1997). See also Mary Grover, 'The authenticity of the middlebrow: Warwick Deeping and cultural legitimacy, 1903–1940', PhD thesis, Sheffield Hallam University, 2002.

51 Humble, *Middlebrow*, pp. 4–5, 11–13; Bracco, *'Betwixt and Between'*, p. 3.

52 Pierre Bourdieu, *Distinction: A Social Critique of the Judgement of Taste* (London: Routledge & Kegan Paul, 1984), pp. 6–7.

53 Ibid., p. 50.

54 Ibid., p. 327.

55 Clement Greenberg, 'Modern and postmodern', in Robert C. Morgan (ed.), *Clement Greenberg Late Writings* (Minneapolis: University of Minnesota Press, 2003).

56 Leavis, *Fiction*, pp. 33, 35, 48, 55.

57 *Oxford English Dictionary*, under 'middlebrow'.

58 Leavis, *Fiction*, pp. 38, 36–7.

59 Priestley, *Delight*, p. 70.

60 J. B. Priestley, 'Fifty years of the English', *The Moments* (London: Heinemann, 1966), pp. 207–8: essay first published in *New Statesman* (19 April 1963).

61 Priestley, *Margin*, p. 156.

62 F. R. Leavis, *The Great Tradition* (London: Chatto and Windus, 1948), p. 11.

63 Priestley, 'Thoughts on Dr Leavis', *New Statesman* (10 November 1956) (signed 'Dr Priestley'). Reprinted as 'Dr Leavis' in Priestley, *Wilderness*. See also Priestley's critical but on balance very favourable review of Leavis's *D. H. Lawrence: Novelist*, 'Who will pass his scrutiny?', *News Chronicle* (6 October 1955), p. 8.

64 J. B. Priestley, *Festival at Farbridge* (London: Heinemann, 1951), pp. 375–6.

65 Priestley, *Margin*, p. 156.

66 J. B. Priestley, 'High, low, broad', in *Open House*, pp. 162–7. Originally published in *Saturday Review* (20 February 1926), pp. 222–3.

67 Ibid., p. 165. Surbiton was also a favourite target of the Bloomsburyites.

68 Ibid., p. 166.

69 Ibid., p. 167.

70 For mockery of modernism see J. A. Hammerton (ed.), *Mr Punch and the Arts* (London, n.d. [c. 1930s]).

71 Leavis, *Fiction*, p. 202.

72 F. R. Leavis, *Mass Civilisation and Minority Culture* (Cambridge: Minority Press, 1930), p. 14.

73 Ibid., p. 20.

74 Ibid., pp. 270–1.

75 Bracco, *'Betwixt and Between'*, p. 2.

76 John St John, *William Heinemann: A Century of Publishing 1890–1990* (London: Heinemann, 1990), pp. 28–30; Vivien Allen, 'Caine, Sir (Thomas Henry) Hall (1853–1931)', *Oxford Dictionary of National Biography* (Oxford: Oxford University Press, 2004) (www.oxforddnb.com/view/article /32237, accessed 15 April 2005).

77 Keating, *Haunted Study*, p. 272.

78 St John, *Heinemann*, p. 206.

79 McAleer, *Popular Reading*, pp. 49–50; N. Joicey, 'A paperback guide to progress: Penguin Books, 1935–c1951', *Twentieth Century British History*, 4: 1 (1993).

80 Bracco, *'Betwixt and Between'*, p. 14.

81 Humble, *Middlebrow*, gives a richly informative account of how 'middle-brow' readers and reading habits were depicted in the 'middlebrow' novels they read.

82 F. R. Leavis, 'What's wrong with criticism?', *Scrutiny* 1:2 (September 1932).

83 McKibbin, *Classes and Cultures*, pp. 46–7.

84 Stephen Taylor, 'The suburban neurosis', in Judy Giles and Tim Middleton (eds), *Writing Englishness 1900–1950* (London: Routledge, 1995), p. 238, originally published in *The Lancet* (26 March 1938), pp. 759–61.

85 Ibid., p. 263.

86 See Chapter 4 below.

87 Priestley, *Margin*, p. 177.

88 Priestley, 'Introduction' to *Adam in Moonshine Benighted* (London: Heinemann, 1932 edition), pp. v–viii.

89 J. B. Priestley, *Open House*, endpapers.

90 Priestley, 'Introduction', p. vi.

91 Quoted in Holger Klein, *J. B. Priestley's Fiction* (Frankfurt: Peter Lang, 2002), p. 282.

92 Priestley, *Margin*, pp. 186–7.

93 St John, *Heinemann*, p. 207; John Braine, *J. B. Priestley* (London: Weidenfeld and Nicolson, 1978), p. 41.

94 Priestley, *Midnight*, p. 48. Priestley, 'Introduction' to *The Good Companions* (London: Heinemann, 1931 edition), p. x.

95 Priestley, 'Introduction', p. xi.

96 Klein, *J. B. Priestley's Fiction*, p. 54. This is the best sustained critical account of *The Good Companions*.

97 *The Good Companions* is discussed in more detail in Chapter 2, below.

98 St John, *Heinemann*, p. 207.

99 Klein, *Fiction*, p. 45.

100 Ibid., pp. 76–7.

101 J. B. Priestley, *The Good Companions* (Harmondsworth: Penguin, 1962), back cover.

102 Priestley, *Margin*, pp. 186–7.

103 Anne Olivier Bell (ed.), *The Diary of Virginia Woolf*, vol. 3: 1925–1930 (London: Hogarth Press, 1980), p. 317 (entry for Monday 8 September 1930); Virginia Woolf to Quentin Bell, 12 December 1933. In Nigel Nicolson (ed.), *The Sickle Side of the Moon: The Letters of Virginia Woolf Volume 5 1932–1935* (London: Hogarth Press, 1979), p. 259.

104 Priestley, 'Tell us more about these authors', *Evening Standard* (13 October 1932), p. 11.

105 Virginia Woolf to Vita Sackville-West, 18 October 1932, in Nicolson (ed.), *Sickle Side*, p. 111.

106 Priestley, *The Moments*, p. 207.

107 J. B. Priestley, 'To a highbrow', *John O'London's* (3 December 1932), p. 354.

108 Priestley, *Good Companions*, p. 65.

109 J. B. Priestley, *Wonder Hero* (London: Heinemann, 1933), p. 168; J. B. Priestley, *Let the People Sing* (London: Heinemann, 1939), pp. 204–5.

110 Virginia Woolf, 'Middlebrow', in *The Death of the Moth and Other Essays* (London: Hogarth Press, 1942). The episode is discussed in Melba Cuddy-Keane, *Virginia Woolf, the Intellectual, and the Public Sphere* (Cambridge: Cambridge University Press, 2003), chapter 1 *passim*.

111 Cuddy-Keane, *Virginia Woolf*, pp. 25ff.

112 Virginia Woolf to Quentin Bell, 12 December 1933. In Nicolson (ed.), *Sickle Side*, p. 259.

113 Letter to Dorothy Bussey, 15 December 1936/1 January 1937. In Nigel Nicolson (ed.), *Leave the Letters Till We're Dead: The Letters of Virginia Woolf, 1936–41* (London: Chatto and Windus, 1980), p. 100.

114 Cuddy-Keane, *Virginia Woolf*, pp. 27, 24.

115 Cuddy-Keane, cited in Mark Hussey, 'Mrs Thatcher and Mrs Woolf', *Modern Fiction Studies* 50:1 (Spring 2004), p. 17.

116 Hussey, 'Mrs Thatcher'. Hussey also says that Priestley is denounced for his misogyny in Woolf's *Three Guineas*. In fact he is not mentioned in that essay.

117 Margaret Thatcher, *The Path to Power* (London: Harper-Collins, 1995), p. 22. This is the same page which Hussey references in his article.

118 J. B. Priestley, 'Gay with the arts?', in *Moments*, p. 11. Originally published in *New Statesman* (23 April 1965).

119 J. B. Priestley, *Particular Pleasures* (London: Heinemann, 1975).

120 J. B. Priestley, *Literature and Western Man* (Harmondsworth: Penguin, [1960] 1969), p. 421.

121 Ibid., p. 435.

122 Priestley, *Literature*, pp. 434–5.

123 Ibid., p. 421.

124 Bradbury, *Social Context*, pp. xiii–xv.

125 *Evening Standard* (25 February 1932), p. 7.

126 Quoted in Stuart Hall et al. (eds), *Culture, Media, Language: Working Papers*

in Cultural Studies (London: Hutchinson, 1980), p. 255.

127 For the 'Brecht/Lukács debate' of the 1930s see Ernst Bloch et al., *Aesthetics and Politics* (London: New Left Books, 1977); for the *Days of Hope* debate of the 1970s, see Tony Bennett et al. (eds), *Popular Television and Film: A Reader* (London: BFI/Open University Press, 1981), part 4.

128 Marion Shaw, *The Clear Stream: A Life of Winifred Holtby* (London: Virago, 1999), pp. 258–62.

129 Stefan Collini, *Public Moralists: Political Thought and Intellectual Life in Victorian Britain* (Oxford: Oxford University Press, 1993).

130 Cyril Connolly, *Enemies of Promise* (Harmondsworth: Penguin Books, [1938] 1961), p. 83.

2

Bruddersford and beyond

By the end of the 1930s Priestley was a different kind of writer from the one he had been at the start of the decade. Now society was no longer a backdrop to his novels but the central character, and his journalism had shifted away from literary reviews and *belles-lettristic* essays towards social observation and the forthright expression of political opinions. In this he was part of a new cultural trend, towards social investigation, social criticism and politics, along with the documentary film movement, Mass Observation, *Picture Post* and writers such as George Orwell, and many of those who, along with Priestley, were labelled 'middlebrow'. This trajectory led Priestley to his prominent role in the Second World War, which will be examined in the next chapter. First, before discussing what he wrote in the 1930s, we explore the roots of his social and political critique, in pre-1914 Bradford, the 'Bruddersford' of his novels.[1]

Bruddersford revisited

Unlike many of his contemporaries, Priestley did not come to politics in the 1930s: it was in his upbringing, and in his blood. He grew up in one of the most radical cities in England, the cradle of the Labour movement, and in a household awash with political discussion. As he later declared, with reference to the 1930s public-school Marxists,

> I did not discover 'the proletariat' in late night talks in some tutor's rooms at Oxford. I grew up with the proletarians in one of the grimmest industrial regions in the country, and indeed their blood is mine just as, I hope, their dreams are mine.[2]

It has been suggested that Priestley is romanticising here, suppressing his suburban lower middle-class origins in order to lend credence to his stance as a social critic and supporter of the working class.[3] But however overblown his language may be, the facts are as he states them.

Bradford was an uncompromisingly industrial town, based on one industry, wool, which had caused its rapid growth in the nineteenth century and shaped its character. Priestley's family, like many in such industrial towns, was socially mixed, spanning the working and lower middle classes. His paternal grandfather was a mill-hand, and treasurer of the local Co-op who had managed to send his son to train as a teacher. His mother, who died when Jack was an infant, came from a 'back o't' mill' background, and his stepmother started out as a shop-girl. There undoubtedly were 'grandparents and uncles and aunts who still lived in the wretched little "back-to-back" houses in the long, dark streets behind the mills'.[4] Priestley made no bones about being himself a member of the Edwardian lower middle class, son of an elementary-school headmaster, living neither 'back o't' mill' nor in the 'wilderness of suburban Drives and Groves' beyond the town but in Saltburn Place, among the respectable terraced houses off Toller Lane, a short tram-ride from the town centre.[5] In Bradford, as an official guidebook remarked in 1917, 'the residential districts ... possess in a peculiar degree the characteristics of a mingling of the social grades', so much so that, despite the presence of wealthy businessmen, ill-health and overcrowding spread fairly evenly through the town, and in 1896 every ward in the borough was reported to have at least 40 per cent of back-to-back houses.[6] So despite its bay windows, trees in the street, shopkeepers living next door and views across still undeveloped fields, Saltburn Place was not far from working-class housing, mills and factories, or from some of the town's largest and most opulent suburban villas. 'I had grown up with strikes', Priestley said, 'played football and gone soldiering with warehouse lads and wool-combers' and dyers' labourers, miners and foundry men and fitters', and indeed the huge Manningham Mills, site of the bitter and violent strike of 1891 which helped give birth to the Independent Labour Party the following year, was only half a mile from Priestley's childhood home.[7]

Bradford, then, was the very paradigm of nineteenth-century industrial England. But did Priestley like this England? Not if we are to judge by his bitter remarks at the end of *English Journey*:

> It had found a green and pleasant land and had left a wilderness of dirty bricks. It had blackened fields, poisoned rivers, ravaged the earth, and sown filth and ugliness with a lavish hand ... I felt like calling back a few of these sturdy individualists simply to rub their noses in the nasty mess they had made. Who gave them leave to turn this island into their ashpit? ... What you see just looks like a debauchery of cynical greed.[8]

This is the England of slag-heaps and mill chimneys and doss-houses, back-to-back slums and cindery waste-grounds, and 'grim, fortress-like cities'. It would be easy to set this heartfelt disgust alongside some of Priestley's affectionate praise for the English countryside and conclude that he had trodden a path familiar enough among those who rejected industrial capitalism and all its works, spurning his northern industrial origins and opting for an idealised, rural 'Deep England'.

Any such conclusion would be profoundly mistaken. Lurking in Priestley's long catalogue of nineteenth-century detritus we also find Town Halls and Mechanics' Institutes, Literary and Philosophical Societies, pier pavilions, fried-fish shops and chapels – things which speak of something more positive: a distinctive way of life, a culture.[9] Indeed, even as he denounces the 'sooty, dismal little towns', Priestley lists rather more of their positive features than negative ones. If people have been compelled to live 'like black-beetles at the back of a disused kitchen stove', they have made a life there which embodies something of value – of greater value, in some ways, than the more comfortable one which succeeded it. We are reminded of Eric Hobsbawm's words about the 'traditional' working-class culture which was consolidating itself from the 1870s onwards: 'It was neither a very good nor a very rich life, but it was probably the first kind of life since the industrial revolution which provided a firm lodging for the British working class within industrial society.'[10] In fact, if Priestley idealises anything about the English past, it is not some lost rural Arcadia – or even, as some might expect, the struggles of the working class – but its urban civilisation: Bradford's robust and democratic culture which he conjures up from memory and imagination.

From this culture Priestley took with him two profound ideological influences: socialism and Dissent. 'I was brought up among socialists,' he reminds us, 'not the embittered rebels of today, but the gentle, hopeful theorists of thirty or forty years ago.'[11] His father Jonathan ('both a better and happier man than I') was an elementary teacher, in due course a head-master, and it was in his Green Lane School that the first school meals in Bradford, and possibly the country, were provided.[12] As a 'gentle, hopeful' kind of socialist, 'he did not want too much himself and hated to see others have too little', believed with H. G. Wells that 'we could educate ourselves out of muddle and wretchedness . . . into the sunlight forever', to which end he made speeches and sat on committees, filling his house with friends and colleagues, warm in argument over pipes and hot toddy.[13] As for Bradford itself, Priestley asserted, with pardonable exaggeration, that it was consid-ered 'the most progressive place in the United Kingdom'.[14] Arriving in the town in 1893, the socialist and educational reformer Margaret McMillan had found 'Social Democratic Federationers . . . Swedenborgians . . . old Chartist, Secularists', as well as the newly formed Independent Labour Party.[15] Bradford was one of the earliest cities in which the Labour move-ment became truly independent from liberalism as a political and ideological force. The ILP was founded in Bradford and throve there, partly because of the industrial conflicts in the woollen industry, partly because of the dominance of a reactionary local Liberal Party run by wealthy local Nonconformist employers such as Alfred Illingworth, who believed in financial retrenchment and, unlike Liberals elsewhere, made few concessions to working-class interests.[16] We have already encountered the local ILP paper, the *Bradford Pioneer*, where the young Priestley saw his first published work. From the 1880s, the cross-class alliance between middle-class liberals, radicals, Nonconformists and trade unionists which the Gladstonian Liberal Party represented was breaking down in Bradford, leading to a three-party politics in which ILP candidates polled strongly and won council seats. When Labour won the Bradford West parliamentary seat in 1906, a year of Lib-Lab alliances up and down the country, the successful candidate, Fred Jowett, unlike most of his colleagues, had to defeat a Liberal as well as a Conservative opponent. Years later Priestley wrote a Preface to Jowett's biography in which he demonstrated his own deep affinity to Bradford and its politics.[17]

Bradford was not only one of the most socialist, but one of the most Dissenting cities in the country. The 1851 religious census showed almost two-thirds of its worshippers attending Nonconformist chapels, and, although chapel-going had declined by Priestley's time, it was still the dominant religious tradition, and a vital part of Priestley's heritage.[18] Jonathan was an active member of Westgate Baptist Chapel, which was not only a place of worship but the 'great focal point' of the community.[19] Nonconformity was still a highly politicised culture, with an inbuilt inclination towards Liberalism, radicalism, and now socialism, and a tradition of democracy and popular activism. For men like Jonathan Priestley politics, religion and community could not be separated. As W. Haslam Mills, who came from a similar background in Ashton-under-Lyne, wrote, 'Public prayer with us took the form of a spirited and highly topical review of the field of contemporary events, all the more interesting because it was so allusive and oblique ... It was understood that God had read the *Manchester Guardian* that morning.'[20] Or as Priestley put it, 'they told Him what they expected from Him and more than hinted that He must attend to His work'. More to young Jack's taste than the interminable prayers and sermons were the weekdays when the Sunday School classrooms 'crackled or hummed with life ... sewing meetings, gymnastic classes for the young men, teas-and-concerts, lantern lectures, conjuring entertainments, and – best of all, the bazaars, which kept people busy for weeks and weeks and were then uproarious affairs for three or four nights'.[21] Writing in 1939, when organised religion seemed in terminal decline, he regretted – 'apart from all questions of belief' – the disappearance of this kind of church and chapel activity from people's lives, leaving them with a sense of detachment and loneliness.[22] Despite his unbelief, something of Westgate Chapel rubbed off on Priestley, in the form of a deep attachment to the idea of community, as well as an underlying, though often well-hidden, spirituality.

'All one lot of folk'

For Priestley socialism and dissent were part and parcel of a rich, democratic and self-sufficient cultural life, which is powerfully recreated in his
novel *Bright Day* (1946).[23] The novel's narrator, Gregory Dawson, is in
the 1940s a successful Hollywood scriptwriter. A familiar face and a piece
of music in a hotel dining-room bring flooding back memories of his
youth in 'Bruddersford', and a fragile Edwardian world doomed both by
the War and by more private catastrophes. Only by reconciling himself to
this past, in a narrative which moves between Edwardian Bruddersford
and the film industry of the 1940s, can Dawson resolve the impasse in his
present life and face his future. Although Dawson has much in common
with Priestley himself, *Bright Day* is more than just a slice of fictionalised
autobiography. It is a novel about time and memory, two of Priestley's
recurring preoccupations, and about cultural change: the two contrasting
cultural worlds, divided by the Great War, in which Dawson (like
Priestley) has lived, and which he must attempt in some way to reconcile
and exorcise through the act of remembering. Priestley the social-democratic reformer is the familiar figure with which *Bright Day* ends,
recouping Edwardian optimism in the spirit of 1945, but the novel merges
this figure with Priestley the Jungian mystic, reminding us that it is
memory, and the ever-present past of his lost Arcadia, which is the foundation stone of his social critique. It is this bringing together of Priestley's
two sides which makes *Bright Day* arguably his most accomplished novel
– and, as of 1962 at any rate, Priestley's own favourite.[24]

The novel's Bruddersford scenes evoke a rich cultural world of Free
Libraries, Playgoers' Societies, Hallé Orchestra concerts in the Gladstone
Hall, pantomime at the Theatre Royal and the 'brilliant Indian Summer of
a popular art' at the Imperial Music Hall[25] – a culture inhabited by a spectrum of Bruddersford society from the enchanting but doomed
middle-class Alington family to down-to earth Yorkshiremen in the nether
reaches of the wool trade. It is a deceptively cosmopolitan world, where
modest employees regularly journey to the other side of the globe to buy
and sell wool (Priestley himself went as a teenager to Belgium, Sweden,
Holland, Denmark, Germany), and where a Londoner was a stranger
sight than a German.[26] It is a world in which an uncouth insurance salesman turns out to be a virtuoso classical pianist, and a man speaking broad
Yorkshire gives up an office job in the wool trade to live in a cottage on
the moors and paint 'delicate and precise' landscapes 'in the grand old
tradition of the English water-colour'.[27] Socialism here means not class
warfare but, in the words of the socialist Councillor Knott, 'a chance for
workin' folk to enjoy life the right way – to see their families growin' up
fine and strong – to meet their friends and 'ave a talk and a laugh together
– to walk over the moors at the week-end – to read some books worth

reading – to go to a theatre or to listen to some music. Like John [Alington] and 'is family do 'ere ...'[28]

It is also, as we notice after a while, a world from which the manual working class is absent. All *Bright Day*'s down-to earth broad Yorkshiremen seem to be clerks, warehousemen, buyers, salesmen, small shopkeepers, and the middle-class ones merchants; there is not a Trade Unionist, a factory hand – or even a mill-owner – in sight. In other novels, the cultural life of Priestley's working-class characters – Jess Oakroyd in *The Good Companions*, or Charlie Habble in *Wonder Hero* – revolves around football, the pub and the Sunday scandal-sheet: no English water-colours or César Franck sonatas for them – or at least, not until Councillor Knott's socialist utopia comes about.

This absence is consistent with Priestley's political language, which speaks very little of class, much more of people, community and nation.[29] He regarded himself as 'a classless sort of man, whose work does not represent the outlook of any particular class', and he regarded privilege as a greater social evil than material inequality.[30] Not that he was unaware of class in the economic sense: he bitterly denounced poverty, exploitation and the gulf between rich and poor, and was hardly unaware of the poor housing conditions and industrial conflicts in his native city. But even bosses, he told a Newcastle Communist, could be regarded as prisoners of the system, 'honestly trying to do their duty'.[31] When he described Edwardian Bradford as almost 'a classless society', he was using class in cultural, not economic terms, just as, when he described it as democratic, he passed over the fact that most of its inhabitants could not vote. For him, Bradford was very nearly classless because although 'a few were rich, and a great many were very poor ... they were all one lot of folk, and Jack not only thought himself as good as his master but very often told him so'.[32] There are various reasons why, Priestley felt, 'the usual English class-consciousness did not thrive in Bradford'.

> The upper class was not represented there at all; so without an apex the social pyramid was not a firm structure. Manners were heartily democratic; gamblers on the wool market who suddenly made fortunes were still called Sam or Joe by characters who wore cloth caps and mufflers; they had to buy a title and acquire a mansion well away from Bradford to find deferential treatment ... Of course there were wide differences in what people could earn and spend, but these existed in an atmosphere of social democracy, familiar enough in America but rather rare in Edwardian England. Finally, in a city like this in the industrial North there was little of the class demar-cation by accent.[33]

This last point about accent is crucial, as is the passing reference to America: it is not just that the employers lived in the town and were part of its culture, but they spoke its language too, a language shared with those they employed, and not with the City or the country house. This may not have been a classless society, Priestley concluded, but it was nearer to one than any southerner can imagine; and when in later life he discovered the rest of the English class structure, 'with all its tangle of superiorities and inferiorities', his response was, and remained, 'bewildered ... half-amused, half-indignant'.[34]

Priestley was to project his vision of Bradford on to the nation. The ideal England he would evoke in wartime was not some proletarian paradise but 'all one lot of folk' writ large. In the industrial north, this populist radicalism had deep ideological roots. In *Visions of the People* (1991) Patrick Joyce has argued that underlying the social identity of the nineteenth-century industrial districts was a radical populist tradition 'conceiving of the true England as the industrial north in struggle with Privilege'.[35] The subject of this 'master narrative' is the destiny of the nation itself, bound up with that of 'the "true people" of England, those who have been excluded from their birthright. England and Providence became identified with the history, character and fate of "the people", and in many respects "the people" itself becomes the subject of the narrative, its travail forming the stuff of legend.' The discourse of radical populism can become a vehicle for class consciousness, and some may feel this was its proper line of development. But the preferred reading is of a broader, more inclusive social identity, which is at the same time radical. 'The likes of shopkeepers, teachers, employers and so on would have defined themselves, and been accepted, as part of the people.'[36] So it is with Priestley: the people – replete with 'strength, dignity and fine associations', and bound together by cultural rather than economic ties – are the point of reference, and the significant struggle is not so much between capital and labour – about which Priestley was always sceptical – as between the 'productive' and the 'unproductive' classes, with resonances in nineteenth-century liberalism that echo from John Stuart Mill's 'they grow rich as it were in their sleep' of 1848 to Joseph Chamberlain's 'they toil not neither do they spin' of 1885.[37] In the words of Walt Whitman, which Priestley was to quote during the War, 'everything comes out of the people', and 'we are all the people, so long as we are prepared to consider ourselves the people'.[38]

Priestley and socialism

Priestley certainly regarded himself as a socialist. 'A belief in some form of socialism', said Priestley, 'is not with me, as it is with many persons, an act of rebellion, but almost something belonging to tradition and filial piety.'[39] But his socialism owed little to class-consciousness, and even less to a belief in the benign power of the state. 'The root objection to Capitalism', he wrote, 'is that its values are all wrong, inhuman.'[40] Such 'ethical socialism' has long been a powerful current in the British left. As the ILP's historian has pointed out, the party's programme was always apt to stress community rather than class, and ethical sympathies before class interests.[41] Criticising the 'workerist' political strategy of some on the left, such as Fred Jowett, Priestley rejected the notion that 'socialism would be created solely by a working-class movement'.[42] The new Jerusalem would never be built under trade union rules, because unions are about making the best bargain within the existing system, not building a better one: they would be more inclined to pop in after the job had started to check that the wages and hours were all right. A true revolution would require creativity, gusto and commitment, not regulated hours and wages, and, for this, wider support than the working class and its organisations would be needed.[43] Moreover, it was from his own lower middle class, despite their obsession with respectability, and from the cultured minority of the upper middle class, that the most progressive ideas came.[44] The left especially needed the support of 'highly-trained technicians' who had a vision of a better society, and the enthusiasm and skill to build it. [45] If Fred Jowett had lived to see the 1945 election, Priestley suggested, he might have realised that only with such support could socialism advance.[46] But despite the rhetoric of Jowett and others, British socialism has never been based solely on the working class; middle-class recruits like Priestley's father, inspired by a public service ethic, have always played a vital role, believing, said his son, that 'there were more and more people like himself coming into the world, people who could be trusted to do their duty by the public that employed him, who did not need to be threatened with starvation or inspired by greed'.[47]

It is partly because of the strength of this public service ethic that socialism has invariably been seen as operating through the state. Here Priestley parted company with his father, who 'believed not only in government for the people by the people but also in production ... by the people for the people', and therefore could have happily tolerated living in a collectivist state.[48] Young Jack had been inclined to share this view: once everything was state-run, 'everybody would be knocking off about three o'clock, ready for folk-dancing, wood-carving, lectures on William Morris'.[49] In later life he changed his mind, leaning, he admitted, to the 'wilful individualism' of the writer, 'I set more store by independent lines of thought and by individual experiments in living' (a favourite Priestley phrase) than his father had done. There was, he acknowledged, an internal conflict between individualism and collectivism. 'By temperament, though not by conviction, I am strongly individualist, independent, perhaps a trifle wayward. In practice, though not in theory, I hate the herd instinct.'[50] As he described it in a 1935 radio talk, his ideal society was one with a minimal state, existing only to provide the basic necessities of life. Beyond this, work would be voluntary and motivated only by individual satisfaction and pleasing one's neighbours: no more financiers or politicians, no more class exploitation, bureaucratic oppression or mystical patriotism.[51] This is really a kind of anarchism – and not a very practical kind at that – but it reveals Priestley's deep belief in the individual creativity that lies within everyone – those fiddlers and water-colourists in *Bright Day* – if only it were allowed to flourish.[52]

Like a true radical, Priestley hated money-jugglers and rentiers, and valued people with skill and competence, people who made things, including ideas, relishing their grasp of the minutiae of the wool trade, electricity or engineering, and regarding it as the greatest crime when they are denied the opportunity of exercising their skills. As a writer, he regarded himself less as an artist than an artisan, a master of the technical problems of writing rather than one specially inspired by the muse: 'writers are not persons with the key to some magical backstairs, but are simply people who write'.[53] In the novel *Wonder Hero* we meet a character who personifies the productive/unproductive divide: Sir Edward Catterbird, a former civil engineer who has discovered a talent for financial manipulation and become wealthy. 'You can't make a big fortune by handling things or ideas, you can only do it by manipulating money, by usury and gambling', but 'there's a curse on usury and gambling, on all money-spinning'. Sir Edward ends up losing his mind; he should have stuck to building bridges.

If Priestley rejected both the class struggle and financial capitalism, he was equally resistant to the attractions of communism and the Soviet system. Although our dominant image of 'committed' writing in the 1930s comes from the communist-leaning 'Auden Group', Priestley, as we have already seen, was inclined to be dismissive of public-school Marxists, whose rhetoric of 'the masses' he considered dehumanising: 'any man who seriously considers himself one of the "masses" should go and put an end to his little insect existence'.[54] The Soviet Union no doubt had greater material equality, but, he suspected, this came at the cost of excessive privilege for the functionaries of party and state.[55] Moreover, he was not unaware that 'they have a habit there of liquidating persons, indeed, whole classes of persons, almost masses'.[56] His fictional communists – Kibworth in *Wonder Hero*, Blair in *They Walk in the City* – as well as Bob, a real one, in *English Journey* – are sympathetically drawn, but narrow, naive and unimaginative, their politics an understandable but mistaken response to social evils, and wilfully or stupidly blind to the real nature of the Soviet Union.[57]

Lost Arcadia

Bright Day gets its title from a line in Shakespeare's *Julius Caesar*: 'It is the bright day that brings forth the adder'. The Nixeys' arrival in

Bruddersford announces the doom not just of John Alington's firm and family but of a whole bright world. If pastoral is about a past state of peace and harmony, and a simpler, more authentic life, then Priestley's account of provincial culture before the Great War could be called an urban pastoral. And as with all pastorals, the world it yearns for is lost, and perhaps never existed. Priestley left Bradford when he joined the army at the age of twenty in 1914, and never settled back there again. For him, as for many of his generation, the war was a 'smoking canyon' which separated him from his youth: especially as, while he enlisted early on, most of his boyhood friends joined up later, in the Bradford 'Pals' Battalion, and were massacred on 1 July 1916, the first day of the Battle of the Somme, 'killed by greed and muddle and monstrous cross-purposes, by old men gobbling and roaring in clubs, by diplomats working underground like monocled moles, by journalists wanting a good story, by hysterical women waving flags, by grumbling debenture-holders, by strong silent be-ribonned asses, by fear or apathy or downright lack of imagination'.[58] When he wrote these words he was not yet forty, but 'sometimes I feel like a very old man ... I have many vivid dreams, and the dead move casually through them'.[59] Only when he was in his late sixties could he bring himself to write directly of his wartime experiences, to bridge the gap between before and after.

After the War, 'we had to move into a world largely alien to the English temperament'.

> The [Edwardian] age somehow created an atmosphere in which English genius, talent, generosity of mind, could flourish ... an atmosphere of hopeful debate which never survived the great War ... And something alien, belonging in a new spirit – harshly derisive, intolerant, arrogant, ultimately dehumanising – already breaking through from 1910 onwards, could still be softened, intuitively transmuted, by the English temperament ... .There is illusion here, of course, but it is not all a cheat: something *did* go, something *was* lost.[60]

Even so, Priestley never fully bought into what Samuel Hynes has called 'The Myth of the War', 'that the world before the war was a lost Eden ... [and] that the world after the war was a ruined place, where dishonourable forces had triumphed'.[61] He was fully aware of the deficiencies of the old society: a class system that was designed to keep the common people in their place, with a 'shallow, self-indulgent, stupid' ruling class, and a working class not much better, all in thrall to an arrogant and boastful imperialism.[62] What had gone wrong since the war was a closing down of possibilities rather than the destruction of a lost Eden. This 'hopeful debate' is what Priestley meant when he said that Britain had been closer to true democracy in 1912 than it was in 1939, and that, if the war had not happened, 'it is certain that I should be writing, if at all, about another and better England'. After 1918, 'the ranks of privileged persons closed up and common people had to keep their distance'.[63] But there must have been something rotten at the heart of the old society, or else there would not have been a war. 'I believe that many of us, all young, had a feeling, never put into words, that a time was running out, that *something was coming to an end.*'[64]

The same feeling informs two of Priestley's best-known plays, which, far from wallowing in nostalgia, reveal the defects of Edwardian society, and show that it was those internal problems, not just the War, which ended the illusion of a golden age. *An Inspector Calls*, set in 1912, was written in 1945–46, and was very much of that moment, and so will be discussed in a later chapter. *When We Are Married* (1938), one of Priestley's best-loved and most-performed plays, is at one level a knock-about Yorkshire farce, complete with drunken photographer (played in several performances by Priestley himself) and a knowing, disrespectful housemaid straight out of the Figaro tradition. Set in 1908, it concerns three middle-aged couples from the aldermanic ruling elite of a Yorkshire town similar to Bradford, who gather to celebrate their joint silver wedding, only to discover that they were never properly married in the first place. Priestley presented it as a 'Yorkshire Farcical Comedy', which he enjoyed writing because he could plunder his memories of Bradford life and manners.[65] But, as Judith Cook wisely observes, 'Priestley comedies are purposeful'.[66] What we see here, should we choose to look beneath the broad comedy, and the affectionately drawn complacent pomposity of the characters, is respectable post-Victorian society rotting in its very core, the institution of marriage itself.

Like *Bright Day*, *Lost Empires*, published in 1965, has a Bruddersfordian as its main character, but is set in a darker version of the rootless theatrical world of *The Good Companions*. *Lost Empires*, which Priestley described as a symbolic rather than a sentimental narrative, is set in the months leading up to the outbreak of war in 1914, and the 'Empires' of the title could be the Edwardian political world or the variety theatres which bore that name – both of them doomed.[67] Richard Herncastle takes a job as assistant to his uncle, who is a successful illusionist on the variety stage. The story follows them on their tours up to the outbreak of war, when Richard announces his intention to enlist, and Uncle Nick, disgusted, goes off to America to make a fortune in munitions. For Priestley, music-hall artistes stand for a lost world of authentic popular culture, and stage magicians, paradoxically, stand for honesty – honest deceit. 'Doctors and lawyers and politicians and financiers. What are they doing half their time? Tricks – pulling the rabbit out of the hat – sawing the lady in two – asking you to watch their right hands while their left hands are making your money disappear – and not telling you anything about it. We're honest. We tell you.' So says the conjurer Alf in *They Walk in the City*.[68] So too says Uncle Nick: 'I'm an honest illusionist ... not like these big illusionists in Westminster, Whitehall and the City, expensive bloody hypocrites'.[69] His illusions work by misdirecting the audience's attention, but Uncle Nick's attention does not stray: 'I earn a living by deceiving other people, but I don't have to deceive myself', he declares, when denouncing the sentimental rituals of Christmas.[70] The tricks with flags which he introduces into his act when war finally comes are nothing more than 'children's party conjuring', the enthusiasm of the audience a sign that we are headed for the madhouse.[71] So the brutal but honest Uncle Nick is the one who can see things coming: he knows there will be war, that it will be bloodier than people think, that it will be no good for old Europe, and that America will be the place to be. But his immunity to deception also leaves him deaf to 'the magical element in life ... all the enchantments of love and art'.[72]

Some, at least, of this symbolism is to do with society in 1914 and its imminent destruction, not just by war but by forces from within. Through the novel's intricate plot of suicide, murder and doomed love, the dark sense of foreboding builds up, more and more sinister characters and events enter the scene. The central figure of the illusionist, Uncle Nick, is the one who can see where things are headed, but he has paid the price in lost enchantment; meanwhile, everyone else, like his audience, takes pleasure in having their attention directed elsewhere.

Priestley was quite right to say that there was much more than nostalgia in his elegiac accounts of the Edwardian age.[73] What he took away from Edwardian Bradford was a sense of society, of history, of politics, which lay fallow for a while, but from the end of the 1920s, when he found fame and a public platform, became increasingly important. We must not forget that he had got his start as a writer in the socialist *Bradford Pioneer*, nor that, to the bafflement of his literary biographers, he had switched direction at Cambridge from English to Modern History and Political Science.[74] From the early 1930s, his novels, as well as his non-fiction, became increasingly, though not exclusively, vehicles for his social concerns: society, as he later said, should be the main character in the modern novel.[75] The broad historical narrative which underlies much of this social and political critique is very much that of Joyce's provincial radicals. It is a narrative of local and regional autonomy superseded by the dominance of London, and by the kind of capitalism for which London stands: financial as opposed to productive capitalism, 'this money-lending England', as he put it in *English Journey*.[76] It is a story, ultimately, of globalisation, in which the national is superseded by the blandly international, a phenomenon which he observed with some acuity in its early stages. But it is also a story of solidly democratic, cross-class communities betrayed by the greed and social ambition of their leaders; a national ruling class surviving well past its usefulness; a people whose attention was increasingly diverted by shallow amusements and hollow consumerism. 'Their lives were narrow,' he says of the Edwardian working class, 'but somehow they contrived to bring to them a great deal of zest, humour, innocent excitement.'[77] As one of his characters in *They Walk in the City*, himself a former music-hall performer, laments, 'That war did something. It's never been the same since. There isn't the fun and the easiness and the character. Too many machines. Too much of this American stuff.'[78] All these motifs we will encounter in the rest of this chapter, and the rest of the book, as we chart the development of Priestley's social and political engagement in the 1930s.

English journeys

We begin with a book which, for most readers, is anything but a political tract – and so much the better, most of them would say. *The Good Companions*, Priestley said, was a fairytale, albeit set against a realistic backdrop.[79] This is not entirely true, or fair to the book. It contains fairy-tale events, and happy if not fairytale endings, and it has no overt social or political axe to grind. But the starting-point of the book is real enough for its time: each of its three main characters has suffered in some way the dislocations of the age. Jess Oakroyd, the Bruddersford working man, has lost his job, his favourite daughter and now he thinks – mistakenly – his reputation. Miss Trant, thirty-seven, and possibly 'on the shelf' after spending fifteen years looking after her father, who has now died, has let the family home, sold its contents and driven off into the distance in search of the rest of her life. Inigo Jollifant, a drifting young Cambridge graduate, trying to be a writer but better at playing the piano, has just been dismissed from his job at a very minor prep school, somewhat like Paul Pennyfeather in Evelyn Waugh's *Decline and Fall*. Only when the three fortuitously link up with each other, and with the failing concert party the Dinky Doos, can they become functioning members of a community again – albeit a temporary, mobile and often fractious one. Each is able to find a way of being useful to that community, and re-estab-lishes within it the meaningful social relationships which have eluded him or her in normal life. In the end the touring concert party becomes their route back into settled life; but for each of them it is a very different life from the one they left behind. As for happy endings, only Miss Trant, who discovers an old flame and gets married, could be said to achieve one unequivocally. Inigo doesn't get the girl, and Jess, while he is reunited with his daughter, has to emigrate to Canada and leave his beloved Bruddersford United behind.

But let us not be too snooty about happy endings, or about the novel's many coincidences: they come with the picaresque genre, and, in any case, sad ones would not change the novel's message much. Like many mainstream 1920s novels, *The Good Companions* deals with social and cultural dislocation and its effect on the individual. The Great War is not mentioned: a singular fact, because everybody in the book must have been touched by it in some way. But this absence reflects Priestley's oblique approach to the War and his own experiences in it, which he did not deal with directly in print until after 1945. In any case, the War was in many ways a symbol of wider and deeper disruptions which were under way before war broke out. A typical, but very different, novel of the 1920s which dealt with these individual experiences of loss and disruption is Warwick Deeping's best-selling *Sorrell and Son* (1925).[80] In this novel an ex-army officer down on his luck, unemployed and abandoned by his unfaithful wife, engages in an intensely individualistic struggle to carve out a future for himself and his son. *Sorrell and Son* restates Victorian middle-class values of personal responsibility and social and sexual hierarchy almost to the point of parody, and certainly beyond that of plausibility, but it is not difficult to see its appeal to middle-class readers who were anxious about modernity. The war was the least of their worries: they also had to contend with anxieties about the rise of Labour, the insubordination of the working class, the emancipation of women, the rise of modernism and the questioning of hitherto-accepted social and moral values.

Sorrell and Son seems to confirm Bracco's view that the role of best-sellers in the 1920s was to combat these dangers, 'to provide reassuring explanations of the present reality, and to counteract the disturbing developments of the modern world by re-asserting well-established values and attitudes' by upholding traditional attitudes and values in a modern context, providing their readers with a reassuring sense of continuity with the past.[81] Many of these readers came from the lower middle class of white-collar clerical and administrative workers, sales people, small businessmen, minor professionals, who had been growing in numbers since the 1870s. This group had never experienced stability: status anxiety was endemic in them, an unavoidable consequence of their 'betwixt and between' position in society.[82] As with Priestley's father, their social detachment and extended education could make them natural recruits for socialism (one thinks of H. G. Wells) – or alternatively, they could swing the other way, their anxieties expressed in fear of the mob, of the working class, of immigrants, emancipated women, intellectuals, making them the *Daily Mail* and *Daily Express* readers of the 1920s and 1930s, and the mainstay of the Conservative supremacy of those years. They had been satirised by the Grossmith brothers in *Diary of a Nobody*, and their fears had been vividly described by the Liberal journalist Charles Masterman in 1911:

> He has difficulty with the plumber in jerry-built houses needing continuous patching and mending. His wife is harassed by the indifference or insolence

of the domestic servant ... He would never be surprised to find the crowd
behind the red flag, surging up his little pleasant pathways, tearing down the
railings, trampling the little garden.[83]

The Good Companions addresses the issue of dislocation, but it does so
in a completely different way, and with the opposite political implications, from Deeping's novel. Dislocation is not blamed on the stock
bogeymen of lower middle-class nightmares and the *Daily Mail*, but
comes in some obscure way out of the uncertainties of the age. The 'happy
endings' do not offer the reassurance that everything can still be the same
as it was in 1900, rather that people can move on; nor does this happen
through the fiercely individualistic striving of *Sorrell*. Instead, they find a
microcosmic community to belong to, and make themselves useful in it. In
a short piece written in his eightieth year Priestley acknowledged that
what he had really always wanted was 'to be a member of a small intimate
community of persons who, though individually they may have separate
strong interests ... happily share a great deal of common ground'.[84] In
Bright Day the jaded and bitter screenwriter Gregory Dawson is rejuve-
nated when he throws in his lot with a new independent film group,
recreating the sense of being part of just such a small, creative community
which he had experienced, years earlier, with the Alington family – itself
modelled on families and groups whose inner life Priestley had envied in
his Bradford youth.[85] This recognition of interdependence between the
individual and the collective, and the creation, or re-creation of community, whether on this face-to-face scale or at the level of a town or even
the nation, became an increasingly powerful theme in Priestley's writing,
paving the way towards his popular wartime collectivism. It makes *The
Good Companions* something more than the mere 'fairytale' of Priestley's
apologia.

The eponymous concert party of *The Good Companions* is a travelling,
rootless community. Postwar England is no longer a nation in which you
have a fixed social and geographical place, like Arnold Bennett's Five
Towns, but a shifting backdrop to your search for one, revealed in the
book through a series of local vignettes – some cosy, some not, like the
depressed and depressing failed industrial town of Tewborough, depicted
in the language of dereliction that will be mobilised again for *English
Journey*.[86] Travel became part of the Priestley repertoire: already in 1932
the London and North Eastern Railway was promising to 'bring you to
Priestley's England'.[87] In March 1929, *The Good Companions* written
but not yet published, Priestley began a series for the *Sunday Dispatch*
entitled 'I Want to Know' in which he travelled around Britain, as his
characters had done, and reported on what he had seen: the series may
even have been a by-product of his research for the novel. But what he
'wanted to know' was whether Nottingham really was 'crammed with
pretty girls', and whether Wigan really did have a pier. He may have

beaten Orwell to the punch with his discovery that Wigan 'has an undoubted flair for the ugly', but the tone of the articles is bland and joky, and they say little of the problems that places like Wigan were already experiencing in the late 1920s.[88] Nevertheless, 'I Want to Know' marked a significant shift from essays and sketches towards the reportage which would come to dominate his writing later in the 1930s.

But for the time being it was the novels which led the way into a deeper social critique. When *The Good Companions* made him famous, Priestley was already working on his next book, *Angel Pavement*, published in the summer of 1930.[89] By now, the trade depression was deepening and turning into the Slump, and this book is altogether a more gritty affair than its predecessor, implying far more strongly 'all the social criticism directly stated in my later non-fiction books'.[90] Once again, rootlessness and insecurity are key themes. *Angel Pavement* concerns the impact on a small City of London firm, and those who work for it, of a crooked adventurer, Golspie, who arrives in London from nowhere in particular, and in the space of a few months comes to dominate and reinvigorate the firm, and then robs and ruins it, departing at the end of the story to South America. While *The Good Companions* is a novel of escape, for the characters in *Angel Pavement* there is no escape: as Priestley put it, 'They are victims of circumstance and they have little to enjoy but the bitter though not unrefreshing brew that a sense of irony can offer'.[91] At the end they all lose their jobs, and, although one way or another most of them have learned something from the experience, this could not be described as a happy ending, especially in 1930 with unemployment rising, and 'boys ... lining up in their hundreds for the chance of a mere beginning at ten shillings a week'.[92] In contrast to *The Good Companions* which was far too cheerful for sophisticated tastes, *Angel Pavement* was criticised by some for its negativity.[93] Although it contains comic passages and much Priestleian wit, it is difficult to see how George Orwell, still writing as Eric Blair, and perhaps not yet attuned to the book's social critique, could describe this story of wrecked lives as 'genuinely gay and pleasant', and mainly intended to set forth 'the romance of London'.[94] Whether it lacked beauty, profundity and humour, as Orwell judged, may be open to debate; his review was for the highbrow *Adelphi*, and no doubt told the readers what they wanted to hear: as Orwell's biographer notes, 'Priestley-baiting was a popular literary parlour-game' in such circles.[95]

The characters who work at Twigg and Dersingham are depicted in the round, some fully equipped with homes, families, friends, pastimes, and others who lack these things feeling their absence. In other words, although scattered about London's residential districts, they are rooted, or want to be. Golspie, on the other hand, is rootless: he has a daughter but no wife is mentioned, and we are told nothing of his past: 'I don't live anywhere. That's me', he declares 'with a kind of grim relish' on arriving in London, like a buccaneer sailing into harbour.[96] Like the Nixeys, who disrupt the lives and business of the gentle and decent Alingtons in *Bright Day*, Golspie represents the 'rootless, parasitic and acquisitive' forms of late capitalism, which enter the scene before 1914 as a 'tiny fifth column' but by 1946 would have become a 'familiar army of occupation'. [97] By contrast Twigg and Dersingham, dealers in furniture inlays and veneers, are, like John Alington, representative of an older, fixed and located form of capitalism, with a stable relationship with their workers and their customers, but vulnerable to being looted by the money-juggling, predatory forces that are now loose in the world. But those veneers in which Twigg and Dersingham deal are more than a little symbolic. Beneath the surface the firm and the system it represents – though not its ordinary employees – are in a bad way, and bear some responsibility for their own vulnerability. Dersingham, the firm's owner, is the typical image of gentlemanly ineptitude – an ex-army officer from a second-rate public school, who inherited the business from his uncle, and is unable to take decisions or do anything at the denouement other than deny responsibility for what has happened – denying even that his cashier, Smeeth (a man far more dedicated to the firm) has warned him against Golspie. 'He thinks he's a gentleman amusing himself', says Golspie, 'Too many of his sort in the City here'.[98] Dersingham may deserve to lose out, but do Smeeth and the others? On his way home after losing his job, Smeeth reflects bitterly not on the guilty individuals but on the system: 'You go on for years and years building up a position for yourself until at last you have a place of your own, a little world of your own ... if this is what could happen at any minute? My God – what was the good of it all?' 'Not good enough,' he repeats to himself, 'not good enough.'[99]

In *Sorrell and Son* all problems and their solutions are seen as individual. The system is unchallengeable, because invisible: carping about it is for Bolsheviks and weaklings, you have to get on with your life. The characters in *Angel Pavement*, the ordinary people who are at the heart of the book, are individuals, and no doubt they will do their best to get on with their lives as individuals must. But the firm is a microcosm of the nation: between inept rulers and predatory speculators, ordinary people have to take their chances. Priestley is quite clear where the blame lies: not in petty crooks like Golspie but in the system that opens the way for the Golspies and Nixeys. It is not capitalism as such that is the problem but capitalism gone wrong – as he was to write at the other end of the 1930s, 'favouring England the money-lender, the receiver of interest from all parts of the world, at the expense of the other England, the producer, the manufacturer, trader'. This tendency was not only 'against the general happiness of the English people' but was 'partly responsible for the present lethargic and uncreative mood of the country'.[100] 'Not good enough', as Smeeth would say. Priestley's voice, if not Smeeth's, is that of industrial radicalism: the productive classes against the unproductive, an ideal of settled communities rooted in making and trading, set against the fluidity and insecurity of internationalised financial capitalism, with a hint of anti-imperialism thrown in. *Angel Pavement* is not a work of political or economic analysis, and it proposes no solution to the problems it highlights, but, by acknowledging their existence, and suggesting that things could be otherwise, it sets itself apart from the supposed reassuring conservatism of the stereotypical 'middlebrow' novel. It announces Priestley's engagement with the social and political issues of his time, which was to continue for the rest of his life.

Angel Pavement points the way towards the central work of Priestley's 1930s, and arguably of his whole career: *English Journey* (1934), a book which will continue to resonate through this study, especially in the next two chapters, for what it has to say about national identity and the experience of modernity. Here I will look at it chiefly as one of the cluster of works in which Priestley responded to the deepening social, economic and political crisis of the 1930s. But first we need to establish what kind of book it was.

Priestley's first non-fiction, non-literary book (unless we count essay collections) was promoted as a major publishing event, just as if it was his latest novel. The *Bookseller* reported a publicity campaign of 'unprecedented scale' in advance of the book's publication in April 1934, including 'what must be a record advertisement display for any single book' in the Sunday papers, featuring quotes from the provincial newspapers, who had already responded to the book's local and regional appeal with extensive coverage – in the case of the *Birmingham Gazette*, for example, a leader, a feature article and a news column on the day of publication.[101] *English Journey* rose almost immediately to the top of the *Bookseller*'s best-seller list (overtaking P. G. Wodehouse's *Thank You Jeeves*), where it remained for much of the summer. By 1956 Heinemann and Gollancz, who published *English Journey* jointly, had sold 96,000 hardback copies, making it Priestley's best-selling book in that format between *Angel Pavement* in 1930 and *Bright Day* in 1946, a period during which he wrote eight novels.[102] It has rarely been out of print since its publication, and has been not only a popular read but a standard source for social historians of the 1930s, featuring in numerous footnotes, bibliographies and student reading lists. Later writers have referenced it, alluded to it, and queued up to re-enact it.[103]

This esteem, however, does not mean that there is any universal agreement as to how the book should be read. Reviews quoted on the 1934 dust-jacket saw it variously as socio-political documentary ('brings home ... the shameful condition in which millions of the English people are now living' - Robert Lynd in the *News Chronicle*); as *Good Companions* part two ('full of amusing characters, unexpected happenings, shrewd, humorous and racy' - *Harper's Bazaar*); as personal testimony ('a thrilling tour with an incomparable guide' - *Daily Herald*); and as an evocation of cosy Englishness ('gives a fair and rounded picture of contemporary England ... its people and its landscape, its towns and country' – Howard Spring in the *Evening Standard*). Denys Thompson, in the Leavisite *Scrutiny*, described the book as 'one large sop for the complacent', by which he meant that Priestley had failed to parrot the *Scrutiny* line on popular entertainment.[104] Historians have tended to read *English Journey* alongside *The Road to Wigan Pier*, as a work of social investigation, bringing together the Slump with the emerging consumerist England. Angus Calder, however, describes the book as a 'popular travelogue', establishing Priestley's 'credentials as a sturdy patriot' through its 'celebration of English landscape and character'.[105] As this verdict shows, it is still possible to read *English Journey* (though somewhat perversely, I would argue) as one of the deluge of cosy English travel books which poured from the presses in the 1930s and are now found in profusion on the shelves of the second-hand bookshops.

I suggest that there are three plausible approaches to reading *English Journey*, each of which will be explored in this and the next two chapters. It can be seen as a study of England and the English character; as an exploration of twentieth-century modernity and its impact; or as a social-reforming stepping-stone on the 'road to 1945'. As this range of choice suggests, it is a useful feature of travel narrative that the writer can turn it to a whole range of different purposes, all the while protesting that they are doing no more than simply describing what they saw and where they went. So it is with *English Journey*. The book has no introductory declaration of the journey's aims. Nor is there a giveaway title: Priestley is not on the road to anywhere (e.g. Wigan Pier), nor is he going in search of anything (e.g. England): he's just journeying. The book's extended and somewhat arch subtitle almost warns us off having any preconceived ideas as to what it may be about:

> Being a rambling but truthful account of what one man saw and heard and felt and thought during a journey through England during the Autumn of the year 1933.

This deliberate archaism implicitly (and disingenuously) tells us not to expect too much in the way of structure and purpose: this is not a sociological survey, simply a truthful account of a journey. Priestley himself we are invited to regard as an honest Everyman, just accurately recording and honestly responding to what he sees. The self-deprecating 'rambling' leads us to expect the artlessness which guarantees authenticity but demurs at drawing challenging conclusions. We may be in for an amusing time, but we mustn't expect to learn too much.

Priestley seems to confirm this when he begins the book merely by

telling us where he is going first and what he takes with him. Having no
destination but 'England', where he already is, he boards a motor coach
for Southampton, on no stronger grounds than that that is where many
visitors arrive in England. This opening section which describes his
journey there seems composed of chance encounters and rambling reflections.[106] He is astonished at the coach's comfort, which he compares to
that of the new picture-palaces: in travel as in pleasure, provided you have
just a little money, the distinction between rich and poor has been anni-
hilated. He looks out of the window at West London, and the new Great
West Road – looking more Californian than English – and at the line of
new factories on either side, not 'real' factories, built of brick with a
chimney at the corner, but pretty glass and concrete façades with painted
signs and coloured lights, housing little luxury trades, the new industries
that have moved south. But how pleasant it would be if we could all work
there. And then he starts a conversation with a fellow-passenger: a down-
at-heel but ever-optimistic small businessman, looking for an 'opening':
tea-rooms (no good, on account of the Slump), hairdressing, electric light,
wireless (all booming now). Depressed Newcastle isn't doing the business
it once did. All over, big companies are cutting out the small man. The
coach stops at Winchester, where the businessman gets off: these small
cathedral cities, how attractive they are, but who could spend a whole day
there without getting bored? And then off into the Hampshire countryside, so redolent of England, so lovely to look at, yet so incapable of
earning its living.

Inconsequential and artless these first few pages may appear, but how
many of the themes of *English Journey* are foreshadowed in them? North
and south, the shifting economic geography of England, the rise of
consumer goods and services, the Slump and the decline of heavy industry, the rise of corporate capitalism and the decline of the small business,
the cultural impact of new technologies, Americanisation, the democratisation of culture, English identity, 'old England', its landscapes and towns
and its irrelevance to the modern world: Priestley's England summarised.
All these themes crop up again and again through the book, and are
drawn together in its conclusion. If Orwell in *The Road to Wigan Pier*
makes his agenda clear by thrusting the squalor of poverty straight into
our faces at the start of chapter one, Priestley sets his out in a few random
glances through a motor-coach window and a desultory conversation
with a stranger.[107]

English Journey, like any other travelogue, presents us with two narratives: a story about a journey, and a story about the place the journey
passes through. The first story is carefully constructed by the route that
Priestley, apparently randomly, decides to follow. He begins in the soft
south, whereupon he prepares himself for what is to come, and makes it
very clear what the central motivation of the book is: 'I know there is deep

distress in the country. I have seen some of it, just a glimpse of it, already, and I know there is far, far more ahead of me.'[108] Proceeding through the relatively prosperous industrial midlands to his own West Riding, shaken but still standing, to Lancashire, its cotton industry in collapse, he finally hits the climax of the book in the dereliction and despair of the north-east, which completely overshadows and trivialises the bucolic charm of the 'heritage' route back to London via York, Lincoln, Norwich and Cambridge. But before he gets there he has already laid down a set of themes and ideas which he will mobilise in analysing and explaining their situation: themes such as industrialism and anti-industrialism, beauty and ugliness, the nature of work, popular culture, civic culture, social inequality.

By the end of the book, in the remarkable concluding chapter, he is ready to declare his second, larger narrative, a historical one. This is a narrative about north and south, about industry and finance, about the productive and the unproductive, about the drawing of wealth away from those who produce it, and about the concealment of all this beneath a carapace of traditions and institutions that are identified with the nation. This is a theme for which his readers are by now thoroughly prepared. In Bradford, Hull, Gateshead he has deplored the decay of the civic culture of his Edwardian urban Arcadia:

> The richer merchants and manufacturers [of Bradford] no longer live in the city. They work there, but live well outside ... Throughout the north ... the wealthier industrialists are busy turning themselves into country gentlemen and are leaving the cities to the professional, clerking and working classes ... When I was a boy, we had certain wealthy families of manufacturers who came as near to forming an aristocracy as such a democratic community as ours would allow. Now they are gone, and their places have not been taken by other families. That chapter is closed.[109]

Similarly, the substantial citizens of Hull have moved out into the countryside, leaving the town's cultural life to those too poor to support it properly; while 'if anybody ever made money in Gateshead, they must have taken great care not to spend any of it in the town'.[110] In what is arguably the book's climactic moment Priestley gazes on the giant slag-heap of the Durham pit-village of Shotton and muses on

> all the fine things that had been conjured out of it in its time, the country houses and town houses, the drawing-rooms and dining-rooms, the carriages and pairs, the trips to Paris, the silks and the jewels, the peaches and iced puddings, the cigars and old brandies; I thought I saw them all tumbling and streaming out, hurrying away from Shotton – oh, a long way from Shotton – as fast as they could go.[111]

But Priestley is writing in 1934: the Slump is at its worst. The problems of industrial England were more immediate than the abiding 'filth and ugliness' that had been laid down in the Industrial Revolution, or even the desertion of those who had profited from it. In those who were left behind, Priestley found another England, 'the England of the dole', where everything that had made nineteenth-century industrial England not just bearable but even a source of pride and identity had been left to rot: 'it is not being added to and has no new life poured into it'.[112] Here were men rendered useless through no fault of their own, their self-respect in shreds, 'their very manhood' going under.[113] Priestley visits Bradford for a bois- terous regimental reunion, a scene 'alive with roaring masculinity', only to find that some of his old comrades could not even attend, unable to afford decent clothes and too proud to appear without them. These men had been heroes in the war, but heroism had been undercut by a postwar life which left 'their manhood stunted, their generous impulses baffled'.[114] The War, the collapse of 'real men's work' in shipbuilding or mining, the decline of the civic public sphere: all amount to the collapse of an old masculine world. Young men of this generation, he has heard, are far less enterprising than the girls; perhaps, he muses later, 'masculine pig-head- edness' is part of the problem, and we will have to turn to women for an answer.[115]

Throughout the north, he has found the same: a series of personal tragedies which adds up to a collective national tragedy. What is to be done? Priestley acknowledges that he is no economist, but he can see that the dole is a palliative, not a solution: it will not bring these people and their communities back to life. So there must be a plan – what kind of plan he is not sure, but something constructive and creative, involving the whole nation. 'The whole thing is unworthy of a great country that in its time has given the world some nobly creative ideas. We ought to be ashamed of ourselves.'[116] But he is fairly sure who is to blame for all this, and his answer refers us back to the repertoire of provincial radicalism. Why is the City still doing so well, 'treated as if it were the very beating red heart of England'? It must have got its money from somewhere – in large part from the toil of the industrial north, which it bled dry and now abandoned to its fate, doing to it 'what the black-moustached glossy gentleman in the old melodrama always did to the innocent village maiden'.[117]

If *English Journey* encompasses the nation as a totality, that totality has an absent centre: London. Although the capital is where he starts out from, apart from glimpses of the western suburbs it is rarely mentioned; significantly, when he returns home at the end of the book, his car crawls into London through thick fog, through which nothing can be seen. But London is present throughout *English Journey* a distorting and parasitic force on the rest of the country. Before the War, it was not like this. In the north there had been 'a kind of regional self-sufficiency, not defying London but genuinely indifferent to it'. His father, he remembers, rarely saw a national newspaper: he read the Bradford-based *Yorkshire Observer*, and occasionally C. P. Scott's *Manchester Guardian*. 'What happened "down south", outside politics, was no concern of his.'[118] Despite moving to London, living and working there for much of his life and developing a great deal of affection for the city, Priestley remained deeply suspicious of London's influence on the national life, which he considered to have increased, and not to the good, since 1914. Above all, London stood for the 'moneylending England' which was bleeding the north dry – 'For generations, this blackened North toiled and moiled so that England should be rich and the City of London a great power in the world' – and its geographical proximity to political power: 'The City is much too near Westminster,' he later wrote, 'they can hear each other talking.'[119]

Denys Thompson, reviewing *English Journey* in *Scrutiny*, couldn't imagine why Priestley wasted time fiddling about in Cotswold pubs while on the Tees and Tyne there were perfectly good slums waiting to be described.[120] I hope we can now see why Priestley's journey had to cover the whole of England, and not just the 'depressed areas'. His interpretation of the Slump, and of everything about 1930s England, is holistic, and historical. In the conclusion, famously, he identifies 'three Englands' – 'Old' rural, 'Nineteenth Century' industrial and 'New' consumerist – not separate places on the map, but successive layers of national history: crudely speaking, agrarian, industrial and consumer capitalism, representing in Raymond Williams's terms, the residual, the dominant and the emergent Englands of the 1930s.[121] History is uneven, and these phases did not succeed each other in an orderly procession but overlapped, interacted and lingered on, 'variously and fascinatingly mingled in every part of the country I had visited'.[122] It is by understanding this 'mingling', the interplay between these 'Englands', that we can understand the multiple, unevenly developing and contradictory nation Priestley saw in 1933 – the product of its uneven and contradictory history. In seeking a way forward, Priestley develops themes of community and social responsibility, the importance of self-respect, the unequal relationship between wealth-creators and money-jugglers, and the nation as a single community with shared responsibility for all its members. This is why his central, indignant question about England in 1933 is not 'why are these people so poor', but 'Was Jarrow still in England or not?'

A fashion for fact

Significantly *English Journey* was commissioned by the left-wing publisher Victor Gollancz, who went on to publish Orwell's *The Road to Wigan Pier* and to underwrite Mass Observation's work, and the book was published by Gollancz jointly with Priestley's regular publisher, Heinemann. In its social-democratic impulse, and its attempt to create or contribute to a public sphere of debate, *English Journey* can be seen as part of the 1930s shift towards social documentation which affected a wide range of media from journalistic and fictional writing to photography, radio and cinema, and embraced projects like Mass Observation and magazines such as *Picture Post*. In the 1920s, at odds with the prevailing atmosphere of modernist experimentation, Priestley had stuck out like a prematurely aged leftover from 1900. Now his increasing politicisation and engagement with social issues was converging with the new documentary trend, and he was suddenly up to date, with a whole new persona as a serious commentator on society and current affairs. As the title of one of his review articles in 1934 declared: 'Fact is now the fashion, but it must be disguised as fiction'.[123] But just as the 'documentary impulse', when closely examined, tends to fragment into a number of diverse and conflicting trends, so Priestley's relationship to this new wave was a complicated one.

In 1934, when *English Journey* was published, the documentary impulse was only just getting going. Key developments such as Mass Observation (founded in 1937) and the photojournalism of *Picture Post* (1938) – for which Priestley himself was to write – were still in the future. Moreover, there were other, less political, impulses in the wind, which were also feeding the appetite for domestic travelogues, the 'fashion for fact', as Priestley and his publisher were surely aware. The new domesticity of the 1930s expressed itself in an unprecedented demand for books about England, ranging from the rather cosy travelogues of H. V. Morton and others to the many guide books which announced the arrival on the scene of the motoring public.[124] And even politically engaged 'state of the nation' books could be conservative in tone: for example those of Priestley's fellow Heinemann author Philip Gibbs, whose *European Journey* was intended as a companion piece to Priestley's. Books like Morton's, and most other investigations of English landscape and character, were also conservative in their depiction of the nation, reaffirming its pre-industrial heritage rather than challenging its current condition. [125] What this suggests is that in the early 1930s the impulse to document and describe the nation was politically ambivalent, just as likely to come up with a conservative and backward-looking redefinition of England as with demands for political and social reform. Priestley's book, a direct response to the Slump, was anything but cosy and reassuring about the state of the nation, but its success also reflects the 'fashion for fact' amongst a middle-class, suburban reading public – the novel-readers to whom *English Journey* was so energetically promoted, and at whom the blander reviews were aimed. But Priestley was determined to go beyond the bland expectations of these readers.

Later in the decade, over beer and ham sandwiches in the saloon bars of Soho, he would encounter the documentary film-makers, admiring 'their contempt for easy big prizes and soft living, their taut social conscience, their rather Marxist sense of the contemporary scene', and work briefly with Grierson and Cavalcanti, sharing the social-democratic impulse which motivated much of their work. He liked their enthusiasm, their exploration of cinematic technique, and their willingness to 'work like demons for a few pounds a week', while the moguls of Hollywood and the Savoy Grill were spending money like water on films that never got made. Above all, he felt they represented the future, a generation ahead of the 'old-fashioned theatrical types' who were running the film studios. Characteristically, and prudently, he did not spurn Hollywood or the Savoy Grill, but kept a toe-hold in the commercial cinema, although like the documentarists he deplored its version of national life, 'taken from a few issues of the *Sketch* and *Tatler* and a collection of Christmas cards'. He was also sceptical of some of the more extreme claims made on behalf of documentary, and like most of its practitioners knew that it was not a window on the world but an aesthetic strategy deployed to construct a particular effect: 'It is not the raw material but the treatment that counts', and for realism you could not beat the printed word. 'Nearly all documentary films', he wrote in 1939, 'seem to me a very romantic heightening of ordinary life, comparable not to the work of a realistic novelist or dramatist, but to the picturesque and highly-coloured fictions of the romancer.' Film as a medium 'cannot help dropping out all the dull passages, beautifying and heightening the rest, and then giving the whole thing a kind of glitter and excitement'. The results can be entertaining, dramatic, moving. But 'for plain truth they cannot compete with the printed word': by which he meant not just simple reportage but realistic fiction.[126]

What we have here, no doubt, is the writer's puritanical mistrust of the emotional seductiveness of the visual image, and of film's ability to conceal its constructed nature behind a 'naturalised' visual rhetoric, while the writer has no option but to construct his world by putting marks on paper. Priestley would never have agreed with his fellow novelist Storm Jameson, who, writing in the magazine *Fact* in 1937, urged writers to imitate the documentary makers. Instead of dressing up facts as fictions, or going on 'visits to the distressed areas in a motor-car', the writer should keep himself and his feelings out of the picture, while selectively deploying the facts, as documentarists do visual images, in such a way that they, not the author, would elicit the readers' emotional response.[127] This was not Priestley's way. For one thing, he did not know how to write without putting himself in the picture; even the third-person narrators in his novels cannot forbear to let you know what they think about characters, events and situations. For another, he was at heart a rationalist, preferring argument and persuasion to emotional manipulation. *English Journey*, as the subtitle tells us, is about where he went, and what he 'saw and heard and felt and thought'. This is Priestley's England, and there is no pretence that he is letting it speak for itself. But his interpretations are so openly presented that the reader is virtually invited to argue with them: and indeed he often argues with himself. In this way we are drawn into a debate, instead of being presented with an unchallengeable version of the world.

Nor was Priestley's notion of the 'plain truth' ever all that plain. Strict realism bored him: never a fan of Arnold Bennett's approach, he needed a touch of 'the fantastic, the philosophical, the symbolical' in his work.[128] In an article written in 1932 he wrote that the only way the contemporary novel could avoid becoming 'lost in subjectivity' was through 'some kind of dramatic symbolism, in narratives that would move in more than one world at once'.[129] In many of his plays, as he pointed out, while the initial setting and characters are usually naturalistic enough, very often the naturalism starts to fade, and something strange and fantastic starts to happen; much the same could be said of his novels, which are full of premonitions and symbolic events.[130] In the work of the painter Pieter Bruegel the Elder, Priestley found a parallel to his ideal mode of representation: an art which is 'not aristocratic but essentially anonymous and democratic, what films would be if they really were works of art and not products of a cynical industry', and a model for those writers who 'do not wish on the one hand to whisper to a few, or on the other hand merely to tickle the mob'. Bruegel's paintings are realistic on one level, full of sharply observed detail, but 'somewhere just around the corner is a fairy-tale country. We are poised on the edge of marvels and miracles.' This is 'not a plain realism ... but a realism merging into the magical. And as you stare again, feeling a trifle haunted, the realistic-magical turns into the symbolic', revealing a 'rich and complicated' world, 'beautiful and faintly tragic'.

> He had as we have a desperate, foundation-cracking world as his scene and background. Then as now in man's spiritual life the seas were dark and heavy and the steering-gear had nearly gone. There was still colour and gaiety in the foreground, but in the background it looked as if doomsday were breaking ... a great artist with a broad appeal of the popular, tragicomic, democratic kind, showing the crowd a vision of their own life; and those of us who ask to do nothing better than this, for we cannot see that there is anything better to do, whether we are painters, authors, producers of plays and films, should turn to him for refreshment and confirmation.[131]

This seems to me one of Priestley's most important aesthetic statements, and he is talking about himself – or, rather, himself as he would like to be. He avows his 'democratic' aim of 'showing the crowd a vision of their own life', but acknowledges that a straightforward documentary realism would not do this. Only some form of magical realism could do justice to the 'plain truth' of the world and what lurks behind its surface appearances.

Bruegel's art as Priestley describes it achieves this truth by combining a surface realism with a deeper mystery and symbolism. If the possibilities of film were to be realised, it too must work on more than one level. A start would be for documentary and entertainment film to come together. Soho Square would provide the enthusiasm, the 'social conscience and knowledge of the English scene', while the Savoy Grill would provide the resources and the popular dramatic techniques, the capacity to entertain. This would probably not produce Bruegel-like work, but it might achieve a much-needed 'strengthening and *thickening*' of the 'social texture' of English cinema.[132] According to one narrative of British cinema history, this is exactly what happened: the 'realist' movies of wartime, and the British 'New Wave' of the 1950s and 1960s, brought together the methods of documentary and feature film to create a national cinema which could finally deal properly with national life. It is a narrative which favours the high seriousness of documentary realism over other, and often more popular national genres, such as Hammer horror, or Gainsborough romance.[133] Nevertheless, it does reflect what some novelists, including Priestley, were trying to achieve in the 1930s.

Another writer who wrote both fact and fiction in his attempts to grasp England in the 1930s was, of course, George Orwell; although, as we have seen, he did not appreciate Priestley's first shot at social realism in *Angel Pavement*. Reviewing Orwell's first book, *Down and Out in Paris and London* in 1933, Priestley was rather more generous, greeting it as 'uncommonly good reading and a social document of some value', and congratulating its author because unlike so many swaggering writers of 'the down-and-out species' he was prepared to regard his readers as his equals.[134] This remark perhaps indicates how commonplace the chronicles of squalor had become even by this time. In later life Priestley expressed his exasperation at Orwell's booming reputation, complaining that everything Orwell had done he had done first.[135] This is not all that far from the truth: whatever their relative merits as writers, in the 1930s the kind of things they wrote were, in fact, very similar: contemporary novels in the realist mode, and personalised reportage, sustained by essays and book reviews. But of course, Priestley wrote in the *Evening Standard* and the *Sunday Chronicle*, while Orwell's writing appeared in the more 'literary' (but less lucrative) surroundings of the *Criterion* and *New English Weekly*, which may supply some clue as to their respective reputations.

As Valentine Cunningham has pointed out, Orwell's – and even the decade's – most celebrated work of documentary reportage, *The Road to Wigan Pier* (1937), owes a debt to *English Journey* which it resolutely fails to acknowledge, with the result that (like much of Orwell's work) it is 'sometimes wrongly taken as a wonderfully unique achievement'.[136] *English Journey* had hit the road first, inspiring as well as latching on to the new realist spirit – as the photographer Bill Brandt, who went north after reading it, generously acknowledged. Orwell's book echoes not just the structural form of the journey but the continuous, opinionated authorial voice, the personal encounters with representative natives, the occasional injection of facts and figures, and a descriptive mode which turns the industrial landscape itself into a vehicle of moral indignation. However, there are also significant differences between the two books. Documentary film, Mass Observation and *Wigan Pier* all have in common a particular construction of the relationship between the implied readers, the subjects of the investigation and the writer/film-maker. Narrative structure is important to this, because it establishes, literally and figuratively, where the author is coming from. *English Journey* begins with a departure and ends with a return home, its narrative space completely occupied by the journey. In chapter 1 of *The Road to Wigan Pier*, however, Orwell is already at his destination, waking up in a grim northern lodging-house: he is 'there', having got there, we take it, from somewhere else. *Wigan Pier* is structured around this dichotomy between origin and destination, as its title itself announces. Normality is the familiar middle-class London life which lies at the beginning of the road; but at the other end, 'when you go to the industrial north you are conscious, quite apart from the unfamiliar scenery, of entering a strange country'.[137] This 'you', the book's hypothetical reader, is, we therefore assume, not an inhabitant of this 'strange country'. In emphasising his own social and cultural distance from what he was observing, Orwell was, of course, being nothing less than honest. The sympathy he felt for the northern working class was not based on any populist pretence of common experience on the part of a south-eastern, Old Etonian, 'lower-upper-middle-class' writer. But everyone comes from somewhere; and, in constructing his narrative as a journey from a familiar place into the unknown, Orwell excludes the possibility that where he came from and where he arrived at are really (or ought to be) both the *same* place: their people, though different and unequal, members of the same community, who all owe each other the same duty of fellowship. A similar problem of social distance has been identified in the documentary film movement and Mass Observation, and, to be fair, Orwell does not fail to address it. In the tortured discussion of class and socialism which makes up the second half of the book, we can see him striving, and failing, to construct and believe in this sense of common fellowship. However, for all its vividness of description and human sympathy, *Wigan Pier* is as lacking in explanations and solutions for the problems it describes as any middle-class Victorian expedition into 'darkest England'.

Priestley's destination, on the other hand, is 'England', which means that he is already there. He knows and likes some bits of it better than others, but there is no sense that he is alienated from whole chunks of it, or that he is coming into it from somewhere else. Nor does he make Orwell's semi-conscious assumption that the people the book is about are distinct from the people who are reading it. With Priestley, though he does not shirk, and indeed emphasises, social division and inequality, we are all 'us', all members of England: which makes social exclusion particularly unacceptable: 'Was Jarrow still in England or not?' In this respect, Priestley succeeds where Orwell fails: partly because he himself comes from 'out there', the industrial north; but also, and more significantly, because of the kind of book he is writing, aimed at a broad market – more Book Society than Left Book Club – and therefore necessarily more inclusive in tone. Such are the consequences of the 'fashion for fact' and the reconciliation of entertainment and documentary.

On the road again

Indeed, it can be argued that the Book Society and its kind contributed at least as much as the Left Book Club or the documentary film movement to opening up a new public sphere of debate in the 1930s, through the combination of fact and fiction which was characteristic of the despised 'middlebrow' novel. Take, for example, A. J. Cronin's *The Citadel* (1937), which follows the career of a young doctor from early practice in the south Wales valleys to Harley Street and beyond.[138] The protagonist's life story and moral struggle provides the narrative thrust, but the book is also a comprehensive critique of the health system of the time, supported by a huge amount of information about its operation at every level. The book's semi-documentary content and political purpose did not prevent it selling ninety thousand copies in eight weeks; nor did its huge sales stop it from contributing to the ongoing debate about health care which was to culminate in the Beveridge Report and the foundation of the NHS.[139]

'After all, you know, I have certain quite strong political convictions, and I tend more and more to bring them into my writing.' So Priestley wrote to his friend Hugh Walpole in 1936, disappointed at the latter's lukewarm response to *They Walk in the City*.[140] Much of Priestley's output in the 1930s attempted in a wide range of different forms – novels, plays, film scripts, journalism – to grapple with the rising social and political crisis of that decade. Rather than adopting Cronin's preferred form of the lengthy *Bildungsroman*, these novels picked up on the journey theme of *Good Companions* and *English Journey* (and also *Faraway* (1932)), and the 'crisis' plot of *Angel Pavement*. *Wonder Hero* (1934), the film script *Sing As We Go* (1934) and *They Walk in the City* (1936) all deal with the misadventures of young working-class people whose lives are disrupted for one reason or another: they go on their travels, undergo a series of hazards and trials and ultimately gain success and return home to a happy ending. In short, they are quest romances. In *Hero* and *They Walk*, most of the hazards which threaten the young provincials are found in London, and, in an echo of earlier Priestley writings, London itself is portrayed as the villain of the piece, the source of disruption, danger and moral decay, and it is the provincial industrial town which stands for safety and solid values. In Priestley's other major Slump fiction, the script he wrote for the Gracie Fields film *Sing As We Go*, Gracie goes to Blackpool rather than London, as appropriate for a Lancashire comedy, but she too undergoes many adventures and returns home with a solution to the problem which began her travels, the closure of the local mill.[141]

Wonder Hero's Charlie Habble, a young Midlands factory worker, prevents an explosion in the factory where he works, and the newspaper he reads, the *Daily Tribune*, takes him off to London, and turns him into a temporary media hero. Through Charlie's eyes, we see the futility and corruption, moral, sexual, financial and political, of metropolitan life; and we also meet Ida, another temporary and therefore so far uncorrupted celebrity, who comes from a neighbouring midlands town. Then Charlie hears that his aunt is seriously ill, and hurries off to the north-eastern town of Slakeby, which has been devastated by the collapse of the shipbuilding industry, and where only the banks seem to be doing well. With the money the *Tribune* has given him, Charlie can help his aunt, but he can do nothing about the disintegration of the town and along with it his aunt's family. Back in London, he finds everyone has forgotten all about him; meets up with Ida again, falls in love, gets his old job back, and the couple return home together. Formally speaking, Charlie's successful romantic quest is for Ida, but this love interest is perfunctory. The novel's real focus of interest, and what Charlie really discovers, is the condition of England; or rather, three Englands: the relatively prosperous midlands; the stricken north; and London, the nexus of corruption and exploitation, which starts the whole process off by drawing Charlie and Ida into its maw, and then spits them out again when they have served its purposes. While the London scenes are painted in lurid colours, the Slakeby chapter, ironically entitled 'This other Eden', adopts a documentary mode, with plenty of physical description and factual information about the dole system and the impact of unemployment on the people, much of it delivered, like the novel's direct political message, through the crusading Dr Inverurie.[142] *Wonder Hero* is a critique of Britain on the dole, but it is also a critique of the popular press, which should be telling people what is going on but prefers to focus its attention on beauty queens and imaginary heroes. 'We don't like putting the spotlight on that part of the country', says the journalist Hughson, when he hears that Charlie is going to Slakeby.[143]

Priestley was clearly now in crusading mode, and, after *Wonder Hero* appeared in August 1933, he set off on the tour which was to result in *English Journey*. But he did not regard *Wonder Hero* as a success. In *Margin Released* he describes it as one of his 'deliberately polemical, journalistic, social-moral fables', intended to make a quick impact on a public more likely to read a novel than a non-fiction book, rather than to make a lasting contribution to fiction – in effect, a fictional version of *English Journey*. In retrospect, he felt, *English Journey* did the job better. Priestley is not entirely fair to his own work here. While no one is likely to claim *Wonder Hero* as a great novel, and in fact it sold fewer copies than *English Journey*, its combination of social *actualité* and robust satire, within the framework of a conventionally romantic story, is unusual and worthwhile. The London scenes at the newspaper, in a nightclub, at Lady Catterbird's fashionable party and at a semi-fascist meeting, have comedy and immediacy, with more than a touch of caricature, and exploit a vein of genuine disgust at the condition of metropolitan society, which we will see Priestley developing further during the War. The contrast in style between the comic satire of these passages and the sombre semi-documentary chapter set in Slakeby conveys in aesthetic terms, much as he hoped the British cinema would do, the fractured nature of English society in 1933. Ironically, one of *Wonder Hero*'s admirers, in a letter to Priestley, was Ramsay MacDonald, the former Labour Prime Minister, who was currently heading a Tory-dominated 'National Government' following the collapse of the Labour administration in 1931 under the impact of the Slump.[144] MacDonald came from a poor background in Scotland, and represented a Durham mining constituency, but was notorious for his friendships with Lady Londonderry and other London aristocratic hostesses. No individual could have better embodied the fractured nation of *Wonder Hero*.

Sing As We Go (1934) was a very different proposition: a musical comedy, and a vehicle for Gracie Fields, then the country's biggest variety and recording star, whose fee took up half the film's budget. The director, Basil Dean, brought Priestley in as scriptwriter not just for his skill with plot and dialogue, recently demonstrated in his first two successful plays, but because it was thought his regional and class background would enable him to write a more convincing story for the Lancastrian Gracie. But he was also now a celebrity, with box-office appeal in his own right. Advance publicity for the film proclaimed Fields and Priestley ('author of *The Good Companions*') as its two main attractions.[145]

Priestley had long been a fan of Gracie Fields, whose persona embodied the down-to-earth qualities of the northern people.

> Listen to her for a quarter of an hour and you will learn more about Lancashire women and Lancashire than you would from a dozen books on

these subjects. All the qualities are there: shrewdness, homely simplicity, irony, fierce independence, an impish delight in mocking whatever is thought to be affected and pretentious.[146]

In June 1939, when Gracie was dangerously ill and the nation was holding its breath, Priestley expanded on this theme in the Manchester-based *Sunday Chronicle*:

> The secret of Gracie Fields' popularity is that not only does she know, because of her genuine genius for the task, how to entertain people, but she knows, too, how to represent the people. In a country in which privilege is still the rule and snobbery is the most characteristic weakness, the people do not get much of a chance to express themselves. But in Gracie Fields for once they are expressing themselves, and that is why she is at one and the same time an admired artist, a symbolic figure, and a beloved woman.[147]

Priestley's populist understanding of Gracie's cultural significance, and the interplay between the artist, the symbol and the woman, explains a lot about *Sing As We Go*, and why it was, perhaps surprisingly, a movie about the Slump. The plot follows a familiar pattern of crisis, quest and redemption, seen through the eyes not of some imperial hero but of a Lancashire mill-girl, and played out not on some distant battlefield but in the working-class holiday resort of Blackpool. Lancashire cotton is collapsing, and Greybeck Mill closes. Nothing daunted, Grace Platt (Gracie Fields) cycles off to Blackpool to look for work. Here, against a carnivalesque background of funfairs and holidaymaking, she finds a variety of jobs, including waitressing in a boarding-house, performing as a human spider and a vanishing woman, and singing in a promenade song-plugging establishment, and she rescues the pretty, innocent and middle-class Phyllis from an evil seducer. She also meets a benevolent millionaire, who, with the aid of a new textile process, is able to reopen the mill. Grace is appointed welfare officer, and in a rousing finale leads the workers back into the mill singing the optimistic title song.

No wonder serious critics like Paul Rotha ticked off Dean and Priestley for making comedy out of 'social unhappiness'.[148] In fact, though, the film was more popular amongst the northern audiences who were actually experiencing the problems it depicted – including Bolton where the factory-closing scenes were shot – than it was in the south where unemployment was low.[149] Perhaps this was because of Gracie Fields herself, nationally popular, but more so in the north, thanks to her strong working-class northern persona. Perhaps it was because the film worked off a recognisable version of northern working-class life, at work in the factory and on holiday in Blackpool, including locations such as the Pleasure Beach, which northern audiences would have recognised. If the latter, then the unusual semi-documentary style of *Sing As We Go*, is partly responsible for its success. Despite being a star vehicle, and a musical comedy, the film avoided the glamorous spectacle associated with the Hollywood musical, and with British versions of it such as *Evergreen*, the Gaumont-British musical starring Jessie Matthews which also came out in 1934 and was successful in the south of England and the United States, but far less so in the north.[150] A more down-to-earth approach, rooted in older British popular cultural forms such as the music-hall and the funfair, rather than the newly dominant Hollywood pattern, suited Fields's persona. Real locations and, for crowd scenes, non-professional actors were used, making the film a hybrid of traditional popular entertainment, star-vehicle musical and documentary realism, with a rich mix, in Andrew Higson's words, of 'voices, forms and cultures, both high and low, respectable and vulgar', including montage sequences in the factory and at Blackpool which can be traced back, via the documentary movement, to Eisenstein's *Battleship Potemkin*. [151] For this mix, of course, Dean, and the editor Thorold Dickenson, who devised the montage sequences, were at least as responsible as Priestley. Nevertheless, in the story we can spot what by now were trademark Priestley themes: the celebration of popular energy and 'gusto', the affection for popular art and above all the film's focus on community, one of its running themes.

The strengths of Greybeck life before the mill closes are depicted as communal – the concert party, the football team – unemployment is seen as a misfortune endured collectively, even by the boss's son, and the workers march out of the mill as they will march back in, singing together. In Blackpool we see the collectivity of working-class pleasure – including, bizarrely, the appearance of a Friendly Society, complete with procession, banners and secret rituals, on its annual outing to the seaside. And in the final shot of the film, when we have seen the workers march back into the mill, Gracie sings the closing lines of the title song directly to the camera, incorporating the cinema audience into the community of the factory. Grace herself is, of course, a strong individual, but her ultimate role, welfare officer, represents the collective interest of the workers, and at the climactic moments we identify with the crowd just as much as with her. This emphasis on the collective owes a lot to Priestley's understanding of working-class life, and it also chimes in with his developing political stance in *English Journey* and elsewhere. This does not turn the film into a radical text, but it undercuts the conservative, consensual effect which some have detected in its 'stirring and patriotic reassurance that all will be well in the end'.[152] As with the 'middlebrow' novel, we must not make too much of 'happy endings'. The film ends well because all musicals end well, with the resolution of the characters' problems, but this does not fool audiences into thinking that real life is like that. The important thing is exactly how 'all' comes to 'be well in the end'. In *Sing As We Go* it is because the people (not just the workers but the boss too) pull together to solve their problems. This image of solidarity is not revolutionary, but nor is it conservative: it is best described as social-democratic, and it would come into its own in the next decade.

In the stone forest

They Walk in the City was in many ways the most ambitious thing Priestley attempted in the 1930s, an attempt to write a major novel comparable to *Angel Pavement*, and by general consent (including the author's) it was not altogether successful. After it had come out, Priestley explained what he had been trying to do:

> To take two simple young people, typical specimens of the exploited and helpless class, to bring them together, part them, bring them together again, in the fashion of the oldest and simplest love stories, but to place them and their little romance within a strong framework of social criticism. The two youngsters would be symbolic figures rather than solidly created characters. Much of what happened to them would be symbolic of the special difficulties and dangers of the large class they represented ... .The reader's mind would be constantly yanked away from their viewpoint to a wide and critical survey of the social scene.[153]

And so Rose and Edward, two young people from Yorkshire, in love but separated by fate, end up in London trying to find each other again, and on the way are 'threatened by various forces – some old, like capitalist imperialism, etc., others new, like the Fascists and the Communists', personified in the various events of the novel.[154] The love story would provide the narrative thread, told alternately from each character's point of view, but it would be necessary to break off from their story to relate each episode to 'a sharp analysis ... of our modern urban life'.[155] In the end, either the technical problems defeated him or he ran out of time and patience: either way, he failed to realise his idea, and, anxious to finish the book somehow, he resorted to 'melodrama, and not even good melodrama' in a lurid conclusion involving white slavery and contract killers.[156] He never really solved the problem, either, of how to get his 'sharp analysis' across through two simple and unintellectual characters, without making the narrator's commentary intrusive. Nevertheless, there are good things to be salvaged from the book. The treatment of Yorkshire working-class life in the early chapters is vivid and affectionate. Running through the book is a sympathetic account of the impact of mass culture on the lives and thoughts of people like Rose and Edward. There are extended accounts of aspects of London life, including tea-shops, offices, hotels, domestic service. There are some rewarding minor characters, including fascists, communists, a thinly disguised cameo appearance from Priestley himself, and a rather pretentious (though not unsympathetic) young intellectual with a private income, named, in a sly dig at Bloomsbury, Francis Woburn.

What *They Walk*'s panorama of London life does not add up to, though, is the sharp analysis which Priestley was aiming for. Priestley's ambitions are similar to those of Balzac in *La Comédie Humaine*, but he lacks Balzac's totalising vision. In its place he has a series of Priestleian themes familiar to anyone who has read the other books discussed in this chapter: not without value, by any means, but not enough to carry the novel. He has not cracked the perennial problem – which, after all, has perplexed novelists and historians alike through the ages – of reconciling the particular and the general, rounded individual characters with social types, detailed and concrete realistic description with general patterns of society and history. A sure sign of this is that, instead of letting the actions, experiences and thoughts of his characters reveal the working of society and history, he is for ever taking us on one side to explain it to us. His next novel, *Let the People Sing*, which will be discussed in a later chapter, is the lesser work in many ways, but it gives a clearer account of Britain on the eve of war, paradoxically because it is less realistic: a simpler novel, with people and society drawn in bold strokes, it conveys a social and historical analysis more clearly through comic allegory than *They Walk* does through serious realism.

'Britain wake up!'

Priestley began the last year of the 1930s, and the last year of peace, with a series of six articles in the centre-left popular daily the *News Chronicle* entitled, somewhat portentously, 'Britain wake up!'. The national danger which Priestley was referring to came not from abroad, the rise of fascism and the ambitions of Hitler, but from within. The articles, whose arguments are further developed in *Rain Upon Godshill*, depict a nation which has lost its way. Proud inheritors of a great cultural and intellectual tradition, we have lost our own energy and creativity, and are in danger of losing the freedom we prize. Britain has become a national of inheritors rather than creators, a rich tired old country, led by rich tired old men.[157] Democracy itself has gone backwards since the War, the same small privileged class in charge, cut off by their lifestyle from the mass of the people. Events like the Abdication and the Munich Crisis have shown that government has become as secretive and unresponsive as any dictatorship, while the complacent and deferential people have lost their zest for politics, and 'have not had the energy and courage and public spirit to be true democrats'.[158] Snobbery runs through our national life: we have lost the virtues of aristocracy without acquiring those of democracy, and we need the true bourgeois democracy of France or the United States, to make us a more honest, gayer and more intelligent people.[159] Priestley renews his attack on the 'moneylending' Britain, and the private-income, dividend-drawing class which lives off it, many of them idlers, the rest congenitally hostile to the risks which productive enterprise requires, most knowing more about the Empire than about industrial Britain. Since the rallying-cry of *English Journey*, nothing has been done for the unemployed, no relief work along American or even German lines.[160] What is the way forward? The left, to which Priestley gives his guarded allegiance, is crippled by its workerism and class-consciousness, unwilling to recruit the new middle classes to its cause; but its greatest weakness is not extremism but tameness: 'They lack wide vision and the ardent creative mind.'[161] As for the middle classes, from whom the ideas should come to sort out this mess, they have retreated into a 'car and wireless life', cut off from the wider community, from politics and culture. We need real democracy to release the dammed-up talent of the people, starting with reform of Parliament and the electoral system, continuing with the abandonment of snobbery and exclusiveness. The British, Priestley concludes, are at heart a good people, who believe in co-operation and fairness and dislike intolerance and violence. They should be wide awake, instead of 'mumbling and grumbling in their sleep'.[162]

Through the 1930s, Priestley had moved from the tentative social commentary of *Angel Pavement* to a scathing critique of British society and its institutions, and a programme for change based upon a belief in the inherent qualities of the British people. This critique looked back to Bradford's industrial radicalism, and forward to Priestley's wartime agitation, and his hope that 1940 would awaken the people from their slumbers. But also, for the first time since writing about *English Humour* a decade earlier, he had taken up the question of England and the English character, which we go on to explore in the next chapter.

Notes

1 Parts of this chapter previously appeared in John Baxendale, '"I had seen a lot of Englands": J. B. Priestley, Englishness and the people', *History Workshop Journal* 51 (2001), pp. 87–111.

2 Priestley, *Rain*, p. 253.

3 Chris Waters, 'J. B. Priestley: Englishness and the politics of nostalgia', in Peter Mandler and Susan Pedersen (eds), *After the Victorians: Private Conscience and Public Duty in Modern Britain* (London: Routledge, 1994), pp. 213–15.

4 Priestley, *Margin*, p. 12; Cook, *Priestley*, pp. 3–5.

5 Priestley's own accounts are in *Margin Released*, part one; *The English* (London: Heinemann, 1973), pp. 105–9; and *Rain* pp. 252–3. The 'suburban drives' come from *Bright Day* (London: Heinemann, 1946), p. 26. For secondary sources on Priestley's life see Cook, *Priestley*, and Peter Holdsworth, *The Rebel Tyke: Bradford and J. B. Priestley* (Bradford:

Bradford Libraries, 1994), which is particularly informative about Priestley's childhood. A visit to Bradford is also recommended. For his avowal of lower-middle-classness see, for example, *The Edwardians* (London: Heinemann, 1970), pp. 104ff.

6 *Bradford Corporation Official Guide*, 1917, quoted in Henry Pelling, *The Social Geography of British Elections 1885–1910* (London: Macmillan, 1967), p. 298.

7 Priestley, Rain, pp. 252–3.

8 Priestley, *English Journey*, p. 400.

9 Ibid., pp. 398, 400

10 Eric Hobsbawm, *Industry and Empire* (Weidenfeld and Nicolson, 1968), p. 137.

11 *Midnight*, p. 132.

12 J. B. Priestley, 'Preface' to Fenner Brockway, *Socialism Over Sixty Years: The Life of Jowett of Bradford (1864–1944)* (London: George Allen and Unwin, 1946), p. 7. Keith Leybourne, '"The defence of the bottom dog": the Independent Labour Party in local politics', in D. G. Wright and J. A. Jowitt (eds), *Victorian Bradford: Essays in Honour of Jack Reynolds* (Bradford, City of Bradford Metropolitan Council, 1982), pp. 237–9.

13 Priestley, *Margin*, p. 11; *Midnight*, p. 133.

14 J. B. Priestley, 'Born and bred in Bradford', *Listener* (27 December 1945), p. 753.

15 Margaret McMillan, *The Life of Rachel McMillan* (London: J. M. Dent, 1927), p. 77.

16 Leybourne, 'Defence'.

17 Priestley, 'Preface'.

18 Tony Jowitt, 'The pattern of religion in Victorian Bradford', in Wright and Jowett (eds), *Victorian Bradford*, pp. 37–61.

19 Priestley, *Rain*, p. 269.

20 W. Haslam Mills, *Grey Pastures* (London: Chatto and Windus, 1924), p. 17. Priestley reviewed this book in the *Daily News* (23 October 1924), p. 8.

21 Priestley, *Outcries*, p. 142.

22 Ibid.

23 See also Priestley, *Margin*, part 1.

24 Priestley, *Margin*, p. 195.

25 Priestley, *Bright Day*, pp. 43–4; *Margin*, pp. 28–9.

26 Priestley, *Margin*, p. 30; *English Journey*, p. 160.

27 Priestley, *Bright Day*, pp. 92–8; 114–16.

28 Ibid., p. 68.

29 Priestley, 'Masses, workers and the people', *Star* (31 July 1935), p. 4.

30 Priestley, 'Born and bred', p. 754.

31 Priestley, *English Journey*, pp. 299.

32 Ibid., p. 159.

33 Priestley, *Edwardians*, p. 97.

34 Priestley, *Margin*, p. 7

35 Patrick Joyce, *Visions of the People: Industrial England and the Question of Class* (Cambridge: Cambridge University Press, 1991), p. 329.

36 Ibid., pp. 332–3.

37 Priestley, 'Masses, workers and the people'.
38 J. B. Priestley, *Out of the People* (London: Collins/Heinemann, 1941), pp. 111, 33.
39 Priestley, *Midnight*, p. 132.
40 Priestley, 'Masses, workers and the people'.
41 David Howell, *British Workers and the Independent Labour Party 1886–1906* (Manchester: Manchester University Press, 1983), p. 165.
42 Priestley, 'Preface' to *Socialism Over Sixty Years*, p. 11.
43 Priestley, *Rain*, pp. 256–7.
44 Priestley, *Edwardians*, pp. 106–8.
45 Priestley, *Rain*, pp. 256–7.
46 Priestley, 'Preface', p. 11.
47 Priestley, *Midnight*, p. 135.
48 Ibid.
49 Priestley, *Outcries*, p. 120.
50 Priestley, *Midnight*, p. 135; Priestley, 'What is freedom?', *News Chronicle* (5 June 1939), p. 10.
51 Priestley, *Midnight*, pp. 135–43.
52 An important influence on Priestley's thinking in the 1930s was the Christian Socialist philosopher John Macmurray: Macmurray, *Creative Society: A Study of the Relation of Christianity to Communism* (London: SCM Press, 1935).
53 Priestley, *Rain*, pp. 175–6; see also *Midnight*, pp. 9–10; *Margin*, p. 180.
54 Priestley, 'Masses, workers and the people'.
55 Priestley, *Midnight*, pp. 102–3.
56 Priestley, 'Masses, workers and the people'.
57 Priestley, *Wonder Hero*, pp. 16–27; J. B. Priestley, *They Walk in the City: The Lovers in the Stone Forest* (London: Heinemann, 1936), pp. 417–18; *English Journey*, pp. 297–301.
58 Priestley, *Margin*, pp. 79, 81; *English Journey*, p. 166.
59 Ibid., p. 167.
60 Priestley, *Edwardians*, pp. 289–90.
61 Samuel Hynes, *A War Imagined: The First World War and English Culture* (London: Pimlico, 1990), 352.
62 Priestley, *Edwardians*, pp. 78, 61, 84, 53.
63 Priestley, *English Journey*, p. 166; *Rain*, p. 224.
64 Priestley, 'Fifty years of the English', in *The Moments and Other Pieces* (London; Heinemann, 1966), p. 201. First published in *New Statesman* (19 April 1963).
65 Priestley, *When We Are Married* (1938), in *The Plays of J. B. Priestley*, vol. 2 (London: Heinemann, 1949), pp. 149, x.
66 Cook, *Priestley*, p. 250.
67 Priestley, *Outcries*, p. 85.
68 Priestley, *They Walk*, p. 383.
69 J. B. Priestley, *Lost Empires* (London: Heinemann, 1965), p. 33.
70 Ibid, p. 146.
71 Ibid., p. 287.
72 Ibid., p. 262.
73 Ibid. pp. 85, 101.

74 Brome, *Priestley*, p. 64.

75 Priestley, *Literature*, p. 92.

76 Priestley, *English Journey*, pp. 409–11.

77 Priestley, *The Edwardians*, p. 288.

78 Priestley, *They Walk*, p. 385.

79 Priestley, *Margin*, p. 185.

80 Warwick Deeping, *Sorrell and Son* (London: Cassell & Co., 1925). On Deeping see Mary Grover, 'The authenticity of the middlebrow: Warwick Deeping and cultural legitimacy, 1903–1940', unpublished PhD thesis, School of Cultural Studies, Sheffield Hallam University, 2002.

81 Bracco, *'Betwixt and Between'*, pp. 6, 17.

82 Crossick (ed.), *The Lower Middle Class in Britain*.

83 George and Weedon Grossmith, *The Diary of a Nobody* (1892) (London: Penguin, 1999); C. F. G. Masterman, *The Condition of England* (London: Methuen, [1909] 1960), p. 59.

84 Priestley, *Outcries*, p. 85.

85 Priestley, *Margin*, p. 21.

86 Priestley, *The Good Companions* (1929) (Harmondsworth: Penguin Books, 1962), p. 397.

87 Cited in Leavis, 'What's wrong with criticism?', p. 143.

88 J. B. Priestley, 'I want to know', *Sunday Dispatch* (17 March 1929), p. 1; 'On the pier at Wigan', *Sunday Dispatch* (21 April 1929), p. 8.

89 J. B. Priestley, *Angel Pavement* (London: Heinemann, 1930).

90 J. B. Priestley, Introduction to the US Readers' Club edition of *Angel Pavement* (1942); cited in Klein, *Fiction*, p. 104.

91 Ibid., p. 2; cited in Klein, *Fiction*, p. 103.

92 Priestley, *Angel Pavement* (London: Mandarin, 1993), p. 593.

93 S. P. B. Mais in the *Daily Telegraph*, quoted in Klein, *Fiction*, p. 104.

94 George Orwell, *Collected Essays, Journalism and Letters, Vol. 1: An Age Like This 1920–1940*, eds Sonia Orwell and Ian Angus (London: Penguin Books, 1970), pp. 47–50. Orwell's review originally appeared in *Adelphi* (October 1930).

95 D. J. Taylor, *Orwell: The Life* (London: Vintage, 2004), p. 111.

96 Ibid., p. 3.

97 Priestley, *Bright Day*, p. 150.

98 Priestley, *Angel Pavement* (1993), p. 417.

99 Ibid., pp. 591–3.

100 Priestley, *Rain*, pp. 245–6.

101 *Bookseller* (11 April 1934), p. 1.

102 'Complete analysis of the works of J. B. Priestley' (dated 1956), in Random House Archive.

103 See, for example, Beryl Bainbridge, *English Journey, or The Road to Milton Keynes* (London: Duckworth, 1984); Andrew Cross, *An English Journey* (London: Film and Video Umbrella, 2004), with accompanying DVD, and Richard West, *An English Journey* (London: Chatto and Windus, 1981), which despite its title fails to mention Priestley at all.

104 Denys Thompson, 'Comments and reviews', *Scrutiny* 3:1 (June 1934), pp. 68–9.

105 Angus Calder, *The Myth of the Blitz* (London: Cape, 1991), p. 198.
106 Priestley, *English Journey*, pp. 3–11.
107 George Orwell, *The Road to Wigan Pier* (London: Gollancz, 1937), chapter 1.
108 Priestley, *English Journey*, p. 62.
109 Ibid., p. 196.
110 Ibid., pp. 358–9, 302.
111 Ibid., p. 337.
112 Ibid., p. 399.
113 Ibid., p. 407.
114 Ibid., p. 172.
115 Ibid., p. 201; J. B. Priestley, 'Give women a chance', *Star* (27 March 1935), p. 4.
116 Priestley, *English Journey*, p. 411.
117 Ibid., pp. 410–11.
118 Priestley, *Edwardians*, p. 178; *Margin*, p. 30.
119 Priestley, *Rain*, p. 251.
120 Thompson, 'Comments and reviews', p. 68.
121 Raymond Williams, *Marxism and Literature* (Oxford: Oxford University Press, 1977), pp. 121–7.
122 Priestley, *English Journey*, p. 406.
123 *Clarion* (19 May 1934).
124 H. V. Morton, *In Search of England* (London: Methuen, 1927), and *The Call of England* (London: Methuen, 1928). Michael Bartholomew, *In Search of H. V. Morton* (London: Methuen, 2004).
125 Philip Gibbs, *European Journey: Being the Narrative of a Journey in France, Switzerland, Italy, Austria, Hungary, Germany, and the Saar in the Spring and Summer of 1934* (London: Heinemann, 1934); *England Speaks* (London: Heinemann, 1935); *Ordeal in England (England Speaks Again)* (London: Heinemann, 1937); Morton, *In Search*.
126 Priestley, *Rain*, pp. 78–84.
127 Storm Jameson, 'Documents', in *Fact* 4 (July 1937), quoted in Valentine Cunningham, *British Writers of the Thirties* (Oxford: Oxford University Press, 1988), p. 330.
128 Quoted in Cook, *Priestley*, p. 151.
129 J. B. Priestley, 'Some reflections of a popular novelist', *London Mercury* 27: 158 (December 1932), p. 140.
130 Priestley, *Outcries* p. 98.
131 Priestley, *Rain*, pp. 111–14.
132 Priestley, *Rain*, p. 83.
133 Andrew Higson, '"Britain's outstanding contribution to the film": The documentary-realist tradition', in Charles Barr (ed.), *All Our Yesterdays: 90 Years of British Cinema* (London: British Film Institute, 1986), pp. 72–97.
134 J. B. Priestley, 'The truth about a tramp's life', *Evening Standard* (12 January 1933), p. 11.
135 See Angus Calder's account of an interview with Priestley in Calder, *The Myth of the Blitz*, p. 187.
136 Cunningham, *British Writers*, pp. 239–40.
137 Orwell, *Wigan Pier*, p. 141.

138 A. J. Cronin, *The Citadel* (London: Gollancz, 1937).

139 Bracco, *'Betwixt and Between'*, p. 72.

140 Quoted in Cook, *Priestley*, p. 151.

141 *Sing As We Go* (1934: dir. Basil Dean). John Baxendale and Christopher Pawling, *Narrating the Thirties: A Decade in the Making* (London: Macmillan, 1996), pp. 70–8; Andrew Higson, *Waving the Flag: Constructing a National Cinema in Britain* (Oxford: Oxford University Press, 1995), chapter 4; Jeffrey Richards, *The Age of the Dream Palace* (London: Routledge, 1984), pp. 181–90.

142 Priestley, *Wonder Hero*, pp. 199–260.

143 Ibid., p. 197.

144 Klein, *Fiction*, p. 156.

145 Higson, *Waving*, p. 117.

146 Priestley, *English Journey*, p. 253.

147 Priestley, 'I spotted Gracie's genius but others laughed', *Sunday Chronicle* (18 June 1939), p. 7.

148 Ibid., p. 173.

149 John Sedgwick, 'Regional distinctions in the consumption of films and stars in mid-1930s Britain', www.history.ac.uk/projects/elec/sem18.html, accessed 24 May 2005. Basil Dean, *Mind's Eye* (London: Hutchinson, 1973), p. 210.

150 Higson, *Waving*, p. 121; Sedwick, 'Regional distinctions'.

151 Higson, *Waving*, p. 175.

152 Tony Aldgate, 'Comedy, class and containment: the British domestic cinema of the 1930s', in J. Curran and V. Porter (eds), *British Cinema History* (London: Weidenfeld & Nicolson, 1983), pp. 270–1.

153 Priestley, *Midnight*, p. 49.

154 Priestley to Walpole, 12 July 1936, quoted in Cook, *Priestley*, p. 150.

155 Priestley, *Midnight*, p. 49.

156 Priestley, *Margin*, p. 191.

157 J. B. Priestley, 'Britain wake up!', *News Chronicle* (10 January 1939), p. 8.

158 J. B. Priestley, 'Where is our democracy?', *News Chronicle* (11 January 1939), p. 8.

159 J. B. Priestley, 'The big sham', *News Chronicle* (12 January 1939), p. 14.

160 J. B. Priestley, 'Two kinds of unemployed', *News Chronicle* (13 January 1939), p. 17.

161 J. B. Priestley, 'Thunder on the left', *News Chronicle* (14 January 1939), p. 14.

162 J. B. Priestley, 'And, in conclusion', *News Chronicle* (17 January 1939), p. 4.

3

Englands and Englishness

'Was Jarrow still in England or not? Had we exiled Lancashire and the North-east coast?'[1] Priestley's rhetorical question shows that, for him, the condition of society and the identity of the nation were inseparable. It was his ability to bring the two discourses together which turned him from the popular novelist of 1930 to the political figure of 1940. Not all his contemporaries made the connection. Indeed, for some it seemed that the discourses of 'Englishness' were a way of avoiding the problems of the interwar years. As Alison Light has argued, these years saw a shift in the self-image of the English, away from the 'masculine public rhetorics of national destiny' of the era of high imperialism, towards a 'more inward-looking, more domestic and more private' idea of the nation.[2] But this shift could, and did, have a number of different and conflicting meanings, which cannot be lumped together. It has widely been interpreted as a turning away from industry and urbanism towards 'the "timeless" life of the English countryside'.[3] It can be seen as a turning back to the home-land after the grandiose adventure of Empire, or in revulsion against the demonstrative nationalism of the Great War; or as a turning-inwards to the suburban semi away from the rising class conflict outside its garden gates. For Light, it went along with new forms of modernity, located in the domestic sphere rather than in production, and a suburban image of 'pipe-smoking "little men" with their quietly competent partners, a nation of gardeners and housewives'.[4] Priestley's anti-nationalist narrative of the nation also focused inwards, on the ordinary and the small-scale, but not out of complacency or nostalgia – he was no suburbanite and no ruralist – but rather as the foundation of a national self-renewal that was to come from the bottom up: but only if the 'extraordinary ordinary English people' got a fair crack of the whip.

More than anything else, Priestley was an English writer. It is not just that almost all of his novels and plays were set in England, or that he dealt continually with English characters and English situations – with the sole exception of the United States, no other country figured significantly in his writing, either fictional or factual, and even Celtic Britain hardly appeared on his literary radar – but this is true of other writers as well.[5] It is that he always seemed to be trying to encapsulate the nation as a whole: not just English places or characters or situations but 'England' itself. The tour round England, one of his favourite literary modes, provides the narrative structure of three of his most successful books – *The Good Companions*, *English Journey* and *Lost Empires* – and no fewer than five newspaper or radio series, in 1929, 1933, 1939, 1947 and 1949.[6] Several other novels are structured around the journey from one part of England to another: *Wonder Hero*, for example, with its Slump odyssey from the Midlands to London to the north-east and back again; *Let the People Sing* and *Festival at Farbridge*, in which outsiders arrive to shake up an English town, or even the film *Sing As We Go,* in which Gracie Fields gets on her bike and goes to Blackpool. This mobility is not just a device for getting the plot moving: it is the whole point of the plot, as if staying in one place will simply not encompass what Priestley wants to say.

'England' is also tied up with Priestley's identity as a writer, and his estrangement from modernism in the 1920s and 1930s. Modernism saw itself as an international movement, taking up the engagement with European literature pioneered by the previous generation of realists such as Arnold Bennett. From his early days, Priestley pitched his literary tent on English soil, writing about the Englishness of English literature, and its relation to national character.[7] Like Orwell later on, he suspected the high intelligentsia of loving every country but their own: to highbrows, he commented half-seriously in 1926 'a foreign author is infinitely the superior of an English one of about the same standing, because they believe that their fellow-countrymen are little better than idiots'.[8] It is not so much the highbrows' lack of patriotism that he is criticising here as their lack of regard for ordinary English people – a populism that characterises Priestley's patriotism as it does Orwell's.

As we shall see in the next chapter, Priestley was acutely aware that globalisation, 'this queer interdependence of things', was changing national cultures and threatening their autonomy. He had seen it at work even in the South Seas and now Lancashire was learning the lesson.[9] But, ever the anti-imperialist, his response was not a xenophobic one. His vision of England embraced ethnic difference, looking favourably on the mixed-race children of Liverpool, in whom Nature's bounty confounded racial prejudice to give us 'a glimpse of the world of 2433'.[10] He took pride in the hospitality of his native Bradford towards its colony of German-Jewish merchants, destroyed by the Great War, who had made it one of the most cosmopolitan cities in England long before the postwar South Asian migration. Such exchanges of population were good for everybody, and despite 'the leader-writers in the cheap press ... yelping about Keeping the Foreigner Out ... the great England, the England admired throughout the world, is the England that keeps open house, the refuge of Mazzini, Marx, Lenin'.[11] In his teens Priestley had travelled as widely as he could in Europe, later he regularly visited America and the rest of the world, and he was thoroughly well read in European literature.[12] But when his small daughter commented that 'French people aren't true, are they?', he could only agree, finding, like Orwell, that England and its familiarity simply swallowed him up: 'my patriotism, I assured myself, does begin at home'.[13]

Historiographical shifts

Times change, and with them the stories we tell ourselves about the past. In the 1960s and 1970s the dominant narrative of recent British history was social and political, depicting the journey from the dark days of the Slump via the 'People's War' to the postwar settlement, the Welfare State and the new Welfare/Keynesian consensus.[14] Priestley was a key figure in this narrative, one of those who had helped to pave the 'road to 1945'. In the 1970s and 1980s, this narrative of '1945 and all that' lost its lustre. More urgent seemed to be the rising 'sense of crisis about what it has meant to be British', in response to events including migration, globalisation, European integration and the end of Empire.[15] Aided by the 'cultural turn' in the human sciences, interest passed from the nation as a locus of political action and public policy towards the nation as a cultural construct,   a   product   of   the   collective   imagination: towards 'Englishness'.[16] Interest in Priestley shifted in the same direction.

Unfortunately, few took the trouble to look closely at what Priestley was actually saying about Englishness. Consequently, in some accounts he appeared no longer as the progressive of 1945, but as a conservative, almost reactionary figure, a hater of modern civilisation and a 'little Englander', whose ruralist construction of 'Englishness' echoed that of Conservatives such as Stanley Baldwin and Arthur Bryant. For Martin J. Wiener, Priestley was one of those who preached the anti-industrial, anti-modern ideology which lay behind Britain's economic failures in the twentieth century.[17] For Roger Bromley, his 'Little Englander' mentality prefigured Margaret Thatcher's fear of 'being swamped by people from other cultures'.[18] For Angus Calder, Priestley's wartime broadcasts, despite their apparent radicalism, were 'soaked in traditional values', and did little more than promote the restoration of a conservative national mythology.[19] Chris Waters sums the whole thing up: Priestley's lifelong task was to define and defend an 'essential Englishness', deeply rural and nostalgic in character, as a bulwark against the modern world he detested.[20]

This new understanding of Priestley was mistaken, not just about Priestley's views but about the complex and unstable nature of English identity itself, but it is not difficult to see how it arose. After the 1970s, the '1945' ethos with which Priestley was associated was in retreat before the revival of supposed 'Victorian values'. The left was in defensive mode against what it perceived to be a new nationalism, racism and xenophobia associated with Thatcher's Britain. Britain was now a multi-cultural nation in a post-colonial world, and national identities forged in the imperialist past were no longer appropriate. On all sides, early twentieth-century 'Englishness' was out of fashion.

The most widely noticed critique appeared in 1981, in the shape of Martin J. Wiener's *English Culture and the Decline of the Industrial Spirit*.[21] Wiener's book was notable for escaping from the academic ghetto in which historians are normally closely confined into the broader sphere of public debate, and his thesis, which was extensively promoted (though rarely critically discussed) in newspaper articles, political speeches and television programmes, became part of the conventional wisdom of the time.[22] Wiener revived and elaborated the long-standing idea that after about 1850 England became culturally backward, looking to the past, the countryside and gentlemanly values, rather than to industry, urbanism and the future, and that this 'southern metaphor', to adopt Donald Horne's term, has defined the dominant English identity ever since.[23] This analysis appealed to a wide spectrum of opinion: to Thatcherites, who thought they were returning the nation to the Victorian spirit of enterprise; to the left, for whom it encapsulated the 'failure' of British capitalism and the incompleteness of Britain's bourgeois revolution, as argued in *New Left Review* in the 1960s; and to liberal modernisers, for whom sniping at the 'heritage industry' had become a popular sport.[24] Wiener's method took the form of a series of smash-and-grab raids in which a large number of writers were looted for quotes which could be used to support his thesis. Unfortunately, this often meant they were wrenched out of their original context, both historical and textual, to be re-contextualised within Wiener's narrative of the 'decline of the industrial spirit'. However, following Wiener it became commonplace to assert, usually on slender evidence, that the dominant construction of Englishness was one based on the traditions, landscape and social patterns of 'Deep England'.[25]

Critics of the 'Wiener thesis' tended to focus on the question of 'decline', and on the gentrification of the industrialists, which Priestley had criticised in the 1930s. However, in the 1990s, coincident, perhaps, with the decline and fall of Thatcherism, politicians and intellectuals on the left began to call not for an abandonment but for a redefinition of Englishness, and a recognition of its newfound multidimensionality.[26] Historians such as Peter Mandler and David Matless questioned the identification of Englishness with ruralism, and vice versa, while James Vernon, in post-structuralist vein, argued that Englishness 'has always been, and remains, radically unstable'.[27]

Priestley, though no post-structuralist, would perhaps agree with Vernon. After all, the final chapter of *English Journey* concluded that there were at least three 'Englands', each the product of a history, and 'variously and most fascinatingly mixed' to make up an identity which was necessarily contested and unstable.[28] Unlike Vernon, though, he was for ever searching for stability, digging deep to find the bedrock of something securely English on which the nation's future could be built. This he found in the somewhat insubstantial form of the 'English spirit', residing, in true radical fashion, in the English people, and in the radical narrative of their history which was discussed in the previous chapter. This populism was also problematic, but it was a living alternative to an England rooted in imperial glory, national traditions and social hierarchy, and it became an effective vehicle for the social-democratic ideology which, with Priestley's help, was to emerge out of the Second World War. To investigate this, we must first re-examine Priestley's relationship to the backward-looking 'Englishness' described by Wiener and others.

Englishness and the countryside

Priestley loved the English countryside, and wrote very lyrically about it. He deplored the impact upon it of nineteenth-century industrialism and twentieth-century suburbanisation. He edited one book of writings about it, and wrote the introduction to another.[29] To some commentators this is sufficient proof that Priestley was in thrall to the myths of 'Deep England', and further evidence of the centrality of ruralism to English self-identity. Such a conclusion, however, requires interpretative leaps that are rarely justified by the texts being cited, but which even the best historians of Englishness have succumbed to. So, according to Chris Waters, ostensibly quoting a phrase which does not occur in the book, Priestley in *English Journey* finds '"Essential Englishness" ... rooted in the nation's natural heritage'.[30] In similar vein, Angus Calder locates Priestley among the 'Georgians', 'much obsessed with English landscape and countryside', while Iain Chambers finds him standing shoulder to shoulder with the improbable figure of Evelyn Waugh, both finding 'in antique stones, lanes, hills and country houses the true source of England's culture'.[31] Philip Dodd makes Priestley say that the 'real enduring England' is one of 'ministers and manors and inns, of Parson and Squire' – which he can achieve only by spatchcocking together (and misquoting) two phrases from *English Journey* which occur in the reverse order and three pages apart.[32] Paul Rich asserts that *The Good Companions* was set in a 'strong rural and rustic context of the Pennines', which suggests that in 1989 he hadn't read past the first page into the decidedly urban world of Bruddersford. By 1995 he had evidently read a bit further and modified his view, though he still held that, in criticising the ugliness of Birmingham, Priestley was succumbing to the 'Merrie England myth' – an example of the 'excluded middle' if ever there was one.[33] Finally, in their useful sourcebook *Writing Englishness*, Judy Giles and Tim Middleton describe *English Journey* as 'encoding ... the ideology of rural England', and place an extract from its conclusion in a section entitled 'Versions of Rural England', alongside the deep ruralism of Edward Thomas, H. V. Morton and Stanley Baldwin, recklessly disregarding the fact that only one of the 'three Englands' Priestley discusses in the extract is actually rural.[34]

These comments reveal a deep-seated need to believe two propositions, and to stick to them in the face of the evidence: that everyone who mentions the countryside is really talking about the nation; and that anyone who talks about the nation sees it as essentially rural. While there were undoubtedly many people in 1920s and 1930s Britain of whom these things were true, Priestley was not one of them. In any case, the cultural meanings of the countryside are surely a lot more complicated than that, as more recent writing has acknowledged.[35] Alex Potts pointed out some time ago that the meanings of the countryside in the interwar years were multiple and contradictory and its users divided in their purposes and at odds with each other. Rural imagery could promote class struggle or rational modernity just as much as the nostalgic glow of an eternal Englishness.[36] Peter Mandler has argued that only an unrepresentative minority ever really embraced the ruralist view of England, most people being long reconciled to the urban nature of their society.[37] David Matless also has analysed the interwar preoccupation with the countryside as fractured and differentiated along multiple faultlines like the Englishness it is supposed to reflect, not least between planner/preservationists with an affinity to wartime social democracy, and back-to-the-land organicists who set artisanship and folk culture up against urban modernity.[38] If some of Priestley's contemporaries found in the countryside a stirring image of nationhood, for many it was just a nice place to visit in the family car, while others saw a shared heritage that had fallen into feudal hands, over which they would assert their ancestral right to roam, or an image of social harmony, a cosy, domesticated, post-jingo England.[39] For the Tory romantic Arthur Bryant, it stood for a mythic lost England of order, stability and happiness, before the Industrial Revolution and free trade wrecked everything.[40] Yet others worshipped what Patrick Wright has called 'Deep England', a landscape of the mind and of the memory fully accessible only to a few: the point is 'to have *been there* – one must have had the essential experience', preferably both personally and ancestrally.[41] Where in this array of rural discourses do we find Priestley?

Priestley's landscapes

As Susan Cooper rightly observed, Priestley was essentially an urban man and an urban writer.[42] He never wrote at length about rural matters, and set virtually all his novels in towns and cities. He was certainly not a devotee of the cultural formation called Deep England, or a particular admirer of those who inhabited it. Nor did he see in rural England a utopian social model, a Merrie England to which we might return, still less an England somehow more real or essential than the England of towns and industry from which he himself came. He certainly saw in the countryside an England on the whole more beautiful than urban England, threatened by the latter's growth, and therefore in need of protection. But of course, there is nothing ideologically innocent about notions of natural beauty, or of what needs protecting or by what means. How the landscape looks is partly a product of how we look at it, and our gaze is formed within a cultural and historical context, and articulated to other ideological concerns.[43]

Priestley was fully aware of the pitfalls of idealisation. In an essay written in 1926, he compared the rural reality of mud, manure and mortgages, 'actual lumbering beasts ... wet fields and dirty straw' with 'the country that has always existed in our imagination, so clean, trim, lavishly coloured ... always somewhere around the corner'. This Arcadian dream, he pointed out (anticipating Raymond Williams's *The Country and the City*), had been around for ever, so it was not a case of townsmen longing for the fields, rather they projected on to the countryside an eternal yearning for a perfect world, 'an ideal of unchanging beauty which haunts the mind of man everywhere and in every age'.[44]

In *English Journey* Priestley visits the Cotswolds. He finds the Cotswolds beautiful, but in a specific way:

> There were shifting and broken mists below, and somewhere above, a strong sun, which meant that the country was never seen in one blank light. It was one of those autumn mornings when every bush glitters with dewy gossamer. One moved mysteriously through a world of wet gold. Nothing had boundaries or real continuity. Roads climbed and vanished into dripping space. A beech copse was the near end of an impenetrable forest. The little valleys were as remote as Avalon ... We might have been journeying through the England of the poets, a country made out of men's visions.[45]

These 'shifting and broken mists', these hazy boundaries, lead Priestley to call the Cotswolds the 'most English' of landscapes. Haziness, trembling unreality, the light suffused through 'shreds and tatters of mist', are characteristic products of the British climate, bringing to mind the nation's deep mythic history, equally mysterious and unreal, but also the poets and painters who have taught us to see the landscape this way – and, for

Priestley, the English character itself.[46] But much the same could be said of this, very different, landscape:

> There, far below, is the knobbly backbone of England, the Pennine Range. At first the whole dark length of it, from the Peak to Cross Fell, is visible. Then the Derbyshire hills, and the Cumberland fells disappear, for you are descending, somewhere about the middle of the range, where the high moorland thrusts itself between the woollen mills of Yorkshire and the cotton mills of Lancashire. Great winds blow over miles and miles of ling and bog and black rock, and the curlews still go crying in that empty air as they did before the Romans came. There is a glitter of water here and there, from the moorland tarns that are now called reservoirs. In summer you could wander here all day, listening to the larks, and never meet a soul. In winter you could lose your way in an hour or two and die of exposure.[47]

These are the opening lines of *The Good Companions*, the beginning of an extraordinary aerial zoom shot which finally closes in on the cloth caps of the crowd leaving Bruddersford United football ground. We are not in the Cotswolds any more, but in the Pennine landscape of Priestley's youth, where he would stride out onto the moors with his friends, dreaming of a cottage where he could write. But if the northern English landscape was the one he loved best, second only to it was this:

> Everything far away – and you can see scores of miles – is magically moulded and coloured. The mountains, solidly three-dimensional ranges and peaks, are an exquisite blue in the daytime and then turn amethyst at sunset. Things near at hand are dusty green, greyish, brownish, rather drab, but everywhere towards the far horizon rise chunks of colour unbelievably sumptuous. And the nights are even more spacious than the days ... .The spaces are wider than ever, and are lit, night after night, with all the stars of the Northern Hemisphere.[48]

Now we are not even in England. This is the Arizona desert, where Priestley and his family spent time in the late 1930s – recommended, unlikely as it may seem, by John Galsworthy, author of the *Forsyte Saga* – and, after the Yorkshire Dales, the landscape Priestley was most drawn to.[49]

But back in Yorkshire, we don't even need to be in the countryside to find nature working its transformative magic:

> All the spaces of the town were filled with smoky gold. Holmes and Hadley's emporium, the Midland Railway Station, the Wool Exchange, Barclays Bank, the Imperial Music Hall, all shone like palaces. Smithson Square was like some quivering Western sea, and the Right Honourable Ebenezer Smithson himself, his marble scroll now a map of the Indies, was conjured into an Elizabethan admiral. The façades of Market Street towered strangely and spread a wealth of carven stone before the sun. Town Hall Square was a vast palace of golden light; and its famous clock, as it moved to celebrate the

enchanted moments, gave a great whirr and then shook down into the streets
its more rapturous chimes, *The Lass of Richmond Hill*.[50]

This is the Bruddersford of *The Good Companions*, a thinly disguised
Bradford, of which there is a similar description, written over thirty years
later, in *Margin Released*. 'I cannot believe,' declared Priestley then, 'that
the people who see nothing in West Riding towns but unrelieved ugliness
really use their eyes. They are not looking as a painter would look; they
are at the mercy of an idea of Victorian industrialism.'[51] And not only
West Riding towns: in the London of *They Walk in the City*, 'shapes out
of an adventurous dream drift by on a tide of gilded and silvered air. Such
is the City on one of these mornings, a place in a Gothic fairy tale, a
mirage, a vision, Cockaigne made out of faint sunlight and vapour and
smoke'.[52] The sunlight, the mist and the smoke transport Bradford or
London into another time and another world, perhaps the one that lurks
just around the corner in the work of Pieter Bruegel.[53]

There are people in these fairytale landscapes them, sometimes in
harmony with the landscape, sometimes a disruptive contrast. In the City,
'somewhere behind this enchanting façade, directors are drawing their
fees, debenture-holders are being taken care of, loans are being called in
... '. Back in the Cotswolds, Priestley found stonemasons whose buildings, made for centuries out of local stone, seemed to grow out of the very
landscape: 'In their hands, the stone flowers naturally into these mullions.
They can see Cotswold houses already stirring in the very quarries.' The
unexpected images of flowering stone and houses coming to life establishes an organic relationship between people and the landscape, the
connection between the two made by human labour. But in the touristy
village of Broadway, modernity creates discord – 'Ye Olde Shoppes' and
'bright young people who had just arrived from town and the *Tatler* in
gamboge and vermilion sports cars' – but also the potential salvation of
the landscape in the shape of retired urban businessmen who fall in love
with it.[54] But modernity has been here before. Priestley is fully aware that
the Cotswolds are not a timeless Garden of Eden but a failed industrial
district. When these beautiful, harmonious towns were built, they were
wool towns, and, before Priestley's native West Riding, nearer the coal-
fields, took the wool business away, this was one of the most densely
populated areas in the country.[55] Meanwhile, back in those Pennines, we
again find harmony between people and the landscape, but this time they
are present-day industrial people:

> [T]hough these are lonely places, almost unchanged since the Domesday
> Book was compiled, you cannot understand industrial Yorkshire and
> Lancashire, the wool trade and the cotton trade and many other things
> beside, such as the popularity of Handel's *Messiah* or the Northern Union
> Rugby game, without having seen such places ... At first the towns only

seem a blacker edge to the high moorland, so many fantastic outcroppings of its rock. But now that you are closer you see the host of tall chimneys, the rows and rows of little houses, built of blackening stone, that are like tiny sharp ridges on the hills. These windy moors, these clanking dark valleys, these factories and little stone houses ... have between them bred a race that has special characteristics ... who use emphatic consonants and very broad vowels, and always sound aggressive, who are afraid of nothing but mysterious codes of etiquette and any display of feeling.[56]

Despite the superficial dissonance between remote windy moors and busy industrial towns, Priestley makes the two part of an organic whole, in which the buildings, though the product of human labour, seem to grow out of the landscape, and even the people seem to spring from the moorland and take on its characteristics. In all these English landscapes, Priestley finds 'a compromise between wildness and tameness, between Nature and Man': 'whole towns fitted snugly into the landscape, as if they were no more than bits of woodland; and roads went winding the easiest way as naturally as rivers; and it was impossible to say where cultivation ended and wild life began'. A harmony disrupted only by 'cheap mass production and standardised living ... the dirty hotch-potch of today'.[57] So the landscape, rural or urban, has a consistent moral meaning, presenting the a harmony that, without 'nobly creative ideas', present-day society was finding it impossible to repeat.

Of our three landscapes – Cotswolds, Pennines and Arizona – only in the latter does humanity's role seem insignificant. This may be the New World, comments Priestley, but it is 'the oldest country I have ever seen, the real antique land, first cousin to the moon ... There is no history here because history is too recent.' The meaning of this landscape is tied up with these absences.[58] The historic presence of Native Americans is conveniently forgotten in this rhetorical trope, though it is dealt with elsewhere.[59] There is, however, one other semi-legendary presence in this wilderness: the cowboy, 'the solitary heroic figure' who has escaped the economic slavery of urban capitalism and 'contrived to live his life in an epic simplicity impossible to the rest of us'. The cowboy has become the subject matter of pulp fiction, utopian object of the wistful admiration of those who know their own lives are undignified and unheroic, precisely because he is not rooted as they are, and his gravely courteous manner with strangers is perhaps just the way all Americans were when they were newcomers to the land.[60]

There is undoubtedly an idealisation of the landscape in all these different accounts. Each, in different ways, is set up both as an ideal of beauty and as the antithesis of the things Priestley dislikes about modernity. But, Arizona apart, they are not a product of nature alone, but of the interplay between people and nature, an interplay which includes industry as well as agriculture. The landscape is the product of human history, as even the 'almost unchanged' Pennines are identified with the Romans, Domesday Book, the Industrial Revolution. In turn the character of the people who live in these places is either shaped by, or metaphorically expressed in the character of the landscape, so that it is not always easy to see where the history ends and the metaphor begins. Of course, modern people have made a mess of this relationship with nature, but even in the heart of the industrial city, the old partnership is still at work, buildings and sunlight, smoke and mist co-operating to create an unexpected beauty. The thing is to restore the harmony, but not by going back to an imagined past, or an idealised rural life, as so many of Priestley's contemporaries were eager to do.

In 1924 Stanley Baldwin, the midlands ironmaster turned Tory Prime Minister, in the peroration of a speech much quoted as an example of inter war 'ruralist' Englishness, asked what is it most of all that England stands for?[61] Baldwin answers, 'England is the country and the country is England'. The 'things that make England', that 'strike down into the very depths of our nature', are all country things: the sounds, the sights, the smells of rural life. There are people in Baldwin's landscape as in Priestley's, ploughmen and blacksmiths alongside corncrakes and primroses. But what is missing, and what, crucially, we find in Priestley, is history, and, without history, all sense of change or variety is lost. For Baldwin, everything rural is 'eternal', 'imperishable', sights and sounds touching 'chords that go back to the beginning of time and the human race'. The horse-drawn plough, a specific agricultural technology with its own history (shortly to end, as could easily be foreseen in 1924), is for Baldwin a timeless feature of rural life: 'the sight that has been seen in England since England was a land ... the one eternal sight of England', which will endure long after the Empire and industry are gone. If we catch the smell of wood-smoke on an autumn evening, so did 'our ancestors, tens of thousands of years ago ... coming home with the day's forage, when they were still nomads, and when they were still roaming the forests and the plains of the continent of Europe'.[62] Rural Englishness, then, is not only uniform across the whole country (flying in the face of geography) and completely unchanged over the millennia (flying in the face of agricultural history), but even existed before England did. Only recently, we gather, have the English people been deprived of that birthright by being made to live in towns. But their love of gardens, and their settlement of the unspoiled Dominions, show that the countryside is 'innate and inherent in our people'. So everything, even the Empire, goes back to the English countryside.

In similar vein, H. V. Morton, when he goes In Search of England (1927), decides that it is to be found not in the towns and cities where most English people (including Morton) live but in the countryside, and 'the village that symbolizes England [and] sleeps in the subconscious of many a townsman'. Like *English Journey*, Morton's book is the story of a round trip, in which people met and sights seen evoke pithy and some-times weighty observations from the narrator. But where Priestley's is simply a *Journey*, Morton's is a *Search*: there is a real England there to be found, not three of them but one, and the book's brief prologue tells us what it is. Ill and homesick in inhospitable Palestine, Morton summons up the image of an English village at dusk, and resolves to return home, and go in search of England: that is, 'the lanes of England, the little thatched villages of England ... English bridges ... English grass'. And not just any countryside, either, but, as the thatched cottages signal, a southern, lowland one. So the frontispiece depicts not miners' cottages or slag-heaps or city streets, but shire-horses making their way down a country lane past a picturesque thatched, half-timbered cottage. This is not a book about rural England – although the Introduction dwells upon the present-day plight of agriculture, that is the last we hear of the matter – so much as a book about the essential rurality of England.[63]

There was a lot of this kind of talk about in the 1930s. But the motives behind it varied: it cannot be reduced to a single uncontradictory discourse of English ruralism. Morton later wrote a series of articles for the *Daily Herald* investigating slum conditions in six major cities, later reprinted as a Labour Party pamphlet, which illustrates how a ruralist distaste for urban life could be turned to a reforming purpose, whatever the author, himself rather right-wing, had intended.[64] The intended effect of Baldwin's rhetoric was, in Bill Schwarz's words, 'to displace and neutralise the antagonism between the people and the state', and as Ross McKibbin has pointed out, it concealed a political strategy which effec-tively excluded the organised working class from its conception of the nation.[65] At a different level, the innumerable guides to the English coun-tryside and heritage that appeared in the 1930s were written not to construct the ideology of the nation but to inform motorists about the beautiful, interesting or historic places they could drive to, and to tell them what to look for when they got there. Nevertheless, many of them also felt the need to instruct their readers about what it should all mean to them. Thus:

> The Englishman is at heart a countryman; towns do not come naturally to him. Often only one or two generations separate the confirmed town dwellers of today from the completely rural life of their forbears. The call of the country-side was never greater than it has become in recent years, and, with more and more leisure, it is not too much to hope that as heretofore the townsman will turn to 'the sound of the blackbird and the rippling stream, or the keen wind off the misty hills' as to his real home.[66]

So the countryside is not just a good place to visit: it's where you really belong, your 'real home'. This kind of sentiment was commonplace in the 1920s and 1930s; but how far did people really believe it? Tourism is partly about the search for difference, and the attraction of the motor car, as of the excursion train before it, was that you could quickly be whisked off from one way of life in the town to another in the country or at the seaside, just as planes would whisk later generations off to somewhere sunny and foreign. Unlike present-day visitors to the Costa del Sol, though, day-trippers to the English countryside could tell themselves, if they so wished, that their ancestors did live there, that in a historical sense, perhaps it was their 'real home'. Summoning up romantic notions of the naturalness of the countryside, its 'unspoilt' condition, visitors might well indulge the fantasy of being 'countrymen at heart'. But the reaction of some contemporaries to the explosion of rural day-trippers does not suggest that this was the case. Dr C. E. M. Joad regarded the countryside as, in principle, everybody's birthright, but as yet townspeople simply did not know how to use it, dumping their litter in it, 'cackling insanely' in the woods and singing raucous songs, dancing to gramophones and roaring through quiet country lanes in their cars.[67] Every child, said Joad, needed to be educated in the recognition and appreciation of rural beauty, and taught 'country lore and country manners' at school to make them fit to visit the countryside. If the urban English really did feel an instinctive ancestral affinity to the English landscape, we might well wonder why they needed to be instructed on what it meant and how to use it, and we might well conclude that urban life, far from being alien to these day-trippers, came so naturally to them that they cheerfully brought it with them into the countryside.

Priestley was not against people visiting the countryside: indeed, as it could no longer support itself, that was chiefly what it was there for, so he was all in favour of hikers striding out into the moors, and even people rushing along the country lanes in cars, which he felt could give you a whole new perspective on the landscape.[68] So the best bits of it should be scrupulously preserved, not for us to 'brood and dream' over, but so that we could all have 'an occasional peek', to remind us what 'natural or architectural loveliness' was. Leaving the Cotswolds, he calls for the whole area to become a national park, 'to banish from these hills the grimmer realities of our economic life, to make it *artificially* secure in its fairy tale of old grey stones and misty valleys'.[69] In calling for collective action to protect the best of Old England, just as he called for a plan to save the depressed areas, Priestley, like many other preservationists, was looking forwards, not backwards, challenging the *laissez-faire* approach which had allowed nineteenth-century private enterprise ('cynical greed') free rein to transform the countryside into 'a wilderness of dirty bricks', and leading the way to new forms of governance that were to emerge during and after the Second World War.[70] But any such protective action was inescapably 'artificial': left to its own devices, Old England did not have the means to survive. It was not just greed or bad management which

caused the problem but also our sentimental illusions about the countryside. The very cause of creeping suburbanisation was that (echoing the
received wisdom of the time) '[n]early all Englishmen are at heart country
gentlemen', but far from yearning for a return to Merrie England, or even
just a country house, they were quite happy to play this fantasy role in
their suburban villas and gardens. The result is that suburbia, 'higgledy-
piggledy and messy', was eating up the countryside. Not that the
suburban salesman and clerk care, because like all the English they love a
compromise: avoiding the choice between town and country, they have
'contrived to lose the urban virtues without acquiring the rural ones ...
making the worst of both worlds'. 'It might be better', Priestley declares,
'if people who work in the cities were more mentally urban, more ready
to identify themselves with the life of the city proper', leaving the countryside to be properly looked after.[71]

It was not just the beauty of the landscape which attracted Priestley's
contemporaries but the rural way of life, to which a small but vocal
minority thought we should return, a positive alternative to urban civilisation and machine-led modernity .[72] Towards the extreme end of this
'organicist' school of thought, as Matless describes it, was Priestley's host
in the Cotswolds, Charles Wade of Snowshill Manor, an eccentric
medievalist and 'a thorough hater of everything modern', who had
restored the house with the help of a family fortune made from West
Indies sugar.[73] Wade refused electricity and all modern conveniences, and
would return if he could to the pre-machine days of handcrafts and guilds.
Priestley demurs. Surely, medieval life was a lot less merrie for most
people than Wade supposes: machines had lifted from their backs 'a horrible dead weight of miserable toil'. It was not the machines that caused the
problem but the 'shoddy, greedy, profit-grabbing, joint-stock-company
industrial system' which put them to work, and which we had allowed to
dominate us – a view not dissimilar to that of William Morris, patron
saint of the anti-machine brigade, who was a Marxist as well as a crafts-
man. If 'the dear old quaint England' had been so wonderful, Priestley
asked at the end of *English Journey*, why did the populace rush so eagerly
into the towns and mills as soon as the opportunity arose? 'You do not
hurry out of Arcadia to work in a factory twelve hours a day for about
eighteen pence.' And what was it, exactly, that kept the population so
low?[74] No, this was no Arcadia: those old Cotswold stonemasons who
glorified the Old England with their craftsmanship also flattered it in the
eyes of posterity.[75]

Nor, in a running argument which he describes as the *leitmotif* of his
Cotswold chapter, does Priestley have any time for nonsense about
peasant virtues. Earlier, in a hotel, he has encountered an ex-army officer,
who wants to re-establish the sturdy English peasantry. To which Priestley
replies that a 'romantic literary man's peasant' is all very well, but from

what he has seen of real peasants they are by and large 'ignorant, stupid, mean'.[76] Wade expresses his 'contempt for the new urban mob, the products of industrial towns and free education at council schools and cheap books and so forth'. Priestley, who considers himself one of this mob, is having none of it; he would rather have the 'courage, intelligence, eagerness, chivalry, humour, irony' of the urban working men he fought with in the War than any number of peasants. As for Old England today, it is a luxury country that can no longer earn its own living. The people who live there are, at best, custodians, or marginal eccentrics like his host: at worst, they are playing the 'Ye Olde game', turning villages like Broadway into fashionable parodies of their former selves. Country houses are preserved 'unspoiled and exquisite' only with outside money, as places for 'rich men from the black holes of industry' to spend the profits they made from the 'muck and sweat of Birmingham and Manchester'.[77] We can learn something from the Cotswolds, use it as a laboratory for 'experiments in living', but we would not want to return to its past. 'Our business now', he concludes, 'was not to sentimentalise the Middle Ages but to take the whole roaring machine-ridden world as it is and make a civilised job of it.'[78] In this spirit Priestley heads off to the car factories of Coventry, and the distress of the industrial midlands and north.

Gentlemanly traditions

So Priestley, though he loved the countryside, wanted it kept firmly in its place – and the people of England in theirs, which was now the city, and which they should try to improve instead of seeking to escape from it. Unfortunately, however, among those who had been deserting the city were its erstwhile social leaders, lured into the countryside by the siren song of Old England. In Bradford, he found, 'the richer manufacturers and merchants no longer live in the city. They work there, but live well outside, Ilkley, Harrogate, Grassington way ... Throughout the north ... the wealthier industrialists are busy turning themselves into country gentlemen and are leaving the cities to the professional, clerking and working classes.'[79] The lure of rural life had also drawn Hull's more substantial citizens out of the city, with the result that, as in Bradford, the arts, and in particular the theatre, had gone into a decline.[80] In Bristol, by contrast, he found that the big merchant families were still resident, and civic culture was thriving.[81] The decay of civic life is one of the running themes of English Journey, and it is not only the collapse of industry in the Slump which was held responsible but the continued attractions of the gentlemanly life, as well as, ironically, modernity in the shape of the motor car, which had made it possible to live in the country and do business in the city.

Off they go into the country. The directors go first, and then the managers and cashiers, if they can afford it, follow them. One of them is asked to dinner by a peer. A baronet has nodded to another. The County may be calling. A little rough shooting, eh? What about the Hunt next season? And Coketown is nothing but a distant blur of smoke, and its long dark streets are forgotten. I do not say that there is not in many of the English a deep love of the countryside ... But always, over and above this, there is the lure of this absurd tradition, this retracing of the feudal pattern, this gigantic pretence.[82]

By the time Priestley wrote *The English* in 1973, this lament had developed into a full-blown, quasi-Wienerian explanation of the relative decline of British industry.

Because the aristocratic tradition outlasted the downright socially democratic Manchester outlook, grandsons of the original successful mill-owners and merchants were sent to public schools, to Oxford and Cambridge, and too often fell in love with the country-house style of life, probably the most seductive of all styles of life. So time, attention and money too often went elsewhere, not back into business.[83]

So as soon as foreign competition arrived, English industry came to seem 'amateurish and old-fashioned' and was easily overtaken. It is ironical that this succinct statement of the 'Wiener thesis', a decade before Wiener, came from one of the alleged enemies of his 'industrial spirit'.[84] The class system with its lingering aristocratic tradition, Priestley argued, also lay behind the feeling of 'staleness, boredom, vague depression' which constituted the malaise of the postwar years. The trouble was that most of the English felt happier with a class system than with an egalitarian society. But at the same time it was dragging us down: there were too many 'apparently important men, ennobled, decorated and beribboned, who have really never done anything in particular', too many of the 'quaint traditional ceremonies', which used to have meaning, but now only pleased the tourists: the life had ebbed out of them. England should ditch this 'oh-so-English traditional business' and 'discover her own living identity, something better than a tourist attraction'.[85] True to these words, Priestley would turn down Harold Wilson's offers of a knighthood and a peerage.[86]

Priestley had long been averse to 'tradition, that great English hocus-pocus'. In his youth, unlike some schoolfriends, he could not see himself at Oxbridge, 'in courts or quads, under dreaming spires ... Statutes about not playing marbles on the Senate House steps, that kind of thing, never made me giggle cosily; they merely irritated me ... I felt even then alienated rather than attracted by everything that had been long-established.'[87] Brought up in an environment free of 'ladies and gentlemen', it was wartime before he encountered 'various specimens of the English ruling class, and listened to accents so extraordinary that they might as well have been foreigners'.[88] When he finally arrived at Cambridge after the war, he was predictably uncomfortable there, 'being compelled to feel – and quite rightly too – a bit of a lout and a bit of a mountebank'.[89]

In 1939, increasingly radicalised by the experiences of the 1930s, and frustrated by the lack of progress since he wrote English Journey, Priestley launched a polemical attack on the nation's hidebound traditionalism. The conclusion to Rain Upon Godshill prefigured his wartime writings, and was firmly rooted in the English radical tradition: plutocracy, the rotting remnants of feudalism, the failure of democratisation were holding the people down: set them free, and who knows what they could achieve. But the chance of democratic progress after 1918, he argued, had been lost, and we were further from a real democracy than we had been in 1912.[90] We prided ourselves on inheriting institutions that had grown organically, like trees, but now there were cracks in the trees and the smell of rotting wood everywhere. As a nation, 'we wear the face of the inheritor, not the creator. We have amongst us thousands and thousands of Bertie Woosters who do not know that Jeeves is dead.'[91] At the top of the social pyramid was the Crown. The Crown was very popular: and why not? It wielded no power, was agreeably glamorous and did not pretend to be something it was not. But the function of the Crown was to hold together a social pyramid that was nothing more than a gigantic sham: 'a plutocracy pretending to be an aristocracy ... an unreal world of masquerades and disguises', in which rich businessmen could buy peerages and disguise themselves as feudal barons.[92]

> This is called keeping up a tradition. It is no more keeping up a tradition than the auctioning of old armour can be called knight-errantry. It is prostituting a tradition. This is a real country, where men and women have to live out their lives, and not a vast fancy-dress ball ... The tradition of feudal aristocracy and landed gentry hangs over our life like the pall of smoke over wintry London.[93]

It is this, he continued, which stopped us behaving like grown-up people, stopped us abolishing the House of Lords or reforming the electoral system, and kept us glued to the antics of the fashionable and titled in the newspapers and gossip columns. 'And while everybody is still gaping or cheering, no awkward questions will be asked', and the Right People remain in charge. This 'pretence of values that no longer exist' encouraged mental dishonesty, blunted intelligent criticism and promoted indifference to the life of the mind and spirit.[94] Even the cinema was unable to depict more than 'the faintest dribble of real English life', while BBC, stuffy and inhibited on principle, lacked the spontaneity of American radio.[95] Do away with all this feudal baggage, and the people would come back to life, become 'more honest ... easier, gayer, and more intelligent ... turn into real characters, genuine folk'.[96] Instead, they waited in the streets all night to see the 1937 Coronation - 'a ceremony with hardly a glimmer of real significance left, an immense empty shell of a function' – not out of loyalty and affection for the monarch, or because they had been brainwashed by the newspapers, but out of their 'hunger for beauty and joy' in a world of 'empty shows and dingy routine'. 'But to crown at last these people themselves, to ennoble the whole kingdom, where were the wealth and time and energy for this task? Who would, after taking down the bunting and the lights, tear down the streets themselves, and build a nobler, happier, beautiful Britain?'[97] Priestley expressed the same forceful views in the London evening newspaper the *Star* on Coronation day itself, his article running alongside a routinely royalist editorial, unabashed by a royal coat of arms, and a page heading which proclaimed 'God Save the King' in a suitably archaic typeface.[98]

At the end of *English Journey*, Priestley declared himself 'bursting with blatant patriotism', proud of the English heritage: not the Empire and the Crown, but the countryside, the cathedrals, Shakespeare: 'so many great men and great ideas that one's mind is dazzled by their riches. We stagger beneath our inheritance.' But he had also seen a lot of bad things on his travels, and, measured against them, this inheritance was not what really counted: it would not, by itself, put right the nation's problems. There was something far more important at stake. 'Let us burn every book, tear down every memorial, turn every cathedral and college into an engineering shop, rather than grow cold and petrify, rather than forget that inner glowing tradition of the English spirit' – the spirit that will defend freedom and social justice, protect exiled foreigners, and will not tolerate 'an ugly, mean way of living'.[99] If Priestley was searching for a 'real, essential England', he had found it not in the landscape but in this 'English spirit'.

National character

Priestley was a patriot, but a patriot of a particular kind:

> I thought about patriotism. I wished I had been born early enough to have been called a Little Englander. It was a term of sneering abuse, but I should be delighted to accept it as a description of myself. That *little* sounds the right note of affection. It is little England I love. And I considered how much I disliked Big Englanders, whom I saw as red-faced, staring, loud-voiced fellows, wanting to go and boss everybody about all over the world, and being surprised and pained and saying 'bad show!' if some blighters refused to fag for them. They are patriots to a man.[100]

'Little Englanders', of course, were not the xenophobes to whom the label is most often applied today, but rather the opposite – Edwardian anti-imperialists, amongst whom Priestley counted his father and himself. 'Big Englanders', as Priestley called them, stand for a different conception of an Englishman: the Imperial Hero, still extant in 1930s, but in retreat. A turning-point can be identified in Bradford, where as part of his *English Journey* Priestley attended a reunion of his old Great War regiment. The 'roaring masculinity' of the 'woolcombers and dyers' labourers, ware-housemen and woolsorters, clerks and tram-conductors' he had fought with is blunted as an inept rendering of the regimental march mars the toast to the dead, and Priestley remembers the greedy old men and diplo-mats and journalists who killed them in the first place, and the plight of some of the survivors who were unable to attend for lack of decent clothes to wear.[101] These men had performed the ultimate masculine public duty of fighting for their country, but returned to a postwar world where the narratives of manhood, of civic life, of comradeship itself had been violated. What price the Imperial Hero now? And what image of English character would replace him?

'National character' is a way of talking about the nation in terms of individual personality traits. We may define it, in Peter Mandler's words, as 'a cultural, psychological or biological essence that all individuals in a nation share in common, and that directs – somewhat abstractly – all manifestations of national life'.[102] It is a very slippery concept, and indeed many people would doubt whether the 'essence' it refers to actually exists, but discourses of national character play an important part in organising popular ideas of nationhood. These discourses take a number of different forms. National character has been seen as biological, a matter of race and genetics. This usage is largely discredited in more thoughtful circles, but many people would still explain the English national character in terms of the 'mixture of many races' that made up the population.[103] It can refer to the way individual values and behaviour are shaped by a shared culture. Thus, for the popular writer Arthur Bryant, 'the strong tradition of England ... mould[ed] the new-comers to the national pattern'; while at an academic level, cultural anthropologists in the 1930s, such as Ruth Benedict and Margaret Mead developed the idea of 'cultural character': regularities in the individual psyche accounted for by patterns of child-rearing, education, etc.; during the Second World War the British and US governments thought it worth employing anthropologists and psychologists to study the national character of the Germans and Japanese.[104] 'National character' can provide crude stereotypes of indi-viduals from other nations, unsupported by rigorous evidence but immensely powerful in constructing our sense of 'us' and the Other. At a more sophisticated level, social psychologists have applied personality theory to testing and identifying 'modal personalities' characteristic of particular cultures. Historians and sociologists, while more suspicious of assertions about individual personality types, have been prepared to debate national character as a collective phenomenon perhaps susceptible to historical analysis: for example, the contradiction in the American national character between frontier individualism and corporate-capitalist conformity, or the relative influence of romanticism and authoritarianism on the German character.[105]

Whether valid or not, 'national character' has provided nations with a way of talking to themselves about themselves. Peter Mandler argues that this way of thinking about the nation became 'respectable and necessary' in the mid nineteenth century, when liberals projected a vision of the English character as modern and commercial: egalitarian, self-governing, enterprising and adaptable.[106] Imperialism brought with it more atavistic notions of character based on heroism, duty and manliness, which were drawn upon in the early stages of the Great War – the 'big-Englandism' which had sent Priestley's comrades off to die, but which after 1918 was in retreat, as Alison Light argues, and as Priestley's Bradford narrative suggests, though lingering on in the popular fiction of war and Empire.[107] Even Conservatives like Stanley Baldwin renounced the jingoistic past of 'flag-wagging [and] boasting of painting the map red', and insisted that any resemblance between the British Empire and previous enterprises bearing a similar name (the French, the Roman, the Russian) was purely coincidental.[108]

The version of national character that we find in these years is still individualistic and freedom-loving, but lower-key, showing a desire to retreat not just from Empire but also from the expansionist capitalism of the nineteenth century, whose future in any case seemed in doubt. This was not a retreat into the past, or a into rural fantasy, but into the suburban house and garden, where the modernity of the time was most closely encountered. A dissident minority apart, discourses of national character displayed a surprising degree of agreement.[109] For Baldwin the English were creative but anti-intellectual, serene in difficulties but ruthless in action, sympathetic to the underdog and 'the kindest people in the world', and above all a nation of individuals.[110] To the right-wing writer Arthur Bryant, who described the national character as 'probably the most secure asset in our heritage', the Englishman was 'kindly, dogged, humorous, patient', with a self-confidence and inner contentment which arose from a love of home, 'an intense "at-oneness" with his environment' and the 'England of his dreams'.[111] On the left, George Orwell saw the English as unintellectual, and impractical, lovers of personal liberty and privacy, anti-militaristic and gentle, but apt to slip into brutality not out of hypocrisy so much as through their tendency to act on instinct rather than thought.[112] For the Scotsman John Allan the Englishman had an easy but not a humble mind, was reluctant to contemplate radical change and lived 'happily in a certain moral and intellectual confusion'.[113] A. L. Rowse found at the core of the English spirit a deep inner contentment with life, and a profound wish to be left alone.[114] One could go on, almost ad infinitum, but all these examples from the 1920s, 1930s and 1940s point in much the same general direction: towards a peaceful, private, kindly, individualistic people, reliant on instinct more than intellect.

What about Priestley? We find in his writing about national character a similar perspective, but given an added twist by some of his own preoccupations. The English, he wrote in 1929, are a very private people, not to be judged by how they behave in public. The observer 'sees the high walls, but not the gardens they enclose. He watches Englishmen hurrying silently through the streets to their homes, and does not realise that they are hurrying away, out of his sight, only in order that they may unbend at last, turning themselves into persons he would not recognise.'[115] They are an instinctive, not an intellectual people:

> The English do not approach life intellectually; they do not demand that it shall conform to some rigid mental plan; they are not convinced that the universe can be penetrated by thought; ... they are willing to go to work, either in politics or art, without a theory to sustain them ... they do not busy themselves asking reason to find a key when instinct has already shown them that the door is wide open.

Far from being cold and unimaginative as some believe, they are deeply emotional and romantic. They 'float through life on a deep if narrow stream of feeling ... they live in such a deep intimacy with their feelings that they find it difficult and distasteful to reveal them ... feeling to them is the key to the inner citadel, and to lose control of themselves is to reveal the last secret'.[116] There is a strong metaphorical link between Priestley's view of the English mind and his view of the English landscape. In the former, there is 'a haze, rubbing away the hard edges of ideas, softening and blending the hues of passion'; while the latter is 'covered with mists so light that they are nothing but a haze, in which hard edges are rubbed away and colours are softened and blended'. In the English mind, as in the countryside, there are no 'long straight roads down which the battalions of thought must march', reason does not conquer all, but 'mirth and melancholy play like light and shadow, sunlight and mist'. [117]

The Czech exile Professor Kronak in *Let the People Sing* (1939) develops the point, and by this time Priestley has refined his analysis with some Jungian concepts and bolstered its populism. People think the English are hostile to art, the Professor argues, but this is just the official, upper-class tradition, the prejudices of a landed ruling class:

> [A] great many of the English, because they are dominated by what lies in the unconscious, are genuine if only half-developed artists. In this they are the opposite of the French, who are controlled by their conscious minds, and appear to be more artistic than they really are. If England were to be conquered, were suddenly to lose nearly all its wealth and power ... I think

the English would soon be famous throughout the world as a race of poets, painters and actors, and life on this strange misty island, which is essentially romantic in its atmosphere, would seem to the Americans, Russians, Chinese, who by that time would do the world's manufacturing, to be a fairy tale of arts and dreams.[118]

In *The English*, published in 1973, Priestley developed Professor Kronak's Jungian account. In the English psyche, he wrote,

> the barrier between consciousness and the unconscious is not fixed, high and strong, and indeed is not really complete, so that the conscious and the unconscious often merge as if they were two English counties sharing irregular misty boundaries ... It is essentially English not to allow the intellect to go its own way and decide everything: it must submit to some shaping and colouring by the instinctive and the intuitive.[119]

Accounts of the English character with which Priestley disagrees – for example, that they are energetic and practical, or unusually kind and tender-hearted – are dismissed, again in Jungian terms, as self-deception coming from the shadow side of Englishness, an unavoidable result of the overlap between consciousness and the unconscious.[120]

This instinctive and intuitive side of the English character, Priestley is convinced, is 'the essence of Englishness, the great clue, the guiding thread in the maze'. Interestingly, he acknowledges that this points to a feminine cast of mind, not the 'robustly masculine image that Englishmen have projected down the centuries'; a view which fits Priestley's anti-imperialist hostility to 'Big Englanders', and acknowledges a feminisation of the English self-image which, if we follow Alison Light, was well under way in the 1920s.[121] In *The English* Priestley traces this Englishness through many facets of English life and culture. He finds it at work in the arts, humour, hobbies; he studies English women, the upper and lower classes, and seven case studies of individuals (all men!) who represent the central and essential character of Englishness in a variety of ways. The outcome of this rumination is rather surprising. The English character, it seems, is not always to be found in England. There are moments in history where it goes underground, and England follows a path which is inimical to its true nature. One such moment is the eighteenth-century Age of Reason; another is the twentieth-century Age of Admass.[122] Moreover, not only certain English artists (Turner, Blake, Stanley Spencer, Sickert) but a whole litany of revered English leaders, once considered the epitome of English virtues, are found wanting in true Englishness. Cromwell, Fox, Nelson and Palmerston were English enough, as were Bevin and Churchill in later years; but not Pitt, Melbourne, Gladstone or Disraeli, Chamberlain or Asquith, or, surprisingly, the Duke of Wellington.[123] Indeed, despite as an Irishman not really qualifying as English at all, Wellington is held responsible, by his personal example, for creating a new and distinctly non-English type of Englishman, associated with the public-school system: 'the strong, arrogant, silent Englishman of the ruling class', poker-faced, laconic and unaffected by the vagaries of instinct or intuition; steady, reliable conformists brought up to mistrust the imagination, and lacking in any 'enlivening sign of Englishness'.[124] And so, ironically, this 'famous Irishman playing a character part' created a type which was widely but mistakenly assumed to be the essence of Englishness.[125] As Priestley put it in 1939

> [A]bout a hundred and fifty years ago our ruling classes adopted a pretence of being the new Roman stoics, calm-faced, steely conquerors. Wellington, with his habitual cool understatement, was the type. The public schools learned and taught the trick. The Empire Builders carried on and widened the tradition. And now we are the unemotional race, so that some foreigners see us as chilly, reptilian creatures, incapable of feeling. Actually we are a deeply emotional people, and therefore it is neither safe nor sensible to behave as if we were not.[126]

So if the essential upper-class Englishman does not epitomise the English national character, who does? The true home of Englishness, it turns out, is among the 'Uncommon Common People', who for a long time have been 'chockful of Englishness'. This is discovered in their refusal both of fanatical reason and of wild irrationality, their combination of scepticism and credulity, their 'tolerant, rarely unkind, live-and-let-live reasonableness'. Tradition, in fact, was more important to the common people than to the upper class, but it was a tradition passed down not through empty rituals but by way of talk at the fireside or in the pub, in popular memory.[127]

The shadow side of this ordinary Englishness is a tendency to cosy self-deception and lazy self-satisfaction, a 'slow-moving hazy reasonableness' which inhibits the making of sharp decisions.[128] Even in the darkest days of industrial England, the common people were producing 'courageous and independent, odd and richly humorous characters', exemplified in the old music-halls.[129] The ordinary English people were at their best during the Second World War, driven by a sense of great common purpose, but since then they have acquired a reputation for being lazy and bloody-minded, which reflects 'their deep feeling of unease, their underlying disappointment at the way life seems to be going' in the mechanised and Americanised postwar world – an instinctive and intuitive disappointment to which, being English, and therefore open to the unconscious, they are unable to keep at bay.[130] Here, finally, Priestley manages to link all his preoccupations about society and history, culture and class, into the single overriding issue of Englishness and the English character.

Notes

1 Priestley, *English Journey*, p. 411.

2 Light, *Forever England*, pp. 8–9.

3 Krishnan Kumar, *The Making of English National Identity* (Cambridge: Cambridge University Press, 2003), pp. 230–2; Martin J. Wiener, *English Culture and the Decline of the Industrial Spirit 1850–1980* (Cambridge: Cambridge University Press, 1981).

4 Light, *Forever England*, p. 211.

5 For rare exceptions see *Empires*, pp. 35–92; *Sunday Dispatch* (19 May, 26 May, 9 June 1929) (visits to Edinburgh and Aberdeen in the series 'I want to know'); 'Men of steel', *News Chronicle* (19 October 1947), p. 2 (a visit to Llanelli in the 'Crisis journey' series); and his disagreeable remarks about the Irish in *English Journey*, pp. 248–9.

6 'I want to know', *Sunday Dispatch* (March–June 1929); *Sunday Chronicle* (September–November 1933); 'Priestley's journey through the new Britain', *News Chronicle* (September–October 1939); 'Crisis journey', *Daily Herald* (September–November 1947); *Journey Across England*, BBC Home Service, reprinted in *Listener* (November–December 1949).

7 Priestley, *The English Comic Characters*; J. B. Priestley, *English Humour* (London: Longmans, Green and Co., 1929); *The English* (London: Heinemann, 1973). See also his second shot at *English Humour* (London: Heinemann, 1976).

8 J. B. Priestley, 'High, low, broad', in *Open House* (London: Heinemann, 1927), p. 164. George Orwell, 'The lion and the unicorn' (1941), *Collected Essays, Journalism and Letters*, vol. 2, p. 95.

9 *English Journey*, pp. 276–7.

10 Ibid., pp. 239–43.

11 Ibid., pp. 158–61.

12 Priestley, *Literature*.

13 Priestley, *English Journey*, p. 417. Orwell, 'The lion and the unicorn', p. 75.

14 Baxendale and Pawling, *Narrating*, chapter 6.

15 Paul Ward, *Britishness since 1870* (London: Routledge, 2004), pp. 1–2.

16 See, for example, the following pioneers of a literature that has become too extensive to list in a footnote: Patrick Wright, *On Living in an Old Country* (London: Verso, 1985); R. Colls and P. Dodd (eds), *Englishness: Politics and Culture 1880–1920* (London: Croom Helm, 1986); Raphael Samuel (ed.), *Patriotism: The Making and Unmaking of British National Identity*, 3 vols (London: Routledge, 1989); Light, *Forever England*; Linda Colley, *Britons: Forging the Nation 1707–1837* (New Haven: Yale University Press, 1992).

17 Wiener, *English Culture*, pp. 123–5, 166.

18 Roger Bromley, *Lost Narratives: Popular Fictions, Politics and Recent History* (London: Routledge, 1988), p. 124.

19 Calder, *The Myth of the Blitz*, pp. 196–204.

20 Waters, 'J. B. Priestley', p. 210.

21 Wiener, *English Culture*.

22 A two-part treatment by Granada TV's *World in Action*, at the time the most left-wing current affairs programme on British television, featured among

other Wiener enthusiasts the youngish Neil Kinnock, soon to become leader of the Labour Party.

23 Among the literature on the 'Wiener Thesis' see Bruce Collins and Keith Robbins (eds), *British Culture and Economic Decline* (London: Weidenfeld and Nicolson, 1990); W. D. Rubinstein, *Capitalism, Culture and Decline in Britain 1750–1990* (London: Routledge, 1993); F. M. L. Thompson, *Gentrification and the Enterprise Culture: Britain 1780–1980* (Oxford: Oxford University Press, 2001). For an early critique see John Baxendale, 'Anti-industrialism and British national culture: A case-study in the communication and exchange of social values', in A. Cashdan and M. Jordin (eds), *Case Studies in Communication* (Oxford: Blackwell, 1987). The 'Northern' and 'Southern' metaphors are in Donald Horne, *God Is an Englishman* (Harmondsworth: Penguin Books, 1969), pp. 21–3 and *passim*.

24 Perry Anderson, 'Origins of the present crisis', *New Left Review* 23 (1964), reprinted in Anderson, *English Questions* (London: Verso, 1994); Robert Hewison, *The Heritage Industry: Britain in a Climate of Decline* (London: Methuen, 1987).

25 The term 'Deep England' was introduced by Patrick Wright, *On Living in an Old Country*, pp. 81–7, who adapted it from the French. Subsequent appropriations have lost some of the subtlety of the original concept.

26 See, for example, two pamphlets published by the think-tank Demos: Philip Dodd, *The Battle Over Britain* (London: Demos, 1995) and Mark Leonard, *BritainTM* (London: Demos, 1997).

27 James Vernon, 'Englishness: Narration of a nation', *Journal of British Studies* 36 (1997), p. 248; Peter Mandler, 'Against "Englishness": English culture and the limits to rural nostalgia, 1850–1940', *Transactions of the Royal Historical Society*, 6th ser., 7 (1997); David Matless, *Landscape and Englishness* (London: Reaktion Books, 1998). For a recent survey see Ward, *Britishness*.

28 Priestley, *English Journey*, p. 406.

29 J. B. Priestley (ed.), *Our Nation's Heritage* (London: J. M. Dent and Son, 1939); Priestley, 'The beauty of Britain', introduction to Charles Bradley Ford (ed.), *The Beauty of Britain: A Pictorial Survey* (London: Batsford, 1935); Priestley, 'This land of ours', in Anthony Weymouth (ed.), *The English Spirit* (London: Allen and Unwin, 1942).

30 Waters, 'J. B. Priestley', p. 211.

31 Calder, *Myth*, p. 181; Iain Chambers, *Border Dialogues: Journeys in Postmodernity* (London: Routledge, 1990), p. 33.

32 Philip Dodd, 'The views of travellers: travel writing in the 1930s', in Dodd (ed.), *The Art of Travel: Essays on Travel Writing* (London: Frank Cass, 1982), p. 127. See Priestley, *English Journey*, pp. 397, 400. 'Ministers' is presumably a misprint for 'minsters'.

33 Paul Rich, 'Imperial decline and the resurgence of English national identity, 1918–1979', in T. Kushner and K. Lunn (eds), *Traditions of Intolerance* (Manchester: Manchester University Press, 1989), p. 41; Paul Rich, *Prospero's Return? Historical Essays on Race, Culture and British Society* (London: Hanslib, 1994), pp. 36–7.

34 Judy Giles and Tim Middleton (eds), *Writing Englishness 1900–1950: An*

Introductory Sourcebook on National Identity (London: Routledge, 1995), p. 73, and chapter 2.

35 See also, on an earlier period, Keith Thomas, *Man and the Natural World: Changing Attitudes in England, 1500–1800* (London: Allen Lane, 1983), esp. chapter 6.

36 Alex Potts, '"Constable Country" between the wars', in Raphael Samuel (ed.), *Patriotism*, vol. 3: *National Fictions* (London: Routledge, 1989), p. 175.

37 Mandler, 'Against Englishness'.

38 Matless, *Landscape*.

39 Howard Hill, *Freedom to Roam: The Struggle for Access to Britain's Moors and Mountains* (Ashbourne: Moorland, 1980); John Lowerson, 'The battle for the countryside', in Frank Gloversmith (ed.), *Class, Culture and Social Change: A New View of the Thirties* (Brighton: Harvester Press, 1980); Light, *Forever England*, pp. 8–9.

40 Arthur Bryant, *English Saga 1840–1940* (London: Collins, 1940).

41 Calder, *Myth*, p. 182; Wright, *On Living in an Old Country*, pp. 81–7.

42 Cooper, *Priestley*, p. 165.

43 John Taylor, *A Dream of England: Landscape, Photography and the Tourist's Imagination* (Manchester: Manchester University Press, 1994), p. 12.

44 J. B. Priestley, 'The toy farm', in *Open House*, originally published *Saturday Review*, 27 March 1926.

45 Priestley, *English Journey*, p. 50.

46 Ibid., p. 47.

47 Priestley, *Good Companions*, p. 11.

48 Priestley, *Midnight*, p. 91.

49 Priestley, *Margin*, p. 181.

50 Priestley, *Good Companions*, p. 19.

51 Priestley, *Margin*, pp. 19–20.

52 Priestley, *They Walk*, p. 232.

53 Priestley, *Rain*, p. 113.

54 Priestley, *English Journey*, p. 58.

55 Ibid., p. 51.

56 Priestley, *Good Companions*, pp. 11–12.

57 Priestley, 'Beauty', p. 8.

58 Priestley, *Midnight*, pp. 97, 2–3.

59 Ibid., pp. 63ff; see also J. B. Priestley and Jacquetta Hawkes, *Journey Down a Rainbow* (London: Heinemann, 1955).

60 Priestley, *Midnight*, pp. 95–102.

61 Stanley Baldwin, 'England', in *On England and Other Addresses* (London, Philip Allan, 1926), pp. 1–9. See also Bill Schwarz, 'The language of constitutionalism: Baldwinite Conservatism', in *Formations of Nation and People* (London: Routledge & Kegan Paul, 1984); Philip Williamson, 'The doctrinal politics of Stanley Baldwin', in Michael Bentley (ed.), *Public and Private Doctrine: Essays in British History Presented to Maurice Cowling* (Cambridge, Cambridge University Press, 1993); and Sian Nicholas, 'The construction of a national identity: Stanley Baldwin, "Englishness" and the

mass media in inter-war Britain', in Martin Francis and Ina Zweiniger-Bargielowski (eds), *The Conservatives and British Society, 1880–1990* (Cardiff: University of Wales Press, 1996).

62 Baldwin, 'England', p. 7.

63 Morton, *In Search of England*, pp. vii-xi; 1–3.

64 H. V. Morton, *What I Saw in the Slums* (London: The Labour Party, 1933). It is possible that Morton had no control over the later use of his *Daily Herald* articles. Bartholomew, *In Search of H. V. Morton*, pp. 145–7; see also chapters 7 and 8 for Morton's politics, his sympathy for fascism and his later attempt to recreate the hierarchical rural idyll of his imaginary England in apartheid South Africa.

65 Schwarz, 'Language', p. 18; Ross McKibbin, 'Class and conventional wisdom: The Conservative Party and the "public" in inter-war Britain', in *The Ideologies of Class: Social Relations in Britain 1880–1950* (Oxford: Clarendon Press, 1990).

66 W. S. Shears, *This England: A Book of the Shires and Counties* (London: Hutchinson & Co., 1936), p. 8.

67 C. E. M. Joad, 'The people's claim', in Clough Williams-Ellis (ed.), *Britain and the Beast* (London: J. M. Dent and Sons, 1937), pp. 64–85.

68 Priestley, *English Journey*, p. 268; Priestley, 'The beauty of Britain', p. 3.

69 Priestley, *English Journey*, p. 66, italics added.

70 Ibid., p. 400; Matless, *Landscape*, chapter 1.

71 Priestley, 'The beauty of Britain', pp. 6–7.

72 Matless, *Landscape*, chapters 3 and 4.

73 Priestley, *English Journey*, pp. 53–5; The National Trust, *Snowshill Manor* (London: National Trust, 1995).

74 Priestley, *English Journey*, p. 400.

75 Ibid., p. 66.

76 Ibid., p. 49.

77 Ibid., p. 57.

78 Ibid., pp. 49, 65–6.

79 Ibid., p. 196.

80 Ibid., p. 358.

81 Ibid., pp. 30–3.

82 Priestley, *Rain*, pp. 237–8.

83 Priestley, *The English*, p. 124.

84 Wiener, *English Culture*.

85 Priestley, *The English*, pp. 20–2.

86 Cook, *Priestley*, p. 287.

87 Priestley, *Margin*, pp. 4.

88 Priestley, *Edwardians*, p. 56.

89 Priestley, *English Journey*, p. 394.

90 Priestley, *Rain*, pp. 223–4.

91 Ibid., p. 221.

92 Ibid., pp. 232–4.

93 Ibid., p. 236.

94 Ibid., pp. 239–40.

95 Ibid., pp. 84, 127–8.

96 Ibid., pp. 240–1.

97 Ibid., pp. 40–1.

98 J. B. Priestley, 'After the cheering', *Star* (12 May 1937), p. 4.

99 Priestley, *English Journey*, p. 417.

100 Ibid., p. 416.

101 Priestley, *English Journey*, pp. 164–73.

102 Peter Mandler 'The consciousness of modernity? Liberalism and the English "national character", 1870–1940', in M. Daunton and B. Rieger (eds), *Meanings of Modernity* (Oxford: Berg, 2001), p. 120.

103 Arthur Bryant, *The National Character* (London: Longman's, Green and Co., 1934), p. 6; Priestley, *The English*, p. 33.

104 Bryant, *Character*, p. 6; Milton Singer, 'A survey of culture and personality theory and research', in Bert Kaplan (ed.), *Studying Personality Cross-Culturally* (New York: Harper, Row, 1961); Alex Inkless (ed.), *National Character: A Psycho-Social Perspective* (New Brunswick: Transaction Publishers, 1997).

105 David Potter, 'The quest for the national character', in Don E. Fehrenbacher (ed.), *History and American Society: Essays of D. Potter* (London: Oxford University Press, [1962] 1975); David Riesman, *The Lonely Crowd: A Study of the Changing American Character* (New Haven: Yale University Press, 1950); Priestley, 'Lost Germany', *News Chronicle* (24 April 1939), p. 10. See also the work of Jackson Lears, e.g. *Luck in America* (New York: Viking Penguin, 2003). For the other side of the Anglo-German coin see Matthew Stibbe, *German Anglophobia and the Great War, 1914–1918* (Cambridge: Cambridge University Press, 2001).

106 Mandler, 'Consciousness'.

107 See, among others, Mark Girouard, *The Return to Camelot: Chivalry and the English Gentleman* (New Haven: Yale University Press, 1981); J. M. MacKenzie, 'The imperial pioneer and the British masculine stereotype in late Victorian and Edwardian Britain', in J. A. Mangan and J. Walvin (eds), *Manliness and Morality* (Manchester: Manchester University Press, 1987); Graham Dawson, *Soldier Heroes: British Adventure, Empire, and the Imagining of Masculinities* (London: Routledge, 1994); J. A. Mangan, '"Muscular, militaristic and manly": The British middle-class hero as moral messenger', *International Journal for the History of Sport* 13:1 (March 1996); Light, *Forever England*; Michael Paris, *Warrior Nation: Images of War in British Popular Culture 1850–2000* (London: Reaktion Books, 2000), chapter 5.

108 Stanley Baldwin, 'The privilege of Empire', broadcast from 10 Downing Street on Empire Day, 24 May 1927, in Baldwin, *Our Inheritance* (London: Hodder and Stoughton, 1928).

109 Hamilton Fyfe, *The Illusion of National Character* (London: Watts & Co, 1940). See also Jack Lindsay *England My England* (London: Fore Publications, n.d. [1939]).

110 Baldwin 'Empire'; Baldwin, 'On England', pp. 2–5; Lord Baldwin, 'The Englishman', in British Council, *British Life and Thought: An Illustrated Survey* (London: Longman, 1940), pp. 439–62.

111 Bryant, *Character*, pp. 4–5, 16–17, 20.

112 Orwell, 'The lion and the unicorn', in *Collected Essays*, pp. 76–83.
113 John Allan, *England Without End* (London: Methuen & Co., 1940), pp. 6–13.
114 A. L. Rowse, 'The English Spirit', in *The English Spirit* (London: Macmillan, [1940] 1944), pp. 35–6.
115 Priestley, *English Humour*, p. 4. See also *Rain* (1939), p. 218, where he quotes the philosopher John Macmurray to the same effect.
116 Priestley, *Humour*, pp. 18–19.
117 Ibid., p. 8.
118 Priestley, *Let the People Sing*, pp. 292–3.
119 Priestley, *The English*, p. 12.
120 Ibid., pp. 14–16.
121 Ibid., p. 12.
122 Ibid., pp. 47–8, 127.
123 All discussed in ibid., chapter 3 'Lords and masters'.
124 Ibid., pp. 95–6.
125 Ibid., pp. 89–90.
126 Priestley, *Rain*, pp. 205–6.
127 Priestley, *The English*, pp. 108–12.
128 Ibid., p. 120.
129 Ibid., p. 126.
130 Ibid., pp. 137, 127–8.

4

This new England

In 1934, growing up in the interstices of the old, agrarian England and the industrial England of the nineteenth century, Priestley found a new, emergent England, an England not really English, but global, and born in America:

> the England of arterial and by-pass roads, of filling stations and factories that look like exhibition buildings, of giant cinemas and dance-halls and cafés, bungalows with tiny garages, cocktail bars, Woolworths, motor-coaches, wireless, hiking, factory girls looking like actresses, greyhound racing and dirt tracks, swimming pools, and everything given away for cigarette coupons.[1]

This familiar list, which has made its way into many a history textbook, was one of the first attempts to characterise the suburbanised, consumerist way of life which was to carry all before it in the long boom of the 1950s and 1960s, the age of 'You've Never Had It So Good'. To us, these images evoke a distant past, in which we can almost hear the faint strains of Jack Hylton and his Orchestra drifting in from some distant wireless set across the bungalows, lidos and cocktail bars. In 1934, though, they all signalled modernity, bang up to date and moving into the future. But, as Priestley observed, nothing dates like modernity: 'we roar past them in our supercharged roadsters and fast planes ... forgetting that in another twenty-five years people will scream with laughter at the sight of us'.[2] Another thing which strikes us is that nearly all these images are of leisure. Even the factories have been downgraded to exhibition halls, places to visit rather than places to work; while the rest of the list carries the unmistakable whiff of suburbia, a site of consumption where nothing is produced. If the modernity of the nineteenth century was driven by new sites and technologies of production, the factory and the steam engine, that of the 1930s was led by technologies of culture and communication, domestic consumption and popular pleasure. While Priestley's engagement with industrial England and its plight in the 1930s can be seen as paving the way to the collectivism of 1945 and the Welfare State, his analysis of the 'new England' starts us on the road to a different modernity, the consumer society and globalised mass culture which represent the other side of the post-1945 world.

Many of Priestley's intellectual contemporaries were, one way or another, distanced from and hostile to modernity and its culture, a stance which dated back at least to the Industrial Revolution.[3] But while nineteenth-century cultural critics still belonged to a ruling elite, the cultural democracy of the twentieth century threatened the 'cultivated mind' with marginalisation or worse. Intellectuals responded in a number of different ways.[4] Some, as we have seen, lost themselves in fantasies of a pre-modern England. Some, like the modernists and Bloomsbury, retreated to the aesthetic high ground, separating themselves from the market and the instincts of the crowd. Others, especially in the 1930s, embraced Marxism, and denounced modern mass culture as a narcotic for controlling the working class and distracting it from its historic mission: as W. H. Auden put it, 'By cops directed to the fug / Of talkie-houses for a drug, / Or down canals to find a hug / Until you die'.[5] Yet others fought back on the battleground of culture itself, seeking to disseminate their own cultural values and keep debased commercialism at bay: in this category, in different ways, belong John Reith of the BBC, and the literary critic F. R. Leavis and his associates.

Although he was sharply critical of many aspects of modernity, none of these forms of rejection appealed much to Priestley. He was impatient with those who simply denied the modern world instead of trying to sort it out. He regarded the modernist retreat into introspection as inimical to what he wanted to do in his novels, to 'show men in their relation to the outer world'.[6] He regarded the intellectual Marxists as too theoretical, mistaken in their view of the working class and their idea of how history worked. He disliked the paternalism of Reith and company, and he conducted a long-running feud with the Leavisites, who despised his work and whose idealisation of pre-industrial culture he rejected. The problem with all these alternative critical postures was that Priestley did not share their distancing – deliberate or otherwise – from the lives and tastes of the people. 'If there is an elite,' he announced later in life, 'I don't belong to it ... I am not delicate or subtle in my tastes; I prefer artists in the major tradition to minor masters; it does not worry me to have to share my favourites with so many other people; I have enjoyed books, music, pictures, but without despising music-halls and football matches.' Far from avoiding the crowds, he went on, he had sought them out, 'and if they were happy then I was happy too'.[7]

An elite education at Cambridge had left little mark on Priestley: he accepted what he took to be its view that he didn't really belong there. In London, he made his way as a jobbing literary artisan, which suited the kind of thing he wanted to write (having got 'Atlantis' out of his system), rather than seeking patronage in upper-class circles. His political stance remained stubbornly Bruddersfordian, and his conception of the nation rooted in 'the people', out of whom (rather than from the elites) any significant change must come. His approach to modernity and mass culture was populist rather than elitist: critical of them to the extent that they disempowered the people, he could never wholly reject the life and the culture which the people themselves had chosen. Priestley's populism, his rootedness in industrial England, and his rejection of aesthetic elitism, allowed him to bypass the deadends down which so many interwar intellectuals retreated, and make a real contribution to history during the Second World War.

This chapter will develop these arguments around Priestley's attitude to modernity and modern culture – the 'New England' of *English Journey*. We will first look at the way in which that book tackles the 1930s version of the 'modern', and at Priestley's critical approach to suburbia, the location of most of the things he described in his famous list. Next we will investigate his view of popular culture: the old Bruddersfordian culture of football, music-hall and Blackpool, and the new 'mass' culture of cinema, radio and the popular press which seemed to be superseding it. This will bring us to Priestley's deeply ambivalent attitude towards America, with which, on the threshold of the Second World War, the chapter finishes.

'The age itself'

English Journey, which we have already read first as a social investigation of the Slump and second as an exploration of Englishness, can also be read as a commentary on modernity and its perplexities. It concludes with a ringing declaration that the most fundamental 'modernisation' of all, industrialism, had itself been 'the wrong turning'.[8] Nevertheless, the book shows its author to be as besotted with the idea of the modern as any futurist. To explore these contradictions, we rejoin Priestley as he alights from his motor bus, that symbol of technological democracy, in his journey's first destination, Southampton.

When he arrives there, Southampton turns out to be more than just a gateway to England: it is the place to behold one of the most potent symbols and examples of early twentieth-century modernity: the ocean liner. Priestley notes the apparent prosperity and happiness of the town's inhabitants, and rhapsodises about the big ships which have brought this good fortune: 'things not only of formidable size and power, but also of real beauty, genuine creations of man the artist'. What have we built since the medieval cathedrals that compares with them? Their purpose may be to make profits, not to glorify God or the commonwealth, but even so,

having arrived at a time when men have a passion – perhaps the purest of
their passions – for machines, these ships are creations of power and beauty.
I am glad to have lived in their age, to have seen them grow in strength and
comeliness, these strange towns of painted steel that glide up to and away
from this other town of motionless brick.[9]

And so Priestley begins a dialogue with himself about modernity and its
consequences which runs through much of *English Journey*. Much later,
on Tyneside, he will encounter the ruin of the industry and the men who
built ships like these, the waste of their skill and creative powers. But even
here in Southampton, the promise of modernity is undercut. He runs into
an acquaintance, a steward from one of his transatlantic voyages, who
from his below-decks standpoint does not share Priestley's enthusiasm for
the liners: 'Bad quarters. Working all hours. And no proper food and
nowhere to eat it.'[10] Priestley is troubled: perhaps, he muses, the first-class
passengers should give up some of their comforts to allow those waiting
on them to lead a more civilised life. In this modest little allegory we might
glimpse the opening of the road to 1945. Back in 1933, Southampton
suddenly doesn't look quite so bright and prosperous. Priestley starts to
notice squalid sidestreets, junk-yards and fly-blown corner shops: 'one
large clean shed, a decent warehouse' would be preferable, he suggests,
prefiguring the postwar supermarket and reaffirming the unrealised
promise of modernity. Maybe one day Southampton – the town and its
life – will live up to the majesty of its great ships. 'What a Southampton
that would be' – and what an England, we might reflect. But it is not the
rejection of modernity but its embrace which will deliver this new
Jerusalem.[11]

Further down the road, in Bristol, in the Wills cigarette factory,
Priestley first encounters another aspect of modernity: factory work,
transformed from its nineteenth-century beginnings by machine tools,
electricity and new forms of organisation.[12] This theme will fascinate him
for much of the journey. His view in Bristol is a little rosy: yes, the work
is monotonous, but the machines are ingenious, and there is a humanity
in the way the factory is run which dispels the soulnessness of mass
production. Later, in the Daimler car factory at Coventry, his views have
sharpened, and some themes start to emerge more clearly. Here, and later
at a Leicester typewriter factory, he is impressed by the science and technology, the astonishing ingenuity that goes into these modern products,
and the expertise of those who devise and control the production
processes.[13] Himself the child of an industrial town, he wants to get as
close to these processes as he can, where possible trying his own hand at
them. But above all, in all these places, and particularly at a clothing
factory in Leicester where the technology is not particularly advanced, it
is the organisation which strikes him most: 'the strange absence of any
obvious supervision' in a system so intricately well-planned that each

worker knew what they were meant to be doing without needing to have any overview of the whole process.[14] Observing in the Potteries the modern version of an old craft, he reflects on the central role played by electricity. Much like some elderly cyberphobe of our own time, he professes not to understand that which children effortlessly master: nevertheless he is fascinated by it: 'we are definitely *in for* an electrified world'. The factory power-house would make an excellent set for a futuristic movie: while 'essentially of the present [it] looks like a glimpse of the future'.[15]

And above all, this is the age of the expert. In his native Bradford, the laid-back, easy living wool man of the past has been replaced by a new breed, hard-working 'good citizens', well qualified, and with a grasp not just of the technicalities of the wool trade but of languages, finance, transport.[16] Like those who plan and coordinate the factories, they are 'men essentially of the present ... electrical engineers, motor-car designers, aviators, wireless technicians and the like. This is their age and they are completely at home in it.' 'They had that look, that happy absorption in their work, that passion for explaining and demonstrating', though they own no capital and are only employees themselves. In the Potteries, where a modern industry is rooted in a traditional craft, individual skill at handling clay still plays a part on the shop-floor.[17] But elsewhere, the job-satisfaction of the technocrats, 'happy children of our mechanical age', is undercut by the monotony of the ordinary workers' day. Knowing nothing of the overall process in which their labour is just one small element, they are alienated from production in a way never experienced by their grandparents.

Just as Southampton is unworthy of the liners, so the Potteries, in the shape of ugly and undignified Stoke, are unworthy of the potters: one day modernity will arrive and 'a real city, spacious and gay ... [will] rise high and white'.[18] Likewise in Coventry, Priestley concludes that our problems are caused less by modernity than by its absence from important areas of life. 'If we were one half so clever in the matters that lie far outside machinery as we are about machinery itself, what people we should be, and what a world we should leave our children!'[19]

And after visiting Slump-ravaged Lancashire he calls for rational planning, to banish the squalor and 'muddle' left by nineteenth-century industry. 'Lancashire needed a plan, a big plan ... there is a terrible lack of direction and leadership in our affairs ... somebody somewhere will have to do some hard thinking soon.'[20] This is a fairly familiar 1930s theme: competitive capitalism has failed: only some form of socialist planning – some people (though not Priestley) would point to the Soviet Five Year Plans – could deliver on the promise of modernity. But while some saw no further than the decay left by industrial capitalism, for Priestley the 'new England' offered an escape from the 'dark bog of greedy industrialism':

It is a cleaner, tidier, healthier, saner world than that of nineteenth-century industrialism. The difference between the two Englands is well expressed by the difference between a typical nineteenth-century factory, a huge dark brick box, and a modern factory, all glass and white tiles and chromium plate.[21]

'[T]here is such a thing as progress and … it is still happening', Priestley had written in 1928, contemplating the wonders of the London Underground, and impatiently dismissing those who saw the new mechanised life as cold and inhuman: after all, he pointed out, people travelled by tube for much the same human purposes as their ancestors had travelled overground: to go to work, to go to the doctor, to go to the theatre, to meet friends and lovers: their freedom was enlarged, and they 'shed no humanity *en route*'.[22]

But at the same time, there was something in what the old-fashioned wool man Jonathan Crabtree said in *They Walk in the City*:

Trade's gone ter nowt, like all good owd trades. Looks to me as if we'll ha' to get our brass i' this country now by makking bits an' bats o' things – wireless sets an' bathing drawers an' tuppeny toys an' suchlike – that yer gets bits o'lasses makking during time they're not drinking cups o'tea or pahdering their noses. Laking, Ah call it, not working.[23]

Life and work may be easier today, but the old factories, Priestley suspected, had more 'solid lumps of character' inside them than the new glass and chromium boxes like the Keep-Yu-Kozee Underclothing factory where *They Walk*'s heroine, Rose Salter, works:

There it shines and glitters, an almost brand-new, five-storey building, all glass, metal, bright paint … It looks more like a giant greenhouse than an honest mill … Old mill hands, pondering over it, cannot believe that the thing represents a solid commercial enterprise; a parcel of women might have put it up.

Inside, we find an example of modern mass production which could have been (and no doubt was) lifted out of *English Journey*, a female workforce operating 'trumpery gadgets', all scientifically co-ordinated by a few male managers.[24] A female workforce, of course, is nothing new in a textile town, but it is not just the factory floor but the factory itself and what it produces that has been feminised. The heroically male manual labour of the Industrial Revolution, the 'Promethean and Vulcanic grandeur' of shipbuilding – 'the real thing, man's work' – has collapsed in the Slump, and its other classic location, the solid, brick-built factory, four-square with a chimney at the corner, is being replaced with 'decorative little buildings' manufacturing 'potato crisps, scents, tooth pastes, bathing costumes' for 'an England of little luxury trades'. The mocking tone is unmistakable but, as Priestley goes on to say, how much pleasanter the country would be if everyone could work in them.[25]

Gender is never acknowledged as a theme of *English Journey*, but it tells us more about changing gender relations than do most social investigations of the time. Although almost all of his contacts are men – only ten of the seventy or so people he records talking to are female – what they show him is the collapse of an old masculine world. His unemployed Great War comrades, having undergone the supremely masculine ordeal of warfare, were now unable to appear in public to celebrate the fact. Merchants and manufacturers who had towered over their local communities like patriarchal colossi had now either gone out of business or were elsewhere, pretending to be country gentlemen. A woman in Bradford comments on the disappearance of men from the serious public sphere – lectures, theatres, political meetings – and even pubs and cinemas. Priestley is inclined to agree: even amongst the young, the men seem far less enterprising and ambitious, and the girls 'have mysteriously acquired all the dash and virility'.[26]

This is not a bad thing: it was, after all, those heroically male entrepreneurs who had laid waste to industrial England in the name of profit, and male politicians who were in charge of the disastrous politics of the 1930s. Despite women's suffrage, he told readers of the London *Star* in 1935, 'masculine pig-headedness and lack of commonsense seem to be triumphant' in politics. 'Women can only succeed by changing the rules, indeed by stopping the game altogether', he declared, and it's about time they did so: they were 'born arrangers, organisers, negotiators' with 'tough realistic minds', compared to whom most men were 'half-daft'. Most of all, 'they know very well that it is human beings who are really important, and not principles, systems, theories'.[27] In several of his novels it is proactive female characters who set things moving in the right direction: Miss Trant, who rescues and renames *The Good Companions*, the energetic young modern Hope Ollerton in *Let the People Sing*, Rose Salter who takes off for London in *They Walk in the City*. Later, from Priestley's increasing interest in Jungian psychology he drew the notion of a 'female principle', but he did not regard it as subordinate to the male: indeed, as we will see in Chapter 6, he believed that the balance between them had slipped too far towards the male and needed to be redressed.

Suburbia

While the earliest historians of the interwar period such as C. L. Mowat and A. J. P. Taylor recognised that consumption was important, they were not sure what to do with it: they were more at home with class and politics.[28] Since then, it has been widely recognised that although the popular memory of the 1930s has been dominated by hunger marches and street battles, for those with jobs, security and middling incomes the big story was the modernisation of ordinary domestic life.[29] Priestley was among the first of his contemporaries to recognise that something new was being born in suburban England, something 'belonging far more to the age itself than to this particular island'. There was, of course, nothing new about suburbs. In the Victorian city, the development of public transport had encouraged the growth of purely residential areas connected to the city centre and the workplace by buses, railways and tramways. It was in the inner, terraced lower middle-class suburbs of Bradford, a product of the late nineteenth century, that Priestley grew up, and in the more distant suburbs, the 'Drives and Groves', that he placed the idyllic Edwardian world of *Bright Day*'s Alington family.[30] In the 1920s and 1930s, the growth of motor transport in particular encouraged not just an increase in the quantity of suburban housing but its uncontrolled sprawl into the surrounding countryside. Between the wars nearly four million houses were built, the great majority for owner occupation, and the area they covered grew even more: the population of Birmingham, for example, grew by 25 per cent during these years, but its built-up area increased by 68 per cent.[31] The housing boom, electrification, consumer goods, motor cars and the new mass media were not just elements in a better standard of living but the takeoff point for a series of cultural transformations which, interrupted by the war, were to be resumed in the 1950s and 1960s.

But the rise of the suburbs was not universally welcomed. Criticism tended to take two forms: aesthetic and cultural. Suburbia was criticised on aesthetic grounds because its rampant growth was destroying the countryside, and because its buildings were considered ugly.[32] It was criticised on cultural grounds because the way of life that was lived there was deemed to be narrow and unsatisfactory. As we have seen, Priestley liked the English countryside and was as keen as anybody to prevent unrestrained suburban growth from eating it up. But it was on the culture of suburbia that he focused most of his attention. It had its good points. Suburbia may be a poor compromise between town and country, but there was a lot to be said for it: for people of moderate means, those who worked in the city and their families, it offered 'the most civilized way of life' available to them.[33] Care is therefore necessary, Priestley warns us, in evaluating this way of life: 'you can easily approve or disapprove of it too hastily'. And there was much to approve of: indeed, 'after a social revolution there would, with any luck, be more and not less of it'.[34] As John Carey has argued, much intellectual opposition to suburbia was essentially anti-democratic, and Priestley praises the new England as a more democratic England, accessible on exactly the same terms to all who can pay its rock-bottom prices.[35] 'Modern England is rapidly Blackpooling itself', and while Jack and Jill may always have been nearly as good as their master and mistress, now they were 'nearly as good in the *same way*'.

Moreover, declares Priestley, rather optimistically, the 'cheap snobbery' that inspires so much hostility to suburbia is becoming a thing of the past:

> The young people of this new England do not play chorus in an opera in which their social superiors are the principals; they do not live vicariously, enjoy life at second-hand, by telling one another what a wonderful time the young earl is having or how beautiful Lady Mary looked in her court dress; they get on with their own lives.

The new heroes and heroines are film and sports stars, not dukes and duchesses, and so the endless social ladder of snobbery and deference that beset Old England is being levelled, and the new England is 'as near to a classless society as we have got yet'.[36]

The case is more forcefully developed in a newspaper article written at about the same time:

> It is a much fairer world: it offers its advantages to almost everybody. Thus, films and the wireless are new amusements, and there are very few people who cannot enjoy them. Books are everywhere for everybody to read. Millionaires and navvies read the same newspapers. The very housemaids here look as smart as actresses did 25 years ago. The other week I found myself in one of the remotest little market towns in Britain. But I noticed that the girls there had carefully modelled their appearance on that of their respective favourite film actresses thousands of miles away in Hollywood. You may say that you do not want young women in the country to look like film stars. Possibly not, but – and this is the point – *they want to look like that, and what they want they get*. The people who resent these changes most bitterly are either the soured creatures who hate to see others enjoying themselves, or the well-to-do folk who dislike losing what were once their peculiar privileges in the general levelling-up ... The world is more amusing than it was. This is partly because fewer and fewer people are sunk in hopeless, oafish drudgery, leading dreary lives, and looking like ugly, discontented slaves.[37]

That is the case for the defence, and it is a strong one, rooted in Priestley's radical attachment to democracy, and in his optimism about the potential of ordinary people. But then, the doubts come in. The inhabitants of the new England, supplied with easy work and cheap luxuries, certainly have a better life, but didn't they also lack something: 'zest, gusto, flavour, bite, drive, originality'?[38] What about those 'solid lumps of character' who emerged from the cities and factories, and gave Dickens his raw material: what had become of them in suburbia? True, people were not put on earth to provide grist for the novelist's mill, but even so '[t]here is something tepid and passive ... that worries me. I do not see men and women of character emerging in any great numbers from this Americanised urban life'.[39] Weren't these cheap pleasures a little too cheap, in the other sense of the term – 'a trumpery imitation of something not very good even in the original', passively accepted by consumers doing the bidding of commercial interests?[40] And wasn't this an alarmingly depoliticised world, whose people lacked 'any real desire to think and act for themselves, the perfect subjects for an iron autocracy'?

Here Priestley comes close to the left demonisation of 'mass culture' as rendering its subjects passive and easy to manipulate, which Frankfurt School critics such as Theodor Adorno were to develop in response to the rise of European fascism: a theme Priestley would return to after 1945, in his critique of 'Admass'. But he then remembers the younger, idealistic products of the new democratic England, working on behalf of others, from whom a better future might come: 'they have a social consciousness; their imagination is not blunted; they know that we are interdependent . . . They are good citizens and as yet we have no city worthy of them. Perhaps they are building it themselves now.'[41] Perhaps it is the New Jerusalem of 1945.

Priestley was still pinning his hopes on those quintessential suburban-ites, the middle classes, without whom, he believed, British socialism could and would get nowhere. But, increasingly disgusted with the poli-tics of the 1930s, he was starting to lose confidence. If the middle classes had not yet come up with a 'lasting vision of a nobler England', this was because they led 'too trivial and material an existence . . . what I will call a car-and-wireless life'.[42] There was nothing wrong with cars and wire-lesses, or the labour-saving devices and easily prepared food of the modern suburbanites, but these things on their own failed to provide a life as good as that led by Priestley's parents before 1914. What had been lost – and here we return to one of Priestley's key themes – was a 'deep sense of being a member of a community'. Gone were the interests, 'from the welfare of a particular chapel to a love of wild flowers, from a hospital committee to a cricket club', that once brought together people from diverse backgrounds. Instead, people were amusing themselves in ways that depended on spending money rather than on human fellowship: the car, the cinema, the restaurant, the wireless. Gone, too, were the social institutions that once provided a focus for a collective, communal life – in Priestley's parents' case, the chapel. Though Priestley was no Christian, he regretted the decline in spirituality that this loss entailed: the tennis club, the amateur dramatic or musical society, the political organisation were pitiful substitutes for an institution 'dedicated to men's profoundest beliefs and emotions, to their conviction that they need not be lost in the universe'. And so these new people who belonged nowhere led a 'thin, sterile, mechanical sort of existence, cut off from any deep sense of community, rather lonely at heart, and not sustained by any vision of the good life'.

The assertion that suburban dwellers were unhappy almost to the point of sickness was widely believed by contemporary critics. Modern subur-ban young wives, Priestley asserted, had to keep going to the doctor, but they were sick in mind, not in body, 'depressed, dreary, terribly lonely'.[43] Here he was partly echoing the views of Dr Stephen Taylor, who wrote in the *Lancet* in 1938 about 'the suburban neurosis': an ailment afflicting the young suburban wife, and caused by lifestyle and cultural poverty: an excessive focus on the home, the absence of a communal life, and an inability to occupy her mind with anything worthwhile.[44] These young women, Taylor asserted, lacked the intelligence or the education needed for 'the kind of lifestyle successfully led by people to whom books, theatres and things of intellect matter', and so made a fetish of the home, which could never by itself bring happiness. The papers they read and the films they watched were all based on wish-fulfilment, and 'designed to inhibit rather than stimulate thought'; they did not realise that the wisdom of the world awaited them 'on the station bookstall, at sixpence a time' – presumably in the shape of the recently invented Penguin Books. The result was anxiety and a whole range of psychosomatic physical symptoms which the family doctor could do little about.

Priestley was not so lofty or patronising as Taylor, but even so one wonders how much, if any, direct observation of actual suburban life underpinned his critique of its quality, or whether he was merely imagining the lives of those who lived there.[45] Less than thirty years later Peter Wilmott and Michael Young found in the London suburb of Woodford a rich associational life featuring a wide range of organisations and activities; it seems unlikely that this would have been present in Bradford in 1914 and Woodford in 1960, but somehow have gone out of existence in between.[46] Priestley echoed Taylor's concern about suburban cultural impoverishment: 'tired persons', who 'merely want a book to read, a film to stare at, a wireless programme to listen to, not eagerly and critically, but drowsily' – but unless he could get inside their houses, or even their heads, how would he know?[47]

The irony here is that the book, film or programme being so drowsily consumed had quite possibly been written by Priestley himself. Indeed, the terms in which he criticised suburbia's undemanding culture are very similar to those in which the 'highbrows' – Mrs Leavis, for example – condemned Priestley's own readers. Indeed, what could be more middle-brow than Taylor's prescription for finding the wisdom of the world in paperbacks at W. H. Smith's?

To some extent, both Priestley's takes on the 'new England', optimistic and pessimistic, were projections of his own democratic instincts. Where the optimist saw the democratic side of the new culture, the pessimist projected on to suburbia his anxiety that the people had become disempowered and de-energised, the promise of the Edwardian years lost. This anxiety was partly focused on the new cultural forms: cinema, radio, the popular press, which were arriving on the scene before 1914 but which flourished as never before in the 1920s and 1930s. Some intellectuals, like their Victorian forebears, saw this popular culture as inherently bad. For Priestley, though, things were not so straightforward: 'there is nothing essentially wrong with our new popular amusements, such as films and the radio, both of which had done much to brighten people's lives. But they should be enjoyed actively and not passively, attended to eagerly and critically and not used as a kind of mild dope'.[48] His point of reference, not surprisingly, was the popular culture of late Victorian and Edwardian England, about which he wrote with genuine affection and respect for both performers and audiences. About the new popular culture he was more ambivalent: in some ways, he felt, it represented a top-down commercialisation, a decline into passivity, but at the same time he recognised its creative potential, and its genuine appeal to its audiences: nothing was to be approved or disapproved of too hastily.

Blackpool: 'not as good as it used to be'

English Journey takes Priestley to Blackpool, where he first observes the contrast between old and new popular cultures. Blackpool, of course, was the world's first great popular holiday resort, built on the prosperity of the Lancashire cotton industry, but drawing in working-class holiday-makers from all over. 'The democratic and enterprising Blackpool', Priestley declares, had led the way to the new, democratic popular culture: 'you were all as good as one another so long as you had the necessary sixpence'.[49] It is 'a complete and essential product of industrial democracy. If you do not like industrial democracy, you will not like Blackpool.' To show what he means, Priestley produces another of his lists:

> this huge mad place with its miles and miles of promenades, its three piers, its gigantic dance-halls, its variety shows, its switch-backs and helter-skelters, its array of wine bars and oyster saloons and cheap restaurants and tea houses and shops piled high and glittering with trash; its army of pierrots, bandsmen, clowns, fortune-tellers, auctioneers, dancing partners, animal trainers, itinerant singers, hawkers, its seventy special trains a day, its hundreds and hundreds of thousands of trippers . . .[50]

The visitors themselves are part of this carnivalesque parade, the 'vital beings who burst out of their factories for the annual spree as if the boilers had exploded and blown them out', spent every penny they had and returned home having 'rapturously enjoyed their Blackpool'.[51] This feeling of excess and exuberance, a superabundance of pleasures, is captured in the Blackpool-set semi-documentary sequences of *Sing As We Go* (1934), which Priestley scripted at around the same time as he was writing *English Journey*.

But – and it is a big but – 'it is not, in my opinion, as good as it used to be'. This is partly because the rest of the world has caught up with it. But mainly, it is because of what has gone wrong with popular culture since the Great War. It has lost some of its 'old genuine gaiety'. The 'roaring variety turns' have been replaced with talkies. The amusements have become 'mechanized and American'. 'The entertainers are more calculating, the shows more standardised, and the audiences more passive. It has developed a pitiful sophistication – machine-made and not really English – that is much worse than the old hearty vulgarity.'[52] Above all – and this is a recurring theme of the period – it has become Americanised. The language is significant: present-day Blackpool, 'carefully-drilled', 'calculating', 'standardised', 'machine-made', 'passive', 'listless', 'tired' – is set against an old 'genuine' Blackpool, 'roaring', 'energetic' and 'vital', 'fresh' and 'lilting', full of 'gaiety', 'high spirits' and 'hearty vulgarity' – and, of course, 'English'. The smooth organisation and clean mechanisation that Priestley, on the whole, admired in modern factory production is death to a genuine popular culture, which must tap the creative energy of the people. Without that energy, totalitarianism looms: 'it would not be difficult, I feel, to impose an autocracy upon young people who sound as tired as that' (this in the wake of Hitler's recent rise to power). To an extent this is stock 1930s 'mass culture' theory, but it is backed up by Priestley's democratic populism: the carnivalesque gusto of Britain's urban industrial popular culture is offered as a talisman against autocracy.[53] This is why John Carey, selectively citing Priestley's comments on Blackpool, is mistaken in categorising him as one of those who disdained the urban masses and wished they had remained peasants.[54] He was not condemning the popular, as Carey implies, but setting up one version of the popular against another; it was precisely the 'extraordinary ordinary people' whose onetime vitality he celebrated, and hoped to see reborn.

Football: 'Conflict and Art'

The first close-up we see in *The Good Companions* is the grey-green tide of cloth caps flowing down Manchester Road from Bruddersford United's football ground. Times are hard, but thirty-five thousand men can still find a shilling for the match, and Priestley tells us why:

> To say that these men paid their shillings to watch twenty-two hirelings kick a ball is merely to say that a violin is wood and catgut, that Hamlet is so much paper and ink. For a shilling the Bruddersford United A.F.C. offered you Conflict and Art; it turned you into a critic, happy in your judgement of fine points, ready in a second to estimate the worth of a well-judged pass, a run down the touch line, a lightning shot, a clearance kick by back or goalkeeper; it turned you into a partisan ... elated, downcast, bitter, triumphant by turns at the fortunes of your side, watching a ball shape Iliads and

Odysseys for you; and, what is more, it turned you into a member of a new
community, all brothers together for an hour and a half ... cheering
together, thumping one another on the shoulders, swopping judgements like
lords of the earth, having pushed your way through a turnstile into another
and altogether more splendid kind of life, hurtling with Conflict yet passionate and beautiful in its Art.[55]

In Nottingham, he went to a Forest versus County derby match, and was
impressed by the engagement of the crowd with the spectacle. Everything
that could have been done to spoil football had been done, by way of
commercialisation, sensationalism and partisanship, but, he declared, the
game was still not spoiled, and he did not believe there was anything
better these spectators could have done with their free time and their
shillings.[56] Drama, criticism, art, emotion, partisanship, community: these
are what spectators get for their money, and if they were to get all these
things, Priestley well understood, the players must be 'hirelings', professionals. He had no time for the purists of amateurism. In 1926 he
modestly compared his own way of making a living to that of the great
Yorkshire cricketer Herbert Sutcliffe. Both of them, he argued, were
public entertainers, except that Sutcliffe entertained far more people than
Priestley did. Why, then, was it regarded by some as acceptable for him to
be paid but not Sutcliffe?[57] Professionalism was a class issue, and a
regional one. Middle-class amateurs might neglect their businesses to
play, but no one could work in a mill and play cricket all summer; while
Yorkshire, where cricket was a people's game, relied on working-class
professional players, who did not so much play for money as take money
so that they could continue playing. Moreover, as skilled men they
deserved to be paid the rate for the job. 'A footballer of genius may be
worth a hundred pounds a week to his club,' he argued, 'and it seems to
me that he has a perfect right to demand and receive that hundred a week.
His skill may be superlatively rare and valuable, and his football life a
very short one. Let him earn what he can.' We do not know what Priestley
would have thought of a hundred *thousand* pounds a week, but he was
certainly ahead of his time: it would be nearly thirty years before the
maximum wage was abolished and the first hundred-pound-a-week footballer appeared on the scene.[58]

Music-hall: 'for the poor against the rich'

Music-hall and variety crop up in a number of Priestley's novels, which
make good literary use of their detachment from the rest of society. In two
of them – *The Good Companions* (1929) and *Lost Empires* (1965) – the
action takes place within the microcosmic world of the travelling
company, able to move through the social landscape without really being

part of it. In *Lost Empires* the power of the novel derives from the duality signalled in the title, between the world outside rushing headlong into war and the little theatrical world with its own dark themes of violence, sexuality and illusion, both reaching a climax at the same moment, in Blackpool in the late summer of 1914.

But music-hall for Priestley was more than a useful literary device. He wrote out of deep respect for the skill of professional entertainers, especially illusionists and comedians, whose art he analysed in depth while vividly conveying the comedy, the pleasure and the atmosphere of the performance. His obituary of 'Little Tich', an exemplary analysis of comic performance and technique, includes a careful physical description of which brings the man alive before our eyes and makes us smile even at this distance in time, while *Lost Empires*, whose main characters are an illusionist and his nephew-assistant, recreates a whole world of Edwardian entertainment.[59] Priestley was very clear about where music-hall – and its progeny, variety – came from and still truly belonged. The West End halls may have been the best known, but music-hall first took shape, he asserted, where most of its performers came from: in the industrial north and the east end of London. 'Variety came from the industrial working class and never really moved a long way from it ... Music hall humour and sentiment were always at heart working-class humour and sentiment.' Moreover, the halls had 'a fine radical atmosphere: they were always for the poor against the rich', and while their wildly surreal humour 'appealed to some natural incongruity in the working-class mind', its dry and sardonic side working off the irony bred in the experience of working-class life.[60] We might set this positive analysis alongside the view of Gareth Stedman Jones that music-hall was a 'culture of consolation' and an instrument of hegemony, whose comic treatment of everyday experience such as marriage or class encouraged fatalistic acceptance.[61] Priestley's view is closer to that of Peter Bailey, who sees music-hall as a highly charged social space, an arena in which the audience held sway, new roles and identities might be tried out, and 'small but relishable gains' wrested from the dominant powers in society.[62]

Indeed, a sense of place is central to Priestley's own memory of music-hall in Edwardian Bradford. His preferred venue was the less respectable of the town's two halls: 'it was smoky and beery and noisy and vulgar, and if you did not like it, you could lump it or go across the way to the Mechanics' Institute where, no doubt, a lecture entitled "With Net and Camera on the Norfolk Broads" was in progress'. The audience was raucous and critical, demanding an equally raucous band, and artistes with 'stage personalities like a kick from a mule ... but there, in that rich atmosphere, with the stage glowing cavernously through the blue haze, the drums rattling in your very ears, it all seemed tremendously alive'.[63]

By the time Priestley wrote these words, music-hall and variety were no

longer tremendously alive but on their last legs. *They Walk in the City*
(1936) shows us a decaying neighbourhood hall in Islington, warm and
cosy enough, but with an ageing audience and decrepit performers, their
scenery, props, songs and jokes all getting on in years, regretting the old
days of full bookings 'when variety *was* variety'. 'Youth had fled from it.
The sap was drying up; the leaves withering.'[64] This might easily be taken
as a facile symbol for a more general cultural decline: Rose, the young
heroine, is an enthusiastic cinemagoer, who has clearly never set foot in a
variety theatre before. But later in the novel we meet two elderly artistes,
both illusionists, who argue the matter out. Mantoni puts the case: it's
never been the same since the war. Everybody is kidded by the papers and
the wireless and Hollywood that they are having a good time, but 'There
isn't the fun and the easiness and the character. Too many machines. Too
much of this American stuff. Too much of a rush to nowhere, and to hell
with it when you get there ... Too much sex and sex appeal, and not
enough larks and sprees.' We know that at least part of Priestley agrees
with this, but he lets Alf, for the defence, have the last word. 'It's just old
man's talk,' he says, 'the world's moving on and we aren't.' The only
thing wrong with young people is that 'they're twenty and we're sixty ...
There isn't much of your kind of fun any longer, but there's plenty of
another kind. They're just as free and easy in their own way as we were
in ours.' And in any case, the old times weren't all good: 'Lot of dirt
about, all kinds, too much booze, too much bullying, all sorts of nastiness.' We know that Priestley agrees with this too: the argument is within
himself, and it is not resolved.[65]

They Walk's device of two elderly music-hall artistes is reused in *Let
the People Sing*, where we meet the out-of-work comedian Timmy
Tiverton:

> people weren't the same and the world wasn't the same, that was the
> trouble. All machines now. Films – fun out of a tin. Wireless – more
> machines. And now these Hitlers and Mussolinis with *their* machines. It
> wasn't properly human any more. Look at all these new acts – all alike,
> crooning away into mikes, pretending to be Americans: they might all have
> been turned out by a machine. All the real warm liveliness and fun going out
> of the world.[66]

Later in the novel, though, he encounters another retired performer, Daisy
Barley, who has opened an American-style roadhouse outside the town of
Dunbury, and staffed it with fellow music-hall artistes. Timmy dislikes the
American overtones, but, as Daisy points out:

> you've got to move on. Things change, an' you've got to change with 'em if
> you don't want to be left in the cart. I learnt a thing or two in Australia, an'
> when I came back through America ... an' I saw there which way things
> were going. What the Yanks did last year, we'll do next year, y'know ...

> Because somebody's always in the lead an' setting the fashion. Fifty years
> ago it was us. Now it's the Americans.[67]

In the end, the Americanised roadhouse is not just a utopian haven of old
friends and civilised values but stands for qualities that Dunbury itself has
lost, and which the roadhouse helps to restore – energy, vitality, pleasure,
the democratic spirit: qualities which Priestley associates not just with a
lost England, but, paradoxically, with contemporary America.

Old and new

Priestley's ambivalence about the new popular culture runs through his
work and is never really resolved. At one moment, young people who
lapped up the new mechanised entertainments of the age were stigmatised
as passive and listless, potential victims of autocracy; while the next
moment Priestley was creating young characters, invariably female, who
seemed to draw from Hollywood a vitality and energy to match that of
their Edwardian forbears. *They Walk in the City* compares old and new.
Rose Salter comes from a family which represents, almost to the point of
parody, the exuberance of the old-style lower working class, those who
'burst out of their factories' to enjoy prewar Blackpool. The Salters
'belonged to that section of the workers which is the despair of the austere
revolutionary' because of their sheer ability to enjoy life despite its draw-
backs – indeed, they seem to thrive on them: noisy, gregarious, feckless,
immersed in tea, beer, sport, music-hall, radio and Blackpool – hardly
representing a social or political ideal, but with so much more gusto than
the decaying but upright middle-class Fieldings, and full of the 'good
honest vulgarity' which Priestley believed still lived on in the common
people, despite the efforts of the Victorian middle classes.[68] But Rose,
though she is fond of her family, has more to her, and part of this comes
from modern popular culture: 'more and more, inspired by what she saw
in picture papers or at the films, she entertained thoughts quite foreign to
the other Salters'. And so, while middle-class Edward Fielding is stagnat-
ing and depressed in a deadend job, and the other Salters presumably
continue in their feckless way, it is Rose who has the energy to seek her
fortune in London, a place she knows mainly through Hollywood movies.
To know the capital of one's own country through the notions of 'film
scenario writers in Southern California' may seem symptomatic of a crisis
in national culture, but it is this knowledge which gives her the impetus to
go there, and get the plot of the novel moving.[69]

In *Let the People Sing* Timmy Tiverton and the Professor seem to see
eye to eye on the failings of modern culture, though the latter expresses it
in rather more elaborate terms, some of which might have come straight
out of Adorno:

your world, with its clamorous and exacting machines, and its organisation of mechanical little tasks, is draining away their spirit of initiative, making them passive in their leisure instead of active and creative. They drift from the work factory to the amusement factory. Instead of music there is now the strange horrible sound of the cinema organ or the barbaric din of the jazz bands, both of which play on the nerves and do nothing for the heart, the mind, the spirit.[70]

But the pair are joined on the road by young Hope Ollerton, who turns out to be the most proactive of the three characters. The novel partly concerns the machinations of an American plastics company; Americanisation is one of its running themes, and at least one young female character is gently mocked for imitating her favourite film star.[71] Nevertheless, Hope is shown to draw democratic strength from the influence of Hollywood. Visiting the aristocracy at Dunbury Hall,

> she gave no sign of being overawed by the size, age and social grandeur of this room, probably because she was a very handsome, much admired and spirited member of the genuine democracy, now rapidly growing up within the false democracy upon which we are always congratulating ourselves in England ... But if Hope had been sitting down to lunch in the cafeteria of the Paramount Studio in Hollywood, she would have been nearly choking with excitement.[72]

Such are the ambivalences of the 'new England', which we see worked through in Priestley's account of the new cultural forms of the age, cinema, the popular press and broadcasting.

The movies: 'a huge world movement'

It was cinema above all which signalled the cultural transformation that was taking place during the 1920s and 1930s. In 1928, after a visit to the new 'super-super kinema' which had recently replaced the West End's premier music-hall, the Empire, Leicester Square, Priestley reflected on the historical significance of the change and offered some advice to posterity (and perhaps provided himself with the title of a later novel):

> Let nobody imagine it is the same place. These two Empires have their roots in two different continents, for the old music-hall was essentially European, and the new kinema is undoubtedly American. No, they do not belong to the same age, perhaps not to the same civilization. A social historian might do worse than begin a gigantic study of our times with an artful reference to the fall of the old Empire and the sudden rise of the new.

He went on to rhapsodise about the lavish decor of the new cinema, available to anybody, as he points out, for a mere one-and-sixpence. But what was 'all this opulence and effort and superb ingenuity' for? To provide a setting for 'little bits of flickering nonsense ... poor feeble vulgar little shadows ... of an incredible stupidity', more suited to a drill hall with a tinny piano than an Arabian Nights extravaganza.[73] Cinema was not living up to its potential.

Priestley himself worked in Hollywood on a casual basis during the family's extended stays in Arizona during the 1930s – well paid, he tells us, but usually refusing screen credits.[74] Uncredited script work is reported on a Paramount comedy starring Carole Lombard and Fred MacMurray, *The Princess Comes Across* (1936), and he is credited for 'additional dialogue' on Alfred Hitchcock's *Jamaica Inn* (1939).[75] He also worked on a story about a string quartet, and a treatment for W. C. Fields, for which he was handsomely paid but which never made it to the screen.[76] Hollywood he knew in its heyday, and disliked, apart from some of the socialising; he felt that the unreality of the place and its remoteness from the mainstream of life, while it bestowed glamour and mystery, prevented those who worked there from making the very best movies.[77] However, he did not share the dismissive attitude towards Hollywood movies of most of his literary contemporaries. He was impressed by the quick intelligence of the film people he met, and by 'their knowledge of and deep interest in the new art of the film'.[78] At its best, Priestley considered, film was at least the equal of the stage and in some ways superior, with 'a different magic': less literal, quicker to make its points, and in its flexibility closer to the novel, or the Shakespearean drama, than the twentieth-century theatre. In fact, only the Elizabethan drama had experienced such exhilaratingly rapid development as had cinema in the early decades of the twentieth century.[79] Above all, film attracted him because of its huge popularity:

> They actively, almost passionately wanted films, more and more and more of them, and you could no more stop them with a few cultured sneers than you could stop Niagara by telling it it was in bad taste. Here, it seemed to me, was a huge spontaneous world movement, and I saw more in it to wonder at than to despise.[80]

Whatever Priestley said about the quality of most films, and the deplorably low expectations of their audiences, he understood why they meant so much to people. In *They Walk in the City* Rose and Edward go to see a Hollywood musical:

> its world may have been an amusing parody of the world that they preferred to see, a world of quick change, of easy light relations with people and things, without rigid standards and heavy responsibilities, cleansed of despair and madness and death.[81]

Or, as Richard Dyer puts it, 'the image of "something better" ... that our day-to-day lives don't provide'.[82]

Utopian fantasy apart, at their best Hollywood movies, 'with their outspo-

ken democratic feeling, their insistence on the dignity and worth of an ordinary decent man trying to do his job properly', provided a sharp commentary
on contemporary life.[83] This British film-makers, apart from the documentarists, woefully failed to do. Instead they offered stilted glimpses of
upper-crust life, and a meagre diet of filmed novels and plays – including
several of Priestley's own.[84] Priestley admired directors like René Clair, who
created their own cinematic reality, and urged British producers to make
'more satires, more films dealing with our own social scene, more dramas and
comedies dealing with contemporary events'. He had offered them, he said, a
satirical comedy about the British press (probably his 1933 novel *Wonder
Hero* which Clair had been interested in), but they were too afraid to touch it:
then Hollywood came up with *The Front Page* and other tough newspaper
pictures, showing how it should be done.[85] British directors should make use
of the specifically cinematic skills of the documentary-makers, whose tough,
ascetic approach to their craft Priestley admired, rather than leaning on the
theatre and variety all the time. 'Intelligent people who live in large cities . . .
go to a picture theatre to enjoy the unique virtues of film', he declared. 'They
do not want a photographed play, a tinned variety show; they want a film . . .
It is the business of film producers to create masterpieces of their own, and
not to try to borrow importance from other arts.'[86]

Priestley even toyed with the idea of going into film-making himself, an
ambition echoed in *Bright Day* (1946), whose protagonist Gregory
Dawson, a Bruddersford-born Hollywood scriptwriter, resolves his
personal and professional dilemmas by throwing in his lot with a penni-
less but idealistic group of young film-makers. But this was not to be
Priestley's path. One of the fascinations of cinema was that like the
modern factories in *English Journey* it was collective work, combining art
and industry, requiring large-scale co-ordination of many individual
skills: indeed, this could be said of most twentieth-century popular forms,
from popular music to broadcasting. Priestley was not against this, but his
own temperament was that of an individual artisan: even in public life, as
he was to discover in the 1940s and 1950s, he could not work in the
cumbersome world of committees and discussions and arguments, and he
lacked the autocratic impulse of a Chaplin which would allow him to
break through the obstacles and impose his own vision.[87]

It is an indication of his cultural breadth that Priestley's view of the
cinema was so positive – perhaps surprisingly so for one so steeped in
print and the theatre. For him the creative potential of film could even
exceed that of the stage, and he understood both the reasons for its
popular appeal and the important role it could play in the public sphere
of debate to which his own novels and journalism contributed. But he was
frustrated by what he saw as film's failure to realise that potential, a
failure which he attributed to the contrasting deficiencies of British and
American cultures: the former hidebound by class and cultural status, the

latter, which was becoming dominant, in thrall to commerce, meretricious glamour, and the star system – which was less the fault of the producers than of public taste as perceived by the distributors and exhibitors. In the end, 'if the "trade" and their public want stupid nonsense, then they will be given stupid nonsense ... films will improve if public taste improves'.[88] But from another point of view, 'stupid nonsense' could be that other world of utopian fantasy to which popular entertainment held the key, and whose importance Priestley also thoroughly understood.

The popular press: 'Fun City'

Priestley was, among so many other things, a prolific journalist. Throughout his career he wrote a prodigious amount for a wide range of newspapers and magazines, beginning in the 1920s with the low-circulation literary press and traditional 'heavies' such as the *Daily News*, soon branching out into all three London evening papers and after he became famous hitting the large-circulation popular weeklies such as the *Sunday Dispatch*, *Sunday Graphic* and *Sunday Chronicle*. During and after the war he tended towards the leftish mid-market titles, the *News Chronicle*, *Daily Herald* and *Reynolds News*, but was not above the *Sunday Express* and *Sunday Pictorial*.[89] This work, which must have paid very well, ranged in content from ephemeral opinion-spinning about current issues to quite serious political and social analysis, much of which found its way into his books. Popular journalism demanded an ability to present interesting and provocative ideas in an accessible and punchy manner, and Priestley was well able to do this; he identified himself with an age when professional writers were expected to write whatever the market demanded, 'from sermons to farces', and he valued the contact with a wide readership.[90] But he also knew he was taking part in what was, for all its deficiencies, the main arena of public debate at the time, and as we have seen, he had things he wanted to say.

But were the readers paying attention? In *Wonder Hero* (1933) we meet Charlie Habble, a young skilled worker living in the midlands, and a registered reader of the *Daily Tribune*.

> It was to him 'the paper', which is not quite the same as '*the* paper' ... To begin with, he had no particular respect for it. Gone was that reverence which his father and grandfather had had for the news-sheet, the printed page. He did not believe every statement it made, nor did he disbelieve. He read in a curious state of suspended belief or disbelief, the mood of a man at a conjuring entertainment. It left his mind bewildered, in a twilight of scepticism strangely, gaudily illuminated here and there by marvels of credulity ... He felt that it was a grand penny-worth, no matter whether it lied or told the truth.[91]

Later, Charlie is picked up by his favourite newspaper, and quite unjusti-
fiably turned into a temporary national hero. At the end of the novel, the
cynical journalist Hughson explains to Charlie why he is no longer news:

> We've got to keep changing the programme, you know. We're not a news-
> paper in the old-fashioned sense of the word. There are still one or two of
> them left, and they sell about one copy for every ten of ours. No, we're not
> really a newspaper, we're a circus in print, a vaudeville show, a Fun City, a
> daily comic.[92]

In between, we (and Charlie) meet Sir Gregory Hatchland, proprietor
of the *Daily Tribune* – as well as the *Sunday Courier*, *Mabel's Weekly*,
Our Little Pets, the *Boy's Joker* and *Runner Duck Record* – who sees
himself as a visionary, 'two parts Napoleon to one part American
magnate of the type popularised by the talkies', and is given to grandiose
schemes, the latest being the League of Imperial Yeomen, 'out of Militant
Imperialism by Fascism', to which he tries unsuccessfully to recruit
Charlie.[93] Hatchland is a composite 1930s press baron, mostly Lord
Northcliffe, with some of his brother Rothermere's fascist leanings, and a
dash of Beaverbrook's imperialist zeal. Priestley wrote at one time or
another for all three, and justly described Northcliffe's *Daily Mail* (to
which the *Tribune* bears a marked resemblance) as 'the revolutionary
parent of all popular English journalism', the first to recognise that people
wanted something 'easy, bright, exciting' instead of the 'old, heavy, long-
winded journalism'.[94]

But, of course, there was a down-side to this newspaper populism,
which *Wonder Hero* satirises on two counts: its transformation of the
once-sacred printed word into a medium of entertainment; and the
preposterous megalomania of its proprietors. Charlie's entirely spurious
heroism is a nine days' wonder, while the plight of Slump-stricken Slakeby
is not even a story at all. The post-Northcliffe press, Priestley complained,
repeating a familiar charge, did not report news so much as create it,
disregarding the traditional virtues of accuracy and responsibility and
blowing up minor events into major sensations merely to sell newspapers.
The serious role of print in the nineteenth-century public sphere of information and debate, upon which the democratic process depends, and still
very much alive in the Edwardian era, was now being undermined by
commercialism and the search for big circulations, and the consequent
conversion of newspapers into daily entertainments.[95]

The wireless: 'amateurish and patronising'

Priestley was also a prolific broadcaster, and a critical enthusiast for the
new medium. 'I like the wireless', he declared in 1927 – a mere five years

into the life of the BBC. 'It has made life even more fantastic and ridiculous than it was before'. How delightfully absurd to be able to hear in your own drawing room concerts from the Albert Hall, or talks about home life in Baluchistan, and switch them off again at will without causing any offence.[96] He showed a similar enthusiasm for the age's other mechanical aid to listening, the gramophone: how wonderful to be able to construct one's own concert programme, and not have to put up with the 'gasping over-enthusiasm' of the rest of the audience. But even in 1937 progress had only just begun: 'what we need now is a tiny portable instrument, to which one listens through ear-phones, so that it does not disturb anybody else, and whole symphonies and concertos and operas recorded on miniature reels of film, so that they could be easily carried about with us' – imagining the personal stereo before even recording tape had been invented, let alone the silicon chip.[97]

Priestley's own broadcasting career began in the 1920s, and almost ended in 1929, when Hilda Matheson, the BBC's Director of Talks, concluded that he had 'a very unattractive voice on the microphone'. But by 1933 Priestley was back, with a series of personal comments on current events entitled *I'll Tell You Everything*, and he remained a regular and popular broadcaster thereafter, especially during the Second World War, as we will discuss in the next chapter.[98] Matheson's verdict on Priestley's voice would have surprised later admirers of his wartime broadcasting style, and perhaps reflected a 1920s view that northern accents, however 'educated', lacked the gravitas of the 'Received Pronunciation' with which the BBC preferred to discuss weighty issues. If so, it might confirm some of Priestley's reservations about the BBC, which were the opposite of his qualms about the popular press. The way it dealt with issues of commercialism, popularisation and Americanisation was central to the formation of the BBC's distinctive identity. The Corporation, established as a Company in 1922, and given a Royal Charter in 1927, had a monopoly of broadcasting, until the introduction of commercial television in the 1950s, and was financed by licence fee rather than by advertising. The intention was to protect the medium, and the nation, from the 'chaos of the airwaves' and lowering of standards which was perceived to have resulted from unrestrained commercial competition in the United States, although a high-minded monopoly also suited the interests of the commercial entertainment industry, which did not want competition from the new medium.[99]

The BBC under John Reith responded by attempting to define a role for itself as a public service broadcaster, dependent on neither the state nor the market, and came to see itself as representing the entire national culture. According to Reith, that high-minded son of the manse, simply giving the public 'what they want' would be a 'prostitution' of the powers of a medium which should be introducing them to 'the best'. Reith's

notion of 'the best', as LeMahieu has argued, was motivated by Victorian
ideas of morality and 'character', and owed nothing to either the aestheti-
cism of contemporary highbrows, which he mistrusted, or existing
working-class culture, which might as well not exist.[100]

We might expect Priestley to approve of the BBC: it did, after all, fit in
with the interwar progressive ethos of planning, and aimed to avoid the
kind of commercial trivialisation which he had condemned in Blackpool
and the press. However, he was uneasy about the way the BBC was run.
Its social tone and its cultural values, not to mention the 'BBC accent',
were those of the public school and Oxbridge upper middle class, rather
than of the people Priestley had sprung from. In 1929 – during his period
of exile from the airwaves – he used the pages of the *Daily Mirror* to
launch an attack on the BBC's lofty and patronising tone, which he
likened to that of a Nonconformist minister addressing children during
the Sunday morning services of his youth: 'Now we're about to give you
little people a treat. Keep quiet and listen carefully and be good.' The BBC
had turned itself into 'a futile kind of night school', intent on improving
its listeners' minds with talks about 'how glass is made, what vitamins are,
and the number of castes in India'. In his ideal station there would be 'no
talks of any description' – this from a man who was to become one of the
most celebrated radio talkers of all time – and the BBC would stick mainly
to what it did best, which was music – and not just classical music either,
but also cheerful stuff you could dance to.[101] To some extent, of course,
this is simply robust populism tailor-made for the *Mirror*'s readership, at
a time when for its own commercial reasons the popular press was
queuing up to knock the BBC. But the comparisons to the chapel with its
captive audience, and top-down Victorian traditions of cultural improvement, combined with the 'patronising accents' of the 'gentlemen employed
by the BBC', are telling, drawing both on Priestley's hostility to upper-
class domination of English culture and on his instinctive preference for
lower-class 'gusto' and 'honest vulgarity', neither of which found much
place in the early BBC.

In broadcasting as in all the new mass media, the significant 'other'
with which British experience was compared was inevitably the United
States. The *Radio Times* repeatedly criticised American styles of broadcasting, which were seen as incompatible with British culture as embodied
in the BBC.[102] By the mid-1930s Priestley had gained much experience of
American radio, both as a listener and as a broadcaster. The different
styles, he told readers of a popular Sunday paper, were 'really a question
of national taste. The Americans like "pep" and "snap" at all costs, and
on the air they get it at the cost of screaming vulgarity. We like decorum.
We are prepared to risk a little dullness in order to be safe from
outrage.'[103] But the BBC's decorum could be an excuse for amateurish-
ness. If a few months of American radio would make him think kindly of

the BBC, he complained in 1938, after a few months back home he would long to 'hear again a programme that sounds brisk, efficient, professional'. Compared with the Americans, its attempts at entertainment sounded like something got up by the lady of the manor to keep the men of the village out of the public houses. The reason was clear: the BBC's monopoly had been devised when it was expected to be rather a solemn and serious institution, but now it had turned itself into an entertainer, and lack of competition was death to entertainment. In any case, without advertising, the BBC could never afford something as good as, for example, Jack Benny's weekly Sunday night show broadcast from Hollywood – or, for that matter, the excellent orchestra that NBC had specially assembled for a series of concerts by Toscanini. If the monopoly could not be broken, then the BBC should cut down live entertainment to one high-quality evening a week, filling the rest of the time with news and gramophone records – and, perhaps, some of the outside broadcasts done on a shoestring that were one of the delights of the early days.[104]

Priestley's experience as a broadcaster increased his irritation at the BBC's all-round stuffiness. At the BBC you were made to feel that 'just around the corner, in his orderly-room, is some tremendous ex-naval or military big-wig, who is bound to disapprove of all that is being said and done'. In America, where he was often called upon to do a programme at short notice, broadcasting was 'simpler and quicker and more free-and-easy'. In New York, Priestley appeared on the Royal Gelatine Hour, a variety show presented by the crooner Rudy Vallee, in which he talked about his theory of time to a national audience of millions. Even to do a ten-minute talk on the subject for the BBC would have required 'a few months' notice and the exchange of many letters', and they would never dream of popping it into the middle of a variety show.[105]

We can see that Priestley's response to the new popular culture, while anxious and critical, was anything but a simplistic rejection. Unlike most contemporary intellectuals, he was convinced of the potential of the new media, and aware that they meant a great deal to many people; but he was also concerned about who was in charge of them, and how they related to their audience. His idealised view of Edwardian popular culture put the audience in charge: the vitality of music-hall, football or Blackpool derived from that of the paying customers, mediated only by professional performers who were really very similar to themselves, and whom they encountered face to face. Now no such close relationship could be imagined: the performers were in a radio studio, or off in Hollywood: how could they reflect the needs and sensibilities of their audiences? The suspicion was that the producers – or still worse, the businessmen – were now in charge of the culture, manipulating the audience to like what suited them, turning them into passive consumers. At the same time he recognised, and showed in his novels, that many people found this culture just as energising as he had found the music-hall of his youth.

But one phrase from his Blackpool trip comes back to mind: 'not really English'. England was Priestley's frame of reference, the English people the unrealised collectivity that needed to be brought into being. What could be more English than Blackpool, Little Tich or Herbert Sutcliffe? Or more American than ragtime or Hollywood? To someone who recognised the importance of popular culture as much as he did, the threatened loss of its national frame of reference was worrying. But even worse, it was the wrong England, the 'nanny knows best' England that was in charge of the national culture. So while Priestley criticised American popular culture on familiar grounds, he criticised its English versions even more sharply for lacking 'pep' and 'snap', for not grasping the new media with both hands and using them to represent real English life – for being, in short, both insufficiently American and insufficiently English.

'Another kind of life'

One evening in about 1913, 'hot and astonished' in the Leeds Empire, Priestley and his friends had a brush with modernity.

> We discovered ragtime, brought to us by three young Americans: Hedges Brothers and Jacobsen [sic], they called themselves. It was as if we had been still living in the nineteenth century and then suddenly found the twentieth glaring and screaming at us. We were yanked into our own age, fascinating, jungle-haunted, monstrous. We were used to being sung at in music-halls in a robust and zestful fashion, but the syncopated frenzy of these three young Americans was something quite different; shining with sweat, they almost hung over the footlights, defying us to resist the rhythm, gradually hypnotising us, chanting and drumming us into another kind of life in which anything might happen.[106]

Priestley was no great fan of popular music: in the music-hall he preferred comics, and for home listening mainstream classical orchestral music.[107] But he recognised an echo of the future when he heard one:

> Out of these twenty noisy minutes in a music hall, so long ago, came fragmentary but prophetic outlines of the situation in which we find ourselves now, the menace to old Europe, the domination of America, the emergence of Africa, the end of confidence and any feeling of security, the nervous excitement, the frenzy, the underlying despair of our century.[108]

This, of course, was written with the hindsight of half a century. But Priestley was not the only one to whom the arrival of ragtime from America in the years just before the Great War signalled something 'new, strange and curiously disturbing'.[109] To us, after a century of headlong musical change, early ragtime recordings sound jaunty and catchy enough, but to those used to the comic songs, sentimental ballads and sing-along choruses of the music-hall this was music of a hitherto unknown emotional intensity. And it came from America – not just America, but black America (although most of its stage practitioners, like Hedges, Bros & Jacobson, were white).

In *Bright Day* the Nixeys – rootless adventurers from London who are to bring about the downfall of the Alington family – give a party. At the Alingtons' parties, working men from the wool trade play Bach and César Franck on the piano and violin with unexpected virtuosity; at the Nixeys', there is a fat man at the piano 'rattling out ragtime ... the dyed curls on his neck shiny with sweat' while the women cluster round and sing along.[110] Ragtime, its dubious practitioners and its sleazy American lyrics ('*Dog-gone, yew'd better begin – an' play a leetle tune upon your vi-o-lin*') becomes a symbol of the destructive external forces which are breaking up not only the Alingtons but Edwardian Bruddersford and the whole prewar world.

By the 1930s the ragtime era was over, but the American musical invasion continued. *Wonder Hero*'s Charlie Habble is taken to a London nightclub, where a man with 'dark curly hair like a negro, a curious yellow face, and an American accent' sings risqué songs, while 'rolling his black eyes at the nearest women'. 'He may be clever,' comments the journalist Hughson, 'but for all that, he's also a dirty, conceited, damned impudent, doped half-caste who ought to be back where he belongs. The very sight of him and his admirers makes me sick.' Charlie heartily endorses this verdict, complete with its (to us) startling racism, and so, we take it, does his creator.[111] This lurid cocktail of miscegenation, sexual depravity and after-hours sleaziness soon sends Charlie, who has to have it explained to him why the women like this kind of thing, back to clean-living Utterton, where *he* belongs. As with Priestley's caricatured sexually ambivalent highbrows, over whom women also seem to fawn, we must beware of those who cannot be clearly categorised, either in gender or racial terms.

Another occasion on which Priestley mobilises racial discourse to make a cultural point is on his visit to Blackpool in *English Journey*. The vital beings who patronised Blackpool in the past, he tells us, would sing high-spirited songs about 'dear old Charlie Brown and his pals, and the girls, those with the curly curls' – nonsense, true, but 'our own silly, innocent nonsense and not another country's jaded weary nonsense'. Now they were offered 'weary negroid ditties' about 'the woes of distant negroes, probably reduced to such misery by too much gin or cocaine'.[112] Priestley again seems to associate racial difference with moral degeneracy, but that is not his real point. The key word is 'distant': the audience are being invited to wallow in emotion they cannot really feel because it has nothing to do with their own lives. The innocence and exuberance of music-hall was rooted in English working-class life, but Americanisation has replaced it with something to which no authentic response is possible, but only passivity and listlessness, hollow frenzy barely concealing the underlying despair.

The cultural threat may have come from a specific place – America – but it was really part of a process that was general, and global. Priestley's comments on ragtime evoke an age in which the secure bearings of cultures rooted in nations, regions and communities were being loosened by the growing interdependence of the world to which he so often referred. The loss of regional autonomy which so worried Priestley – exemplified by the Nixeys' adventures in Bruddersford – was being repeated on a global level. The incursion of African-American music into English culture had the same causes and the same impact as that of Golspie into *Angel Pavement*: both were a consequence of the increased interconnectedness of the world, and both brought with them 'the end of confidence and any feeling of security': a threatened loss of identity which racial and sexual indeterminacy are used to symbolise. The task, Priestley decided in wartime, was to re-energise – or perhaps reinvent – an English people who could face up to this modern world.

America

But in the vanguard of this democratic England we find Rose in *They Walk*, inspired by Hollywood to seek her fortune in London; and Hope in *Let the People Sing*, re-energising Dunbury from the power-base of an Americanised roadhouse, protected by the movies against the power of dukes and duchesses. Jonathan Freedland has argued that the real English revolution took place in America, and needs to be brought home.[113] Priestley would perhaps agree. His Bruddersfordian Englishness – energetic, democratic, egalitarian – has far more in common with the American social ideal than it has with the traditional hierarchies and class discriminations of Old England. 'I have always been amused', he told a BBC audience in 1945, 'when Americans have pointed out the lack of social equality, real democracy, in England – simply because in the West Riding I knew there was as much social equality and real democracy as I have ever found anywhere in the United States.'[114]

Priestley first wrote about America before he had been there, admiring the kindness and generosity, the energy and enthusiasm of Americans he had met, and comparing them favourably with conceited Europeans, especially the public-school Englishman – but still finding them somehow not quite real.[115] America came more into focus when he paid several prolonged visits there in the 1930s, sometimes accompanied by his entire family, and, needless to say, wrote about it at length.[116] Priestley was

struck above all by two aspects of America: democracy, and modernity –
and, crucially, the two things ran together. In the south-west, where he
stayed with his family, he found a glimpse of a classless society, a 'democracy of good manners': 'the equality may be an illusion, but the manners
do not hint at any suspicions of inferiority and superiority. To return to
England, after a few months of this, is like dropping back into the Feudal
System.' Arizona, he reflected, came closer to 'a free and happy democracy' than the Soviet Union, where wealth and incomes may be more
equal, but Party officials benefited from a system of privileges which
excluded everyone else: beyond a certain point, he decided, distantly
echoing the idealised democratic Bradford of his youth, inequality was far
less damaging than privilege.[117]

As for modernity, New York was surely one of its wonders. After his
first visit in 1931 he wrote:

> If there is a city more foreign than New York – not only to an Englishman
> but to any European – I should like to know where it is. I suspect it cannot
> be nearer than Mars ... Those mad towers, those peaks of steel and
> concrete, so inhuman in the broad light of day, yet so beautiful at dawn,
> sunset and twinkling dusk – what do they mean? He [the New Yorker] does
> not know. And certainly we who arrive there, stare in amazement, and are
> either frightened or strangely moved, do not know.[118]

But life in New York he found stressful and enervating, his initial enchantment invariably succeeded by a feeling of spiritual desolation – perhaps
because of the stresses and strains of the Broadway theatre.[119] It was
Boulder Dam, contemplated in relative tranquillity, which like
Southampton's ocean liners brought out Priestley's infatuation with
modernity.

> Here in this Western American wilderness, the new man, the man of the
> future, has done something, and what he has done takes your breath away.
> When you look down at that vast smooth wall, at its towers of concrete, its
> power stations, at the new lakes and cataracts it has created, and you see the
> men who have made it all moving far below like ants or swinging perilously
> in mid-air as if they were little spiders; and you note the majestic order and
> rhythm of the work; you are visited by emotions that are hard to describe,
> if only because some of them are as new as the great Dam itself.[120]

This is so much more than a 'vast utilitarian device' – it is a thing of
beauty, perhaps a 'massive work of art', 'somewhere in the neighbourhood of Beethoven's Ninth Symphony'. Indeed, perhaps nowadays our
aesthetic emotions are stirred more by creations such as this, than within
'the narrow circles of art'.

The Dam is also 'a symbol of the new man, a new world, a new way of
life', and this thought leads Priestley to reflect on modernity itself, and its
future. There are things he does not like about this future: it will be more

impersonal, too mechanical, too collective – inimical to individuality, eccentricity and whimsy. It will be strange and uncomfortable for people like him, and we may 'have to scrap many things we hold dear to keep the rest secure'. But Boulder Dam, 'that vast impersonal work of utility-art' gave a reassuring glimpse of the new splendours that modernity might bring to compensate for what would be lost.[121]

And Boulder Dam is above all a collective work: 'the soul of America under socialism'. For, despite its individualist ideology, America, he goes on to argue, is further down the collectivist road than even Russia. 'It was not by what a single person can accomplish but by what can be done by collective effort that America had always shown herself so new, formidable and fascinating', excelling at architecture, civil engineering and cinema rather than poetry and painting.[122] The genius of America was 'for concerted effort, for tremendous team-work', and this must surely eventually lead to 'some kind of collectivist state, an ultimate socialism'.[123] But the down-side of collectivism is standardisation, and what the modern American really liked was 'doing exactly what all the others are doing': an anticipation of David Riesman's postwar notion of 'other-directedness'.[124] Priestley had many anxieties about American culture, vaguely expressed in the 1930s but more fully developed, as we shall see, after the War. But he had no doubt that, wherever modernity was going, it was America that was leading the way.

A decade after *Margin Released*, Priestley took another backward look at ragtime. It had arrived, he decided, 'almost like a message from the American working class', from 'a Walt Whitmanish democratic America, that had nothing to do with European culture; it came, though not without a hint of the Deep South, from a Coney Island of hot summers and shirtsleeves, beer and sweat'.[125] In other words (forgetting for a moment the issue of race and the anxieties of modernity) it came from the men who would build Boulder Dam and the New York skyscrapers, and lay the foundations of a new civilisation: as he described them in 1937,'big fellows in blue overalls, Whitman-ish lads, carrying themselves like free men, doing the job but not worrying too much ... [the] new common men who mixed the concrete and threw the rivets'.[126] This was the America Priestley admired: an America of working men and women, who, far from being downtrodden and marginalised, seemed to express more than any other group the spirit of their nation. Just a few years later, in wartime, Priestley would evoke Walt Whitman again to his own compatriots, calling for a new England to be born 'out of the people, everyday people, the people as you find them and leave them; people, people, just people!'[127]

Notes

1 Priestley, *English Journey*, p. 401. Parts of this chapter have appeared in John Baxendale, 'Re-narrating the Thirties: *English Journey* revisited', *Working Papers on the Web* 6 (June 2003) (www.shu.ac.uk/wpw/thirties).

2 J. B. Priestley, 'One man's jubilee', *Star* (8 May 1935), p. 4.

3 Raymond Williams, *Culture and Society 1780–1950* (London: Chatto & Windus, 1958).

4 D. L. LeMahieu, *A Culture for Democracy: Mass Culture and the Cultivated Mind in Britain between the Wars* (Oxford: Oxford University Press, 1988), part 2.

5 W. H. Auden, 'Brothers who when the sirens roar ... ' (1932).

6 Priestley, *Margin*, p. 188.

7 Ibid., pp. 188–9.

8 Priestley, *English Journey*, p. 417.

9 Ibid., p. 14.

10 Ibid., p. 15.

11 Ibid., pp. 15–18.

12 Ibid., pp. 33–4.

13 Ibid., pp. 71–4; 122–6.

14 Ibid., pp. 130–1.

15 Ibid., pp. 213–17.

16 Ibid., pp. 163–4.

17 Ibid., pp. 214–17.

18 Ibid., p. 234.

19 Ibid., p. 72.

20 Ibid., pp. 285–6.

21 Ibid., p. 404.

22 J. B. Priestley, 'Man underground', *Self-Selected Essays* (London: Heinemann, 1932) pp. 78–9: originally published *Saturday Review* (24 November 1928).

23 Priestley, *They Walk*, p. 70.

24 Ibid., pp. 2–3.

25 Priestley, *English Journey*, pp. 311, 4–5.

26 Ibid., pp. 200–1.

27 J. B. Priestley, 'Give women a chance', *Star* (27 March 1935), p. 4.

28 A. J. P. Taylor, *English History 1914–1945* (Oxford: Oxford University Press, 1965), chapter 9. See also C. L. Mowat, *Britain Between the Wars 1918–1940* (London: Methuen, 1956), and the discussion in Baxendale and Pawling, *Narrating the Thirties*, pp. 142–9.

29 John Stevenson and Chris Cook, *The Slump: Politics and Society in the Depression* (London: Cape, 1977); Baxendale and Pawling, *Narrating the Thirties*, chapter 6. See also Martyn J. Lee (ed.), *The Consumer Society Reader* (Oxford: Blackwell, 2000); and Mike Featherstone, *Consumer Culture and Postmodernism* (London: Sage, 1991).

30 Priestley, *Bright Day*, p. 26. For the association between suburban housing and the growth of the lower middle class see Martin Gaskell, 'Housing and the lower middle class, 1870–1914', in Geoffrey Crossick (ed.), *The Lower*

Middle Class in Britain 1870–1914 (London: Croom Helm, 1977).

31 McKibbin, *Classes and Cultures*, p. 81.

32 See Clough Williams-Ellis, *England and the Octopus* (London: Geoffrey Bles, 1928); Williams-Ellis (ed.), *Britain and the Beast*.

33 Priestley, 'The Beauty of Britain', p. 7.

34 Priestley, *English Journey*, pp. 401–2.

35 John Carey, *The Intellectuals and the Masses: Pride and Prejudice among the Literary Intelligentsia, 1880–1939* (London: Faber and Faber, 1992), pp. 46–70.

36 Priestley, *English Journey*, pp. 402–3.

37 Priestley, 'The old Britain is dead – long live the new!', *Sunday Chronicle* (7 January 1934), p. 9 (Priestley's italics).

38 Priestley, *English Journey*, pp. 404–5.

39 J. B. Priestley, 'Foreword' to Ivor Brown, *The Heart of England* (London: Batsford, 1935), p. v.

40 Priestley, *English Journey*, p. 403.

41 Ibid., pp. 405–6.

42 What follows is based on Priestley, *Rain* (1939), pp. 264–70, and 'The new loneliness', *Sunday Graphic* (3 October 1937), pp. 8–9. The former is an extended and partly rewritten version of the latter.

43 Priestley, *Rain*, p. 266.

44 Stephen Taylor, 'The suburban neurosis'. Since the echoes of Taylor's analysis are found only in the second of the two Priestley pieces under discussion, it seems more than likely that Priestley knew the gist of Taylor's argument.

45 Much the same could be said of George Orwell's *Coming Up for Air* (London: Gollancz, 1939); or indeed many another intellectual attack on suburbia: see Carey, *Intellectuals*, chapter 3.

46 Peter Wilmott and Michael Young, *Family and Class in a London Suburb* (London: New English Library, 1967), pp. 79–87. Originally published 1960.

47 Priestley, 'New loneliness', p. 9.

48 Priestley, *Rain*, p. 267.

49 Priestley, *English Journey*, p. 402.

50 Ibid., pp. 265–6.

51 Ibid., pp. 267–8.

52 Ibid.

53 Alan Swingewood, *The Myth of Mass Culture* (London: Macmillan, 1977).

54 Carey, *Intellectuals*, pp. 37–8. Carey's misreading is doubly unfortunate, because Priestley is actually rather more enthusiastic about the popular and the people than Carey's hero, Arnold Bennett.

55 Priestley, *Companions*, pp. 13–14.

56 Priestley, *English Journey*, p. 144.

57 J. B. Priestley, 'Sutcliffe and I', *Open House*, pp. 102–7. Originally published *Saturday Review* (24 July 1926).

58 J. B. Priestley, 'Your world and mine', *Sunday Chronicle* (3 September 1933), p. 9.

59 J. B. Priestley, 'Little Tich', *The Balconinny* (London: Methuen, 1929) pp. 55–61, originally published *Saturday Review* (10 March 1928). Priestley, *Particular Pleasures*, pp. 153–190.

60 Priestley, *Edwardians*, p. 172.
61 Gareth Stedman Jones, 'Working class culture and working class politics in Victorian London', in *Languages of Class: Studies in English Working Class History, 1832–1982* (Cambridge: Cambridge University Press, 1983).
62 See, for example, the Introduction to Peter Bailey (ed.), *Music Hall: The Business of Pleasure* (Milton Keynes: Open University Press, 1986).
63 J. B. Priestley, 'Variety', in *Apes and Angels*. Originally published *Saturday Review* (29 October 1927). See also 'The music halls', in *The Moments and Other Pieces*. Originally published *New Statesman* (28 January 1966).
64 Priestley, *They Walk*, pp. 189–97.
65 Ibid., pp. 385–7.
66 Priestley, *Let the People Sing*, p. 15.
67 Ibid., pp. 164–5.
68 J. B. Priestley, 'Good, honest vulgarity', *Sunday Chronicle* (12 November 1933), p. 9.
69 Priestley, *They Walk*, pp. 12–13, 18.
70 Priestley, *Let the People*, p. 232.
71 Ibid., p. 121.
72 Ibid., p. 194.
73 J. B. Priestley, 'Super-Super', in *Balconinny*. Originally published *Saturday Review* (8 December 1928).
74 Priestley, *Midnight*, pp. 166–201; *Margin*, pp. 215–16.
75 Internet Movie Data Base entry for J. B. Priestley: www.imdb.com/name /nm0697362/, consulted 22 July 2005.
76 Priestley, *Particular Pleasures*, p. 162; *Margin*, p. 217; *Midnight*, p. 166.
77 Priestley, *Midnight* pp. 182–3, 192–3; J. B. Priestley, 'Hollywood debunked', *Sunday Graphic* (7 March 1937), p. 17.
78 Ibid., p. 184.
79 Priestley, *Margin*, p. 213; *Midnight*, pp. 169–70.
80 Ibid., p. 170.
81 Priestley, *They Walk*, p. 399.
82 Richard Dyer, 'Entertainment and utopia', in *Only Entertainment* (London: Routledge, 1992).
83 J. B. Priestley, 'Getting to know one another', *Listener* (7 August 1941), pp. 183–4 – a talk broadcast to the United States.
84 Priestley, *Rain*, pp. 83–4; J. B. Priestley, 'They've slighted Britain', *Sunday Chronicle* (8 October 1933), p. 9.
85 Priestley, *Rain*, pp. 186–7. R. B. Marriott, 'Priestley on British films' (interview), *Era* (6 July 1939), p. 1. *The Front Page*, dir. Lewis Milestone (1931).
86 J. B. Priestley, 'Films and the future', *Star* (23 September 1935), p. 4.
87 Priestley, *Margin*, pp. 214–15.
88 Priestley, 'Films and the future'.
89 This information is gleaned from Alan Edwin Day's invaluable *J. B. Priestley: An Annotated Bibliography* (London: Garland Publishing, 1980).
90 Priestley, *Margin*, p. 180.
91 Priestley, *Wonder Hero*, p. 7.
92 Ibid., p. 288.
93 Ibid., pp. 105–6.

94 Priestley, *Edwardians*, p. 176.

95 Ibid., pp. 177–8.

96 J. B. Priestley, 'Other people's accomplishments', in *Apes and Angels*. Originally published *Saturday Review* (30 April 1927).

97 Priestley, *Midnight*, p. 160.

98 LeMahieu, *Culture*, p. 328; Asa Briggs, *The History of Broadcasting in the United Kingdom*, vol. 2: *The Golden Age of Wireless* (Oxford: Oxford University Press, 1965), p. 134.

99 Asa Briggs, *The History of Broadcasting in the United Kingdom*, vol. 1: *The Birth of Broadcasting* (Oxford: Oxford University Press, 1961). LeMahieu, *Culture*, pp. 148–51. Erik Barnouw, *A History of Broadcasting in the United States Volume 1: A Tower in Babel* (Oxford: Oxford University Press, 1966).

100 LeMahieu, *Culture*, pp. 141–54.

101 J. B. Priestley, 'Wireless without tears', *Daily Mirror* (28 January 1929), p. 11.

102 LeMahieu, *Culture*, pp. 188–9. Valeria Camporesi, 'The BBC and American broadcasting, 1922–55', *Media, Culture and Society* 16 (1994).

103 J. B. Priestley, 'The hocus-pocus of the BBC', *Sunday Chronicle* (4 February 1934), p. 9.

104 J. B. Priestley, 'If I ran the BBC', *Sunday Dispatch* (24 July 1938), p. 10.

105 Priestley, *Rain*, pp. 127–8.

106 Priestley, *Margin*, pp. 66–7.

107 See the list in Priestley, *Pleasures*, pp. 57–102.

108 Priestley, *Margin*, p. 67.

109 For fuller discussion, see John Baxendale, '"... into another kind of life in which anything might happen" ...': Popular music and late modernity, 1910–1930', *Popular Music* 14:2 (1995).

110 Priestley, *Bright Day*, pp. 92–8, 176–7.

111 Priestley, *Wonder Hero*, p. 152.

112 Priestley, *English Journey*, p. 268.

113 Jonathan Freedland, *Bring Home the Revolution: The Case for a British Republic* (London: Fourth Estate, 1999).

114 J. B. Priestley, 'Born and bred in Bradford', *Listener* (27 December 1945), p. 753.

115 J. B. Priestley, 'American notes', in *Open House*. Originally published *Saturday Review* (29 May 1926).

116 America is discussed at length in Priestley, *Midnight* and *Rain*. Each of his visits produced a series of newspaper articles as well as magazine pieces: *Evening Standard*, 4–10 July 1931; *Sunday Chronicle*, 3–24 March 1935; *Sunday Graphic*, 7–21 March 1937.

117 Priestley, *Midnight*, pp. 101–5.

118 J. B. Priestley, 'New York, the nightmare city', *Evening Standard* (6 July 1932), p. 7.

119 Priestley, *Midnight*, pp. 22–4.

120 Ibid., p. 110.

121 Ibid., pp. 111–15.

122 Ibid., pp. 119–20.

123 Ibid., p. 126.

124 Ibid., p. 121. Riesman, *The Lonely Crowd*.
125 Priestley, *Edwardians*, p. 245.
126 Priestley, *Midnight*, pp. 54–5.
127 Priestley, *Out of the People*, pp. 110–11.

5

Priestley's war

September 3 1939 found Priestley on his way to London from his home on the Isle of Wight. He was heading for Broadcasting House, where he was to read on air the first episode of a new novel commissioned by the BBC, called *Let the People Sing*: the first novel it was claimed, ever written specifically for broadcasting. The road was quiet, the day sunny, the journey smooth; but as they reached Staines at about noon, everything changed: noise, traffic jams, screaming sirens, people in tin hats running around shouting: Britain was at war.[1] *Let the People Sing*, 'written during the anxious and darkening days of August', became Priestley's first wartime novel.[2]

It was entirely appropriate that Priestley should spend the first day of the war at Broadcasting House, where he was to spend so much time, one way and another, over the next six years, since his place in history rests to a large degree on what he said there. Broadcasting, journalism and public speaking made him a key wartime figure – perhaps, as Graham Greene would argue at the end of 1940, 'a leader second in importance only to Mr Churchill'.[3] A third of the country or more listened to his Sunday evening *Postscript* talks during the epic summer of 1940, and they now seem as inseparable as Churchill's speeches from the national mood at that critical stage of the war. Throughout the war Priestley's output was characteristically prodigious, across a broad front of novels, plays, films, journalism, broadcasting and political activism. He wrote articles for *Picture Post*, the *News Chronicle*, *Reynolds News* and even the *Sunday Express*. He addressed the nation numerous times on the radio, not just in the *Postscripts*, and seemed to be on permanent call to make overseas broadcasts in the early hours of the morning – thirty-nine in the summer of 1940 alone, at the rate of one every three days.[4] He joined committees, campaigned in by-elections, addressed meetings and spoke with people 'in hotels, camps, factory canteens, hostels, railway trains, bars, restaurants'.[5] He wrote film scripts and narrated propaganda shorts. Almost as an afterthought, he published four novels and five plays. Virtually all of this work in some way addressed the war, how it was being fought and what would happen afterwards. Graham Greene, who hated Priestley's novels and plays, found in his broadcasts something more than morale-boosting propaganda: 'he gave us what the other leaders have always failed to give us – an ideology'.[6]

Priestley's ideology looked to the future, while Churchill's was rooted in the past. So, while posterity reveres Churchill as the great war leader, Priestley has a wider role, not just in the narrative of the war itself – from appeasement to VE Day via Dunkirk and El Alamein – but in the broader narrative of how the postwar world came about – from the Slump to the Welfare State, via the People's War. Our opinion of him depends to a large degree on our opinion of this 'postwar settlement'. Angus Calder, in *The Myth of the Blitz*, sees Priestley as co-inventor of a wartime myth which pretended to be radical but turned out to be nothing of the kind; while in *The Road to 1945*, whose title betrays its rather different stand-point, Paul Addison imagines 'Colonel Blimp being pursued through a land of Penguin Specials by an abrasive meritocrat, a progressive church-man, and J. B. Priestley'.[7]

Either way, Priestley was among those who saw the war as an oppor-tunity for much-needed social and cultural change. For him, as for many others, the hope of radical postwar reconstruction grew out of despair at the condition of the nation in the 1930s.[8] As we have seen, his social and political critique had gathered strength through the decade, from the sharp questions and shrewd observations of *English Journey* to the scathing denunciation of *Godshill*, and it extended beyond the familiar *Wigan Pier* territory of unemployment and social conditions in the depressed areas, to bring in issues of democracy, culture, national identity and the distribution of power and status in British society. During the war, much to the irritation of Churchill and his colleagues, he was the most widely heard spokesman for radical postwar reconstruction, appeal-ing to the oft-expressed desire for 'no return to the thirties'. Even during the 'phoney war', he was already asking why we could not 'learn to plan and spend in peacetime as we do in wartime', to get rid of the slums and the depressed areas.[9] But there was more to his wartime agitation than a shopping-list of legislation, and in any case he had always been sceptical of Five Year Plans, bureaucracies and social reconstruction from above. He was a visionary as much as a social reformer, and his vision was of a nation renewed from below, 'bombed and burned into democracy': 'everything comes out of the people', as he would declare in 1941, echoing Walt Whitman. Like others, he found the war uplifting after the gloom and disillusionment of the 1930s, not least because it at last provided him with a receptive audience and the opportunity to make himself heard, which he seized with both hands and guarded jealously. But he also saw it as a time of fluidity, in which the suppressed energies of the people could at last be freed, and the nation transformed. Above and beyond a new set of policy measures (about whose details he was always rather vague), he was offering a new, almost spiritual vision of a nation at last worthy of itself. It is in this light that his wartime role needs to be understood, as well as his ambivalent response to the postwar world he helped to create.

Let the People Sing

Let the People Sing provides a bridge between Priestley's critical ruminations about British society and politics at the end of the 1930s, and the rather more urgent tasks of wartime. In a *Radio Times* interview he described it as 'a sort of comic novel, with a dramatic symbolism. Centred around an imaginary town, symbolical of England. Present day, with Dictators left out. We want a rest from them. You can read it as a picaresque novel or as a social satire.'[10] And indeed the novel works on two different levels. It is, to begin with, a comic novel, with satirical characters, comic set-pieces, and humorous incidents and dialogue. But it is also a translation into allegorical terms of Priestley's critique of British society in *Rain Upon Godshill*, published just a few weeks earlier. 'The problems seemed to be there still, only now with a deeper despair all round them', he had written then.[11] His complaints – developed at greater length in his series of articles for the *News Chronicle* entitled 'Britain wake up!' – were by now familiar, but expressed with a new urgency: the lack of real democracy, the dominance of the City, a plutocracy concealed behind a 'vast fancy-dress ball' of snobbery, everything run by the Right People in their own interests, and the passivity of the middle classes who could lead the way to change but were not doing so. England was depicted as a tired country living on its inheritance, with no great creative idea to inspire it. But still there were qualities in the ordinary English people, tolerance, kindness, a commitment to human values rather than theories of economics or politics, which could lead the way towards a new and better society, something that was neither communism nor fascism nor a sham capitalist democracy.[12]

Priestley's earlier social novels, such as *Angel Pavement*, *Wonder Hero* and *They Walk in the City*, while not without touches of caricature, described the 'condition of England' in broadly realist mode, as observed by relatively detached and innocent travellers who could do nothing about it except go back home to somewhere safe. *Let the People Sing* has its moments of social realism, somewhat undercut by its Wodehousian comic set-pieces, but it is essentially an allegory, in which the ordinary midlands town of Dunbury stands for England, and the events of the novel act out the crisis which Priestley believed the nation was going through in the late

1930s. The crisis is resolved, in a mood of utopian fantasy, by a spontaneous popular awakening – the kind of renewal from below which Priestley spent the war years hoping and agitating for. As Klein observes, this socio-political theme was hardly a hidden subtext but blazingly proclaimed throughout the novel; even so it seems to have evaded the attention of some British reviewers when the book was published in November.[13] The *Times Literary Supplement*, for example, obtusely dismissed it as 'an easy, good-natured and lightly sentimental fable'.[14] Interestingly enough, American reviewers seem to have got the point: this was a novel, as the *New Yorker* reviewer realised, about 'the outmoded social setup of England', which was perhaps more visible from across the Atlantic than from Printing House Square.[15] Priestley, as ever, set out to entertain his readers, but this was not all he was doing: *Let the People Sing* had a deeper purpose.

The small town of Dunbury has fallen prey to two rival power-groups – the decadent gentry, led by the dowager Lady Foxfield, of cold, damp, decaying Dunbury Hall ('portraits and pieces of armour ... and shredding, moth-eaten lengths of tapestry'), and the town's main employer, a soulless American-owned plastics factory, 'all white and glittering in its modernity'. Both want to get their hands on the Market Hall, which has been bequeathed to the people of the town by one of Lady Foxfield's ancestors: the gentry to turn it into a museum demonstrating the 'great traditions' of the country as a 'bulwark against dangerous tendencies', the plastics firm as a showroom and offices.[16] The people of Dunbury would rather keep it for their town band, but are too cowed and apathetic to do anything about it, until their collective spirit is roused by four itinerant strangers: an out-of-work music-hall comedian, a refugee Czech professor, and a travelling market trader and his energetic and beautiful daughter. After a complex but tightly structured sequence of events, during which many of Priestley's perennial points about Englishness and English society are voiced, mostly by Professor Kronak, the 'collective unconscious Dunburyean' reawakens; there is an explosion of popular radicalism (including a strike at the plastics factory and an outbreak of impertinence towards upper-class residents); and the people regain control of their Market Hall, their town band and, we assume, their historic destiny. The message about England – torn between decadent traditionalism and rapacious Americanisation, and to be rescued only by a national-popular reawakening – is surely not easy to miss, though whether its many readers got the message we can never know.

In many ways *Let the People Sing* set the agenda for Priestley's extraordinary wartime career, which began almost as soon as war broke out, when he was commissioned by the Ministry of Information to tour the new, wartime Britain, *English Journey*-style, and write articles for publication at home and abroad.[17] The tour began in Halifax where Priestley had been inducted into the army in 1914, and covered over three thousand miles in just over a month, producing twenty-six daily articles for the *News Chronicle* starting on 22 September which covered everything from military preparations and war production to evacuation, popular entertainment and civilian morale, and provided a vivid picture, full of telling detail, of Britain in the early weeks of war.[18] Priestley gave free rein to his old fascination with the work process, and readers were treated to detailed accounts of the production of shells, fuses, gas-masks and aircraft, life on board a submarine and in the women's Auxiliary Territorial Service (ATS). But, as in 1934, it was the people, factory workers, army recruits, naval commanders, Observer Corps members and ordinary civilians, who provided him with his most potent raw material: what did they think about the war, and how were they coping with its demands? This was morale-boosting propaganda, conveying the message that we are all in it together, getting on with things, and spirits are high, so the few negative comments were relatively trivial – such as the lack of a theatre for the troops at Catterick Camp. September 1939 was no time for criticising the war effort, but later he reported (perhaps with the aid of hindsight) that even at this early stage of the war he had found discontent:

> Most of the real work was being done by youngish technical men of the so-called middle-classes, men rarely given final authority, and men already feeling restless and dissatisfied because they were hampered by the incompetence, pedantry, lack of drive of the superior persons from whom they were often compelled to take orders. It was as if energy and virtue had been drained away from one strata to reappear, but waiting to be tapped, in another.[19]

Already in September 1939 Priestley's characteristic view of the war was starting to take shape. Like other observers he found the mood of this war more sober and thoughtful than the 'flag-waving jingoism' of 1914. There was no 'crazy Bank Holiday air ... songs, cheers, drinks-all-round, our-gallant-lads, give-'em hell-boys, that sort of thing ... People are now soberly setting about the task. They would much rather be doing something else, but there it is.'[20] It was a professional, industrial war, demanding the sober application of skills and technologies. Even the army officers looked like proper professional military men, rather than the Edwardian dandies of old.[21] And this time it was all right to talk about what the war was for. Two young working men in Halifax wanted to discuss whether a violent war could put an end to violence – '25 years ago no such talk would have come out of their kind'.[22] In Dundee he found that a local paper had criticised people who wanted to discuss war aims, but 'surely this is the time, when we are all prepared (but are not yet fighting tooth-and-nail) to consider what kind of world we want to see'.[23] If a later broadcast to the United States is to be believed, this is exactly what 'hundreds and hundreds' of people he met on his journey were considering: 'what kind of world would come out of this'.[24] The popular mood, he concluded after the first thousand miles of his journey, was 'neither bored nor depressed, but simply bewildered': people were bewildered because they were wondering when the war was going to start, but they were united in quietly and patiently adapting themselves to the new conditions. But the bewilderment needed to be addressed, and here Priestley set out his stall: 'the people should be treated not as a mere donkey-of-all-work but as a sensible partner in a great enterprise ... One reason why we have gone to war is that we believe that the people can be trusted. After all, it's their country.'[25] And so, by the end of October, 'the people' was already established as Priestley's central wartime theme.

Constructing the wartime nation

Nations are, as Benedict Anderson has famously argued, imagined communities, constituted through a continuous collective narrative into which the individual is incorporated and defined as a member of the nation.[26] By the end of the 1930s, with the arrival of mass literacy, universal suffrage and the modern mass media, this national discourse was accessible to virtually everyone and, in wartime more than ever, listening to the BBC or reading a newspaper was a key part of normal everyday life. War requires the mobilisation of people and resources, but it is a crucial moment for generating ideas of the nation which outlast the emergency. Linda Colley has argued that war was a crucial factor in the emergence of a lasting popular idea of Britishness in the eighteenth and nineteenth centuries, and this war too reshaped the national self-image in the decades that followed.[27]

However, discourses of the nation are not straightforward. Although they purport to reflect the essential unity and identity of the nation, they invariably come in different and conflicting versions, evoking contested narratives of history, culture, race and character, and can exclude as well as incorporate. As has been argued, the national self-image inherited from the interwar years was more 'ordinary', domestic and inward-looking than that of 1914: more to do with pottering about in a suburban garden than with seeking military glory in the far outposts of Empire.[28] This low-key and imprecise self-image served to mask social conflicts and divisions in a nation disinclined to assert itself in the world. In peacetime this was all very well, but some found the lack of public demonstrativeness at the start of the war worrying.[29] 'No one knew the names of any generals or admirals', complained the travel writer H. V. Morton: this was 'a nation waiting, almost pathetically, for something to happen'.[30] The Ministry of Information, charged with sharpening up the discourses of the nation, had a torrid time of it at the start of the war, when the nation's class and cultural divides made themselves felt in disputes over the tone of voice in which the people should be addressed. Attempting to tap into what it thought was a core national narrative, the MoI invoked the longbowmen of Agincourt, the defeat of Napoleon and the wonders of the Empire, and urged the BBC to play down the comedy and dance-bands, and broadcast either rousing patriotic marches or British folk music.[31] In a celebrated and somewhat farcical episode, attempts were made to remove the popular singer Vera Lynn from the air, on the grounds that her sentimental programme *Sincerely Yours* was insufficiently virile and warlike to be served up to the troops.[32] But as Vera Lynn herself put it, in reality 'the boys' were fighting for 'the precious personal things', rather than an abstract conception of national duty.[33] This episode illustrates the failure of many in high places to appreciate not only working-class attitudes but the way in which ideas of Englishness in general had become domesticated and democratised since 1918.

These were things which Priestley, though in a rather different style from Vera Lynn, did appreciate, and which brought him to the fore as a radio broadcaster second only to Churchill in his appeal. Priestley's intimate manner, reassuring 'educated Yorkshire' voice, and instinct for vernacular phrasing and delivery, matched the down-to-earth content of most of his broadcasts. A Mass Observation study of early wartime propaganda films found that, while most of them betrayed an 'essentially upper and middle-class attitude' and failed to get through to a working-class audience, the one people remembered most was the seven-minute *Britain at Bay*, for which Priestley wrote and delivered the commentary: Priestley, commented MO's Tom Harrisson, 'provides a bridge between middle and working classes'.[34] Priestley's long estrangement from the upper-class dominance of British culture was starting to bear fruit. He could speak across the cultural divides which hamstrung the early MoI.

The other national performer with near-universal appeal was, of course, Churchill.[35] Both Priestley and Churchill, not unnaturally in wartime, spoke the language of national unity and freedom, but in diametrically opposed but equally effective ways. Churchill summoned up, both in language and in reference points, a deep, historic England under whose heady influence present-day divisions could be forgotten. His version of history was Whiggish in tone, its theme the onward march of free institutions, so that England was now the defender of freedom for all the world. ('Freedom' was not, of course, the same thing as democracy, which was a fairly recent arrival in this national narrative, and had yet to make its appearance in much of the Empire.) Churchill's mode of address rejected the conversational style of most twentieth-century politicians – notably Baldwin, master of the fireside radio chat. Instead, he raised his linguistic register to match the significance of the moment, with vivid touches of the archaic ('the bright gleam has caught the helmets of our soldiers') and a rhetorical style heavily influenced by Victorian and earlier models, so that he could sometimes sound like a Shakespearean actor or an Anglican bishop. Although it did lend itself to parody, the Churchillian style had a huge impact, perhaps not despite but because of its sheer distance from the lives and habits of the people he was addressing. At its best, the effect of this distancing was to make both events and audience sound supremely important, an importance in which all were invited to share: 'This is indeed the grand heroic period of our history, and the light of glory shines on all' (broadcast 27 April 1940).[36]

If Churchill wished his audience to recognise themselves as members of a historic nation, Priestley addressed them as 'the people': 'the kindly, decent, patient folk of this country', for whom 'a nobler framework of life must be constructed' after they had made the sacrifices that war demands.[37] 'The People' is just as slippery a concept as 'the Nation', and likewise has to be constructed imaginatively and discursively, but Priestley's matchless ability to make something special out of vernacular language, coupled with his roots in provincial radicalism, enabled him to produce a discourse in which the people and the nation were one. What is Britain? he asked in 1941:[38]

> Britain is not a sum total of properties, is not a super-trading concern, is not merely another territory where the masses exist: Britain is the home of the British people. Yes, those people whose praises have lately gone round the world, they live in Britain. Before it is anything else, this country is their home. Whatever can be done to make it a better home for the people is right, and whatever makes it a worse one is wrong.[39]

And who are the people? Not 'members of "classes" ... [or] powerful group interests', but 'we are all the people so long as we are willing to consider ourselves the people'.[40] Not just everybody, then, but everybody who was prepared to renounce privilege and subsume themselves in this national collectivity. Although he did not coin the phrase (and no one seems to know who did), Priestley more than anyone became associated with the notion of the 'People's War': that this was a war in which the active participation and commitment of ordinary people was paramount, and that this had implications for what the war meant, for the way it was run, and for what would happen after it was over. Because of these sacrifices, and the betrayals and disappointments of the interwar years, the idea of the 'People's War' carried with it a strong hint of better things to come. But to be part of 'the people' as Priestley saw them meant actively seeking that better life: actively participating in the war effort and in the shaping of the postwar world. This combination of rights and obligations, actively pursued, we might call 'citizenship'.[41] For Priestley, citizenship had been at a low ebb in the Britain of the 1920s and 1930s, but in the summer of 1940 he thought he saw its rebirth.

Churchill's nation, it turned out, had less staying-power than Priestley's. Churchill the war leader continued to be honoured – accorded a spectacular state funeral in 1965, and voted the greatest Briton of all time in a BBC poll as late as 2002. Priestley, though also honoured, became increasingly disillusioned and alienated from the postwar world as it unfolded in the 1950s and 1960s. But if voters in 1945 were choosing between rival ideas of the nation, it was Priestley's and not Churchill's that they voted for. Moreover, the populist construction of national identity which Priestley helped bring to the fore during the war years would dominate the meanings which the war carried in the years after 1945, when it came to be seen as a defining moment of national unity and purpose: the moment when, in the words of two of the period's earliest historians, 'England had arisen', and the British people 'found themselves again', and in due course the Welfare State replaced the Empire as the focus of national pride.[42] The back-story, so to speak, of this postwar rhetoric, Angus Calder's 'myth of the Blitz', leads us straight to the summer of 1940, and the Sunday evening *Postscripts* which Priestley delivered after the nine o'clock news in the epoch-making weeks between early June and late October.

'All of us ordinary people'

In the 'Preface' to the published collection of his *Postscripts* Priestley observed that 'what really holds the attention of most decent folk is a genuine sharing of feelings and views on the part of the broadcaster. He must talk as if he were among serious friends, and not as if he had suddenly been appointed head of an infants' school.'[43] If Churchill's secret was that he spoke from a lofty plane, it was Priestley's lack of remoteness, his common touch, as much as his controversial comments on postwar reconstruction, which made his broadcasts so popular, achieving almost unprecedented audiences of thirty to forty per cent of the adult population.[44] The most famous of them, the one which according to Graham Greene 'began to lead the way out of despair', was the first, broadcast on 5 June 1940, about Dunkirk.[45]

This short piece – less than a thousand words – still stands as a masterpiece of extended metaphor, and an eloquent statement of the 'people's war' vision, in which the 'little ships' which helped to rescue the troops are identified with the ordinary people, and the ordinary people with the nation itself.[46] Priestley achieves this metaphorical linkage through images of popular pleasure, always so central to his conception of Englishness. Centre-stage are the pleasure steamers, called out of the 'ridiculous ... innocent, foolish ... almost old-fashioned' world of the English seaside, all bottled beer, pork pies and peppermint rock, to achieve a heroic destiny. So too, we infer, will the British people themselves, by their nature ordinary, unheroic, rather muddled and blundering, and most unsuited to martial glory, once again conjure up triumph out of near-disaster. History is evoked – 'as if we had turned a page in the history of Britain and seen a chapter headed "Dunkirk"' – not looking backwards but looking forwards, to how this moment will be written about in the future: history is not in some vaguely heroic national past, it is now, and we are in the thick of it. Completely bypassed are the standard ideological markers of nationhood: past glories, tradition, the landscape, and especially military heroism. Instead, Priestley presents a vision of Englishness which is democratic, inclusive, ordinary almost to the point of bathos. His referencing of the English seaside – 'pierrots and piers, sand castles, ham-and-egg teas, palmists, automatic machines, and crowded sweating promenades' – feels more like August 1914 than June 1940, and carries no echoes of his jaundiced take on 1930s Blackpool – no American cocktail bars or 'hot Broadway hits' in sight. This 1940 seaside, in fact, is reminiscent of the opening scenes, set in 1914, of the Richard Attenborough/Joan Littlewood film *Oh! What a Lovely War!* (1969). It was the spirit of the Edwardian English people, energetic and democratic citizens, that he wished to evoke, rather than the listless, demoralised populace of 1939. But even so we are left in no doubt of the capacity of these unheroic people, once roused, to defeat the Nazis, whose Otherness is boldly drawn: ruthless, inhuman, highly organised but unpoetic – making few mistakes but achieving no epics, and with 'nothing about them that ever catches the world's imagination'.

The piece concludes with a return to the prophetic mode, telling how 'our great-grandchildren, when they learn how we began this War by snatching glory out of defeat, and then swept on to victory, may also learn how the little holiday steamers made an excursion to hell and came back glorious'. How far Priestley's listeners on 5 June 1940 really believed this we can never know, but it seems likely that they believed it while he was saying it. He had told them who they were, and constructed the only imaginable narrative of their war which would give them a happy, indeed heroic, ending. In doing so he achieved the remarkable feat, which even Homer did not attempt, of mythologising a war that had scarcely yet begun. The power that this broadcast still has for those who grew up in the war's shadow testifies to the longevity of the myth.

The early *Postscripts* continued the identification of the war and the war effort with everyday life and ordinary people, and when more conventional themes of history and landscape made their appearance, it was in this context. On 16 June Priestley told listeners about his stint with the Local Defence Volunteers at his home on the Isle of Wight, and how this cross-section of rural society dealt with the extraordinary events of wartime by assimilating them to their own familiar lives as they had done for generations – just one more menace like blizzards or floods which country people must deal with. To conclude, Priestley quoted Thomas Hardy's poem 'In time of the "Breaking of Nations"', written in 1915, which presents ordinary life as the one historical universal which outlives the drama of wars and changing dynasties. Priestley's national symbols too insist on their ordinariness – ducks in the park, a Bradford pie-shop, a fat, roaring old woman on a stretcher, Sam Weller from the *Pickwick Papers*, a corny comedian in an ENSA factory show. Even when national leaders are praised, it is for manifestations of ordinariness – a little dig in the ribs and a mischievous grin delivered by Winston Churchill to Ernest Bevin on the Treasury Bench (7 July). And when the national character is discussed – albeit in somewhat sentimental and idealised terms, for this is after all wartime – the virtues are modest and gentle ones: we are 'simple, kindly, humorous, brave', 'imaginative and romantic' (30 June), with 'warmth of heart, and height of imagination' (11 August), 'patience, courage and good humour' (1 September), 'courage and resolution and cheerfulness' (15 September). By contrast, the Nazi enemy are dehumanised and robotic: 'thin-lipped, cold-eyed ... a kind of overgrown species of warrior-ant' (9 June), representing 'the growing corruption, the darkening despair of our modern world' (23 June). Again, history comes in at the side door: Nazis represent the dark side of modernity, while the English virtues (like those of the romantic and philosophical good Germans) are long established.

Nazis apart, Priestley's most scornful words were reserved for that old enemy, the English ruling class. Like the polemical pamphlet *Guilty Men*, published in early July 1940 and selling over two hundred thousand copies despite being blacklisted by the major distributors – or the *Daily Mirror* which called for the dismissal of 'the old loitering gang' of appeasers and was duly ticked off by Churchill and Herbert Morrison – Priestley was catching the current mood, in which the commitment and even the loyalty of the prewar ruling class were questioned.[47] 'In the ascendant demonology of the war period,' Paul Addison has said, 'the upper classes were usually to blame because they were rich, because they were obsolete in their ideas, or because they were both.'[48] Far from being the dynamic public-school heroes of juvenile adventure stories, the top people had become a dead weight. 'Sometimes I feel', Priestley told his listeners, 'that you and I – all of us ordinary people – are on one side of a high fence, and on the other side ... are the official and important personages: the pundits and mandarins', concerned only to order people about and keep them in the dark. 'It isn't woolly, pussy-footed officialdom that will win this war, but the courage, endurance and rising spirits of the British people. And we're still, as we always have been, at heart an imaginative and romantic people' (30 June). As for the propertied classes, backbone of traditional England, they are a waste of space. They have fled the cities to the safety of country hotels, inconveniencing people travelling on war business (6 October) – or to North America, leaving behind country houses and estates which they expect the rest of us to defend for them (21 July) - and even when they have stayed at home, they refuse to make room for city evacuees (22 September).

Priestley's attacks on officialdom and the property-owning classes struck the *Postscripts'* first really controversial note, one which opened up – prematurely, according to his critics – the whole question of war aims and postwar reconstruction. We were being encouraged, he declared, to regard the war merely as an interruption to a normal course of life which would be resumed when peace came. But in the false peace of the 1930s, 'there's nothing that really worked that we can go back to'. Rather, this war was about 'the breakdown of one vast system and the building up of another and better one', and to achieve this we had to think differently. Human creativity must take precedence over the exercise of power; property must give way to community. And meanwhile, owners of property who had gone off to the safety of America must expect to have it expropriated for the war effort (21 July). A week later, on 28 July, he returned to the theme. We had done nothing for those who fought the last war but let them take their chances in a hostile world. Now we must draw on the lessons of war to move from a world of gangsters and tricksters and cut-throat competition to one of co-operation.

Revulsion against the 1930s, 'a stony wilderness of world depression and despair' (28 July) was a theme which Priestley was to pursue throughout the war, in common with many other wartime writers.[49] But looking back in anger was one thing: looking forward was another. Priestley was the first wartime publicist to use popular revulsion against the 1930s as a springboard for moving on to a better world after the war. Concluding his first series of *Postscripts* – at his own request – on 20 October he struck a now-familiar ringing note. The world was watching Britain with admiration: we had weathered the summer storm, and everywhere there was growing hope that civilisation, liberty, democracy could be saved. But 'if apathy and stupidity return to reign once more; if the privileges of a few are seen to be regarded as more important than the happiness of many ... if our faces are still turned towards the past instead of towards the future' the opportunity would be lost.

The *Postscripts*, rightly celebrated though they are, represent only a fraction of Priestley's wartime output. His BBC Overseas Service broadcasts started at around the same time and continued on and off through much of the war, three times a week, sometimes four, recorded late at night and re-transmitted to the Dominions and Colonies and about eighty US radio stations – taken together, he suggested, one of the largest regular radio audiences ever.[50] A BBC colleague remembered him arriving at Broadcasting House, bashing out his *Postscript*, then his North American talk on his typewriter, 'then he'd have a drink [often with the American broadcaster Ed Murrow] and broadcast the Home Service piece. Then at 2.30 a.m. he'd do the other' – never needing to revise what he had written.[51]

The overseas broadcasts covered much of the same ground as the *Postscripts*: once again, the 'ordinary, quiet folk', sleepy and good-natured but dogged when roused (5 June), were ranged against the 'evil empire of machines and robots' (30 May), and a new spirit was said to be emerging from them that might change the world (29 August).[52] But the view of wartime Britain they presented was subtly different. Priestley portrayed an England in which morale was sky-high, and the common people, at last, were setting the pace. 'I shouldn't dream of saying "Britain, Wake Up!" now', he said on 22 August, referring to his prewar articles, 'for the people are not only wide awake but growing visibly in mental and moral stature.'[53]

> [T]he fact that has given me personally more hope for the future, not only of this war but of the world after the war, than any other fact ... is the way in which the ordinary folk of this island have emerged as the real challengers of Nazism. When the real blitzkrieg began and the Nazi sprang like a tiger, then the British people, instead of losing heart, rose at once in spirit to meet the challenger. They came out of a sleep with which several of us had reproached them before this war began ... and roaring with enthusiasm the people waded in and began to show that democracy, when it's a real democracy and not a sham one, is just about as effete and decadent an antagonist as a wounded rhinoceros. They were told to go to it, and they went to it.[54]

This was the 'People's War' story again, but, with its talk of 'real' and not 'sham' democracy, its repudiation of the 'effete and decadent' and its invocation of the 'go to it' spirit, it was a version tailored to an audience in the USA, Canada and Australia, which needed to know that it was being asked not to bale out an old European regime but to lend support to an emerging vibrant democracy. 'The divisions between classes – always England's weakness – are being rapidly rubbed out', he promised them.[55] Critics of the 'men of Munich' were assured that, despite the Conservative Parliamentary majority, 'the real power resides in Mr. Winston Churchill and the labour group, who between them command the full confidence of the country'.[56] If Americans felt that 'the ruling and official classes still cling too much to peace-time privileges' and lack 'the hard drive of leadership', well, Priestley and much of the press thought so too; but the country was now demanding a fiercer tempo: they 'will simply have to get on or get out'.[57] 'The real English people, not a small ruling class, are now taking charge, led by men like Bevin, Morrison, Greenwood.'[58] The key man, for Priestley, was Ernest Bevin: 'Bevin seems to me one of those rare leaders of the people – and probably the finest example of them is Lincoln – who have somehow accumulated in themselves that shrewdness, that deep sagacity, that rich humanity which can be distilled from the experience of the people.'[59] And if the appeal to the Lincoln myth so dear to American hearts was not enough, he reassured them again: 'I know that we often appear an old-fashioned folk, overfond of tradition, but this side of the national medal is exhibited too often, so that many people overseas forget the other side.'[60] Considering that these broadcasts were, in effect, official propaganda, their critical edge is remarkable, contradicting Priestley's jaundiced dismissal of the BBC as a mere 'government mouthpiece'.[61] But this narrative, more than tales of tradition and past glory would have done, served the urgent need of the moment: to keep the Americans and the Dominions on board – a good illustration of how it was the demands of the wartime situation, and not just the opportunism of a few maverick left-wingers, which, willy-nilly, pushed the discourses of the war in a radical direction. But not fast enough for Priestley.

Out of the people

In the last of his 1940 *Postscripts* on 20 October Priestley voiced his anxiety that 'as this high mood passes, apathy will return to some sections of the community and selfishness and stupidity to some other sections'. Two months later, on New Year's Day 1941, he took stock in a 'New Year Postscript' for the *News Chronicle*.[62] In the previous summer, he reminded readers, 'the British people looked danger in the eye and rose to greatness'. It had seemed at that moment that a 'real vital democracy ... a new social order had already arrived ... Old crusts of custom and tradition were cracking.' But since then, there had been 'very definite traces of reaction ... no forward march ... attempts to force the nation to beat a retreat'. Conservative critics too afraid to trust the people accused progressives of putting party before country, but in reality the opposite was the case: only with democratisation and a more equitable social order could the war be won, and this was the task for 1941. For the first time, Priestley began to spell out what this new social order would mean: a minimum and more equal social standard, national control of manpower and property, educational reform, 'the abolition of privilege and worn-out traditions'.

Of course, Priestley was very far from being the only one thinking aloud about postwar reconstruction. Clement Attlee had argued to a sympathetic Harold Nicolson as early as June 1940 that the war needed to have a positive and not just a defensive purpose, which meant 'admitting that the old order had collapsed and asking people to fight for the new order', and even Lord Halifax admitted that, at a time when the war was costing £9 million a day, prewar caution about helping the depressed areas could no longer be defended.[63] Reforming opinion was gaining force across a far broader spectrum than Correlli Barnett's dismissive label of the 'New Jerusalem movement' acknowledges, building on the legacy of progressive 'middle opinion' of the 1930s.[64] In the first week of the new year, the popular news magazine *Picture Post* published a special issue entitled 'A plan for Britain', putting forward a radical view of postwar reconstruction, to which Priestley contributed a piece on leisure and culture anticipating 'a new era of beauty and joy and fun', though rather less specific about how it was to be achieved.[65]

At around the same time Priestley returned, briefly, to the BBC Home Service, for another series of eight *Postscripts*. In the first of these, on 26 January, he demanded a radical declaration of war aims, provoking angry responses from the Conservative backbench 1922 Committee and from Churchill himself, who regarded such talk as premature and unnecessarily provocative. The original contract was for six broadcasts, but he was allowed to do eight, and then the series finished, much to Priestley's ire, and amidst allegations, not least from Priestley himself, that he had been taken off the air on government orders. Sian Nicholas has unpicked what can be known of this tangled story, from which nobody emerges with much credit.[66] It is clear from internal BBC evidence that Priestley was brought back because of his unique popularity, and for the same reason was paid well above the going rate, so, although his original contract was for six broadcasts, he may well have been justified in assuming that renewal was a formality. It is equally clear that Duff Cooper, the Minister of Information, made the decision to take him off the air, and that this decision was prompted by Churchill, and by a deputation from the 1922 Committee, to whom Cooper promised that he would 'give Priestley a rest', within days of the first broadcast in the series. However, Priestley's behaviour was also unhelpful, denouncing Conservative Central Office as a 'political Gestapo', and reacting as if the *Postscript* slot was his by right, and that he was the only personality big enough to fill it – despite his later insistence that the *Postscripts* had been 'ridiculously overpraised'. Nicholas convincingly argues that an important factor was suspicion on the part of both BBC and government of radio personalities who threatened to become bigger than the medium and turn into demagogues: an echo of the BBC's wariness about American broadcasting styles. But one man's demagogue is another man's voice of the people; and, as Priestley frequently pointed out, it was only views outside the conservative mainstream that were regarded as controversial.[67] One of Cooper's motives was surely a desire to restrict critical discussion of postwar reconstruction, as Conservative elements in the government wished – especially after Priestley joined the radical 1941 Committee within a few days of the first broadcast, a development which BBC officials thought 'looks bad'. Although Priestley's reaction was certainly excessive, and egotistical, petulantly refusing to return to the *Postscripts* after a break (although he did do a number of other broadcasts later in the war), it is hard not to sympathise with his displeasure at the characteristically British flavour of this incident: 'stealthy hocus-pocus ... a nod here, a wink there', and somehow nobody quite responsible for the outcome.[68]

Shortly before these broadcasts began, Edward Hulton, a radical Liberal and proprietor of *Picture Post*, called a meeting of likeminded people, including the 'quixotic Christian socialist' Sir Richard Acland, to form a ginger-group under Priestley's chairmanship, called the 1941 Committee, which Addison aptly describes as 'a perfect snapshot of the new progressive Establishment rising from the waves'.[69] The Committee published a nine-point declaration along vaguely socialist lines, followed by number of leaflets and pamphlets, including Priestley's *Out of the People*. In June 1942 the journalist Tom Driberg, supported by a number of Committee members, including Priestley, contested the safe Conservative seat of Maldon in a by-election (the wartime political truce precluding Labour or Liberal candidates) and won, whereupon the 1941 Committee merged with Acland's Forward March movement to form a new political party, Common Wealth, with Priestley as chairman.[70] Common Wealth went on to win three more Conservative by-election seats, but Priestley was by then long gone, having resigned as chairman in September 1942: not because, in the rather trite view of one of his biographers, 'the role of revolutionary sat uncomfortably on his so English shoulders'– after all, he was the one who had urged Common Wealth to repudiate gradualism and make no compromise with capitalism; nor would he would have accepted this conservative characterisation of Englishness – but because, collectivist though he was in principle, and accomplished as a platform speaker, he found the whole machinery of political organisation – committee meetings, policy documents, endless wrangles and compromises – impossible to live with for long.[71] And so, after a (for him) long break, he turned his attention back to the relatively individualistic world of literary production.

But not before he had written, at disconcerting speed, *Out of the People* (1941), the first (and last) in a planned series of 1941 Committee books about postwar reconstruction, which sold over 41,000 copies in a year.[72] Here Priestley elaborated his vision of Britain, present, past and future. His account of the war is familiar enough: it had released 'the free spirit of a creative people taking charge of events' and created the opportunity for change. It had energised a people who had been treated by the media as a passive, featureless mass. It had broken down distinctions of class and emphasised what we all had in common. It had dragged us out of the sterility and decay of the prewar world: the plutocracy pretending to be an aristocracy, power centralised in an inner ring of big business, high finance and Tory politics, behind a tattered façade of tradition.[73] The war would not be won by the old England beloved of sentimental Americans - 'the old Hall, the hunt breakfast, the hunt ball, the villagers touching their caps, all the old bag of tricks' – but by industrial England: 'machines and the men who make and drive those machines'.[74] Now people were feeling the need for great changes, getting back in touch with the democracy that had atrophied in the 1930s, laughing at Blimps and Old School Ties and class distinctions.[75]

Something must be done to consolidate these gains, to make this country 'a better home for the people' – and 'better' did not mean just materially prosperous, if that meant continuing 'a narrow and colourless existence', but the promise of a 'gayer, richer, nobler way of life'.[76] But before this could come into being, there were obstacles to be overcome. One was a loss of interest in the 'larger meaning and purpose of things', reducing the value and dignity of human life and leaving a vacuum in which dictators could arise and people be treated as masses.[77] Another was the centralisation of power and authority, assisted by technology and the propaganda of a centrally controlled press and radio.[78] Finally, the growth of large-scale industry had disempowered people, turning them into dependent 'masses', both at work and in their spare time, in which 'their very dreams come from another mass production factory'.[79] These three forces were making people passive, soft, 'robbed of flavour and edge as characters ... wet clay' in the hands of their masters. Far from removing these obstacles, the war had in many ways made them loom even larger.[80] But permanent change must come from below, from the people: it could not be imposed from above.

This meant that the role of the state, in contrast to the Soviet system, and to the top-down Fabian tradition embraced by many 1940s progressives, must be strictly limited. It was useful for bringing over-mighty organisations and individuals to heel. It should control the financial system, to curb speculation and profiteering. It should supply power and organisation where needed, but where what was called for was originality and enterprise, it should keep out. It should run the railways, but not the press or the radio – though it might have a role in keeping the press barons at bay. Socialism could not be created by setting up a new elite of officials, because without a change of values this would just become another 'masters-and-masses' system. Only 'from the living community itself, out of the people' could the required 'miracles of social and political construction' come.[81]

Priestley's suspicion of the over-mighty state, his belief in a socialism welling up from below and not imposed from above by benevolent officialdom, illustrates the fact that the wartime 'progressives' were very far from being a monolithic bloc of 'new Jerusalemists'. It also explains the shortage of specific policy proposals in his book. What was important was not the introduction of this or that legislative change or state machinery

but the transformation of attitudes and values, the creation of 'a society
in which real people co-operate to provide for themselves': then leadership, if required, would arise out the people, and it would become clear
what needed to be done.[82] This is utopian socialism, growing out of a
humanistic concern for the individual, a recognition of the collective
nature of all human life, and a strong belief in the spiritual purpose of
human existence.

> We are not bees and ants ... but are children of the spirit, with minds, with
> souls. We are not here to multiply ourselves senselessly, but to increase
> knowledge, to create beauty, to experience love. Whatever helps us to do
> these things is right, and whatever stands in their way is wrong. We must
> not try to make our inner life, which is our real life, conform to the outer
> life, but must unhesitatingly reverse this process, making the life of the
> community the true expression of our real inner life ... Nothing matters but
> that the people, not a privileged few individuals but the people, should be
> freely functioning, zestful, unencumbered, thoroughly alive, and know
> something, as they pass through this strange haunted world, of truth, beauty
> and love.[83]

And the book concludes on an almost religious note which prefigures
Priestley's turn towards a more spiritual approach after the war:

> I for one can offer no magic formulas, except the enduring magic of our
> human imagination and will, which may indeed, when working selflessly,
> not be human at all but divine. From now on we may expect hard and bitter
> tasks, and many of us may die long before they are accomplished, but in
> such a struggle and progress, with decay and defeat, fear and cruelty, left
> behind at last, there is no death but an ever-widening prospect of life.[84]

In *Out of the People* Priestley argued that it was the upper classes, the
'uneasy posturing plutocracy', who had let the nation down in the interwar years, and this was a theme he took up with gusto in his second
wartime novel, the melodramatic spy thriller *Blackout in Gretley*
(1942).[85] Gretley is a grim town, existing only to provide absentee
employers with 'country mansions, grouse moors, deer forests, yachts and
winters in Cannes and Monte Carlo' while they blustered on about 'our
traditional way of life'. Its ordinary people are 'patient ... taking what
was given them and asking for no more, except in their hearts'. Much to
the postwar disgust of Evelyn Waugh, its spies, fifth-columnists, defeatists
and black-marketeers are to be found entirely amongst its idle rich,
notable among whom are the black-marketeer Mrs Jesmond, 'a hand-
some, luxurious, lecherous rat', and Colonel Tarlington, authoritarian
local employer.[86] In due course, Tarlington is unmasked as a spy, motivated, in the words of the hero, a Canadian engineer and undercover
agent, by his desire to keep 'yourself and a few others securely on top, and
the common people ... in their place for ever'. As for Mrs Jesmond,

'you're an exquisite, downy sort of creature, but just not worth your very expensive keep. You're one of the luxuries we can't afford.' As Perigo, the undercover Special Branch man, declares, the main obstacle to postwar national renewal will be 'about fifty thousand important, influential, gentlemanly persons', who will have to be told to 'shut up and do nothing'. Significantly, though, none of the villains and Nazi sympathisers is portrayed as unpatriotic: when they sing *Rule Britannia* and wrap themselves in the flag, they are being perfectly sincere. The division is not between patriots and traitors but between those who, like Churchill, Roosevelt and (a sign of the times) Stalin, are on the side of the common man; and those who 'hate the democratic idea and despise ordinary decent folk', and see Nazi victory as a way of preserving their own privileges.[87]

Towards 1945

During 1943 Priestley dramatised conflicting attitudes to the postwar future in two contrasting forms: a highly symbolic play, and a realist, almost documentary novel. The play, *They Came to a City*, takes a group of socially diverse characters, a cross-section of British society, and puts them down in front of a mysterious city, which turns out to be an idealised utopian community of social justice, equality and happiness. The second act is set after they have visited the city, which we never see, and shows their contrasting responses to it. Some find it repulsive because it repudiates their former lives of snobbery, privilege or money-grubbing. Others find it a world they have always dreamed of and decide to stay there. The leading characters, a working-class couple, decide to return home and tell the world about it: people need to know that such things are possible. In his introduction to the play, Priestley describes it as a good example of 'the "symbolic action" on which so many of my plays and novels are built'.[88] The characters do not argue out their respective positions – this would make it a 'play of debate' along Shavian lines, which Priestley was anxious to avoid. Rather they express and exemplify different social standpoints and attitudes to be found in wartime Britain. Despite, or perhaps because of, its didactic quality, *They Came to a City* was a success, and was filmed, though less successfully, with its original cast.[89]

In the third, and by far the best-realised of Priestley's wartime novels, *Daylight on Saturday* (1943), the national microcosm is an aircraft factory, at a low point of the war just before the first significant victory at El Alamein.[90] Production is down: is it because of divided management, bad workers, or just lack of good war news? The factory, the war and the postwar nation are in the balance. The workers are uninspired and apathetic, a patchwork of disparate individuals: something has been lost since the heady, collective days of 1940. Forward-looking leadership is represented by Cheviot, the General Manager, upwardly mobile, classless in tone if a little paternalistic, who identifies with the workers and wants to take care of them. We also meet one of the 'youngish technical men' from the working class (Angleby), as well as an old-style 'rough diamond' works superintendent (Elrick), a languid, anti-industrial civil servant, a communist charge-hand, and a stuffed-shirt government minister (Lord Brixen), upwardly mobile from industry to the City – and a variety of well-observed factory workers. But also on the scene is a modernised authoritarian upper class, in the shape of the gentlemanly but technically proficient Assistant Manager Blandford, arrogantly contemptuous of democracy and the ordinary workers: 'We English enjoy our social hierarchy. We wouldn't be without it.' The old ruling class has made a comeback and may yet seize back the reins of power.

In many ways *Daylight* is the nearest Priestley came to a documentary novel, and it combines a representative panorama of wartime British society, set in the closely observed world of the factory, with a complex sense of social relations and antagonisms. In its ambition of capturing the range and density of real social life, combined with a strong story-line and engaging characters, it is closest of all his novels to *They Walk in the City*, though on the whole more successful. It also reflects its author's continued interest in work and work relations – all too rarely, as he said, the focus of English novels – and he visited several factories to research it. Apart from the very beginning and the very end, *Daylight* takes place entirely within the factory, and there is no main protagonist: as in *Angel Pavement* we see things from the perspective of one character after another – no fewer than nineteen of them – which not only thickens the social texture of the novel but conveys a sense of the factory as a cross-class community in keeping with Priestley's idea of what the war was all about.[91] Linking these impressions together is Priestley's omniscient and often judgemental narrative voice, which makes it clear what we are supposed to learn from them. The *Times Literary Supplement* reviewer praised the novel for its 'exceptionally revealing illustration of social and psychological attitudes in war industry', but concluded that its detailed documentary realism made it lack internal coherence: not for the first time, Priestley was suspected of letting his topical preoccupations loosen his grip on the novelistic imagination.[92] But this is a topical novel: like it or not, Priestley had a purpose in writing it, which was of a piece with *Out of the People*, *They Came to a City* and his other wartime writings. What drives the novel is the conflict over Britain's postwar future, expressed through the discordant styles of the managers. For once Priestley seems less than confident of the outcome. The Elricks and Brixens have certainly had their day, but who will win through – Cheviot or Blandford? At the end of the novel the issue is still unresolved. Cheviot pledges his future to the workers ('there could be for him now no cosy settling down, no easy acceptance of bribe or pension from the moneyed interests ... He had to see them through'), but Blandford too offers change and modernisation, of an authoritarian kind: 'Only machines and highly organised production can save us from the Nazis and ... from a national decline after the war' – clearly a Correlli Barnett before his time. As production picks up after the news of victory at El Alamein, the future of the nation is still in the balance.[93]

Much the same mood pervades Priestley's final war novel, *Three Men in New Suits*, written in the autumn of 1944 but not published until May 1945, after VE Day: a critical failure but a huge popular success, selling according to the publishers well over 250,000 hardback and book club copies.[94] Three demobbed servicemen from different class backgrounds return home only to find that the hoped-for better way of life is not in evidence, nor likely to arrive soon. In the words of Doris, a war factory worker and the author's mouthpiece, 'all that damned stupid greedy self-ishness [is] starting all over again. I tell you, the minute the real danger passed, and people felt safe, out it came.'[95] Resisting the pressures of their old lives, the apathetic and/or reactionary views of their families and the blandishments of worldly success (including another caricatured press magnate), they set off in some unspecified direction to save the world, under the leadership of upper-class Alan. The war has taught Alan not just comradeship but the virtues of the common people: 'an idea of fairness that goes deep, deep down ... kind, patient, forgiving, never arrogant, not corrupted by power'.[96] 'We don't try to return to the muddle of the pre-war time. We don't go on thinking and behaving in the same old way. If it was disastrous before it'll be disastrous again. We don't want the same kind of men looking after our affairs ... Instead of guessing and grabbing, we plan. Instead of competing, we co-operate.'[97] If these passages seem both over-assertive and vague at the same time, it is an indication of Priestley's anxious state of mind as the war drew to its close.

In contrast to the 'high, generous mood' of summer 1940, when anything seemed possible, Priestley's mood in 1945 combined (as Gramsci might have put it) optimism of the will with pessimism of the intelligence. The wartime democratisation and reawakening which he had detected (or in claiming to detect it, tried to persuade into existence) would not continue into peacetime of its own accord: anything was still possible, but everything might be lost. As Priestley warned in his pamphlet *Letter to a Returning Serviceman*, written at about the same time as *Three Men*, if we cannot draw on the bottled-up energy of the people, and rediscover the lost collective purpose of 1940, we may find ourselves trapped, not in a cosy consensus, the prewar 'sleepy Tory Britain', but in the ruthless 'Lord Corporate-State Toryism' of the Blandfords, little different in essence from Nazism.[98]

Priestley had been famous before the war, but the war turned him into a celebrity of considerable proportions: 'if I went into a crowded shop or bar all the people not only had to talk to me but also had to touch me ... as if to prove to themselves that I was more than a disembodied voice'.[99] But the public impact of his wartime work is difficult to assess with any accuracy. Given their popularity, it seems very likely that the 1940 *Postscripts* had a positive effect on home-front morale at that critical time. This is partly for non-political reasons: the language and imagery, Priestley's voice and intimate, homely delivery, his common touch, were at one and the same time inspiring and reassuring, and his affection for the ordinary and everyday, while for him undoubtedly part and parcel of his politics, could easily be read apolitically.

But Priestley also appealed, in words of the BBC Listener Research Department, to 'a very large section of the population who look for a better world but have no party allegiance': which is precisely why Conservatives were so suspicious of him.[100] His reputation for political influence rests not only on his role in boosting wartime morale but on the perception that he contributed to a mood of popular radicalism which culminated in Labour's 1945 election landslide and the social-democratic era that followed. In 1945 Labour and Priestley marched together. He went on the campaign trail, addressing 'three meetings a night, sometimes five on Sundays', wrote newspaper articles and made a Party Political Broadcast, and stood himself, unsuccessfully, and not as a party candidate, for the anachronistic Cambridge University seat.[101]

It has been argued that, despite their reputation for centralised control and planning, Labour also shared Priestley's belief, stemming from the ethical socialist tradition, that 'top-down' reform was not enough, and that the moral transformation and mobilisation of the people was central to the construction of a new society. The so-called 'Apathy School' of historians, challenging what it sees as the myth of 1940s popular radicalism, has argued that the people did not respond to this idealistic call, but continued to be largely cynical and indifferent to politics.[102] However, as James Hinton has pointed out, relationships between activists and voters, political rhetoric and political attitudes, are highly complex. People might appear cynical not because they reject idealism but because, perceiving politicians as less idealistic than themselves, they expect to be let down. What is beyond question is that in 1945 a party speaking the language of ethical socialism and social transformation carried all before it, and despite the privations of the immediate postwar years, retained that public support remarkably well in 1950 and 1951. Whether what that government did transformed British society for good (as the postwar received wisdom had it), for ill (as Correlli Barnett and the Thatcherite right argued) or hardly at all (according to some on the postwar left) will not be debated here, though we will find out in the next chapter what Priestley thought of it.[103]

Notes

1 J. B. Priestley, *Postscripts* (London: Heinemann, 1940), pp. 60–5, broadcast Sunday 1 September 1940.

2 Priestley, *Let the People Sing*, 'Author's note'.

3 Graham Greene, *Spectator* (13 December 1940).

4 J. B. Priestley, *Britain Speaks* (New York: Harper & Brothers, 1940).

5 J. B. Priestley, *Here Are Your Answers* (London: Common Wealth, 1943).

6 Greene, *Spectator* (13 December 1940).

7 Paul Addison, *The Road to 1945: British Politics and the Second World War* (London: Jonathan Cape, 1975), p. 188.

8 For further discussion of this theme see Baxendale and Pawling, *Narrating*, chapter 5.

9 J. B. Priestley, BBC radio broadcast, 'A new English journey' (23 April 1940).

10 'The BBC and J. B. Priestley do something new', *Radio Times* (1 September 1939), p. 9.

11 Priestley, *Rain*, p. 215.

12 Priestley, *Rain*, pp. 214ff; J. B. Priestley, 'Britain wake up!', *News Chronicle* (10–17 January, 1939).

13 Klein, *Fiction*, pp. 440–1

14 [R. D. Charques] 'Let the People Sing', *Times Literary Supplement* (11 November 1939), p. 653.

15 Quoted in Klein, *Fiction*, pp. 440–1.

16 Priestley, *Let the People Sing*, p. 201.

17 Cook, *Priestley*, pp. 176–8.

18 *News Chronicle* (22 September to 26 October 1939).

19 Priestley, *Out of the People*, pp. 105, 31, 106–7.

20 J. B. Priestley, 'Yorkshire stands where it did', *News Chronicle* (21 September 1939), p. 7.

21 J. B. Priestley, 'Two things army lacks', *News Chronicle* (27 September 1939), p. 3.

22 Priestley, 'Yorkshire'.

23 J. B. Priestley, 'Schubert from the sergeants' mess', *News Chronicle* (3 October 1939), p. 3.

24 Priestley, *Britain Speaks*, p. 86 (broadcast of 7 July 1940).

25 J. B. Priestley, 'After the first 1,000 miles', *News Chronicle* (6 October 1939), p. 6.

26 Benedict Anderson, *Imagined Communities: Reflections on the Origin and Spread of Nationalism* (London: Verso, 1983).

27 Colley, *Britons*.

28 Light, *Forever England*, esp. 'Introduction'.

29 For more extended discussion of this theme see John Baxendale, '"You and I – all of us ordinary people': renegotiating "Britishness" in wartime', in Nick Hayes and Jeff Hill (eds), *Millions Like Us? British Culture in the Second World War* (Liverpool: Liverpool University Press, 1999), pp. 294–322.

30 H. V. Morton, *I Saw Two Englands* (London: Methuen, 1942), pp. 280–2.

31 I. McLaine, *Ministry of Morale: Home Front Morale and the Ministry of Information in World War Two* (London: George Allen & Unwin, 1979).

32 Asa Briggs, *The History of Broadcasting in the United Kingdom*, vol. 3: *The War of Words* (Oxford: Oxford University Press, 1970), pp. 569–78; Sian Nicholas, *The Echo of War: Homefront Propaganda and the Wartime BBC* (Manchester: Manchester University Press, 1996), pp. 238–9.

33 Vera Lynn, *Vocal Refrain: An Autobiography* (London: W. H. Allen, 1975), pp. 98–100.

34 Tom Harrisson, 'Social research and the film', *Documentary Newsletter* 1:11 (November 1940).

35 Baxendale, 'You and I', pp. 307–10.

36 W. S. Churchill, *Complete Speeches*, ed. Robert Rhodes James (New York: Chelsea House, 1974), vol. 6.

37 Priestley, 'A new English journey'.

38 Before and after the war the question was 'What is England?': Priestley's shift from England to Britain and back again was so smooth that few people can have noticed it.

39 Priestley, *Out of the People*, p. 45.

40 Ibid., p. 10.

41 Sonya A. Rose, *Which People's War? National Identity and Citizenship in Wartime Britain* (Oxford: Oxford University Press, 2003), pp. 18–20 and *passim*; Sian Nicholas, 'From John Bull to John Citizen: images of national identity and citizenship on the wartime BBC', in Richard Weight and Abigail Beach (eds), *The Right to Belong: Citizenship and National Identity in Britain, 1930–1960* (London: I. B. Tauris, 1998); David Morgan and Mary Evans, *The Battle for Britain: Citizenship and Ideology in the Second World War* (London: Routledge, 1993).

42 Taylor, *English History*, p. 600. Mowat, *Britain Between the Wars*, p. 657.

43 Priestley, *Postscripts*, p. vii.

44 Nicholas, *Echo of War*, p. 244.

45 *Spectator* (13 December 1940).

46 Priestley, *Postscripts*, pp. 1–4. Subsequent dates in the main text refer to the *Postscripts* as reprinted in this collection.

47 Addison, *Road*, p. 108. 'Cato' [Michael Foot, Frank Owen and Peter Howard], *Guilty Men* (London: Gollancz, 1940).

48 Addison, *Road*, pp. 132–3.

49 See the more extended discussion of this theme in Baxendale and Pawling, *Narrating*, pp. 119–24.

50 Priestley, *All England*, 'Preface', pp. xxi–xxii.

51 Norman Collins quoted in Braine, *Priestley*, p. 109.

52 Priestley, *Britain Speaks*, pp. 11, 3, 184.

53 Ibid., p. 170 (22 August 1940).

54 Ibid., pp. 198–9 (3 September 1940).

55 Ibid., p. 127 (25 July 1940).

56 Ibid., pp. 71–2. (3 July 1940).

57 Ibid., p. 75.

58 Ibid., p. 31 (15 June 1940).

59 Ibid., p. 150 (6 August 1940).

60 Ibid., p. 152.

61 Priestley, *Out of the People*, p. 75.

62 'Priestley's New Year postscript: 1940 and 1941', *News Chronicle* (1 January 1941), p. 4.

63 Addison, *Road*, pp. 121–2.

64 Correlli Barnett, *The Audit of War: The Illusion and Reality of a Great Nation* (London: Macmillan, 1986), pp. 11–37; Addison, *Road*, chapters 1 and 6; Arthur Marwick, 'Middle opinion in the Thirties', *English Historical Review* 79 (April 1964).

65 *Picture Post* (4 January 1941).

66 Sian Nicholas, '"Sly demagogues" and wartime radio: J. B. Priestley and the BBC', *Twentieth Century British History* 6:3 (1995), on which the following summary is based.

67 See, for example, J. B. Priestley, 'Beware this Tory grip on entertainment', *Daily Herald* (25 November 1944), p. 2.

68 Priestley, *Margin*, pp. 221–2.

69 Addison, *Road*, pp. 158, 189.

70 Ibid., pp. 158–9.

71 Brome, *Priestley*, pp. 255–61.

72 Priestley, *Out of the People*; Cook, *Priestley*, p. 192.

73 Priestley, *Out of the People*, pp. 13–17, 25–6.

74 Ibid., pp. 31–2.

75 Ibid., p. 37.

76 Ibid., pp. 45–7.

77 Ibid., pp. 50–4.

78 Ibid., pp. 54–7.

79 Ibid., pp. 57–61.

80 Ibid., pp. 61–2.

81 Ibid., pp. 91–101.

82 Ibid., p. 109.

83 Ibid., pp. 123–4.

84 Ibid., p. 127.

85 J. B. Priestley, *Blackout in Gretley: A Story of – and for – Wartime* (London: Heinemann, 1942).

86 Ibid., pp. 173, 158. See Waugh's attack on *Blackout*, *Spectator* (13 September 1957).

87 Priestley, *Blackout*, pp. 207, 194–5, 82.

88 J. B. Priestley, *Collected Plays*, vol. III (London: Heinemann, 1950), p. xi.

89 Brome, *Priestley*, pp. 266–8.

90 J. B. Priestley, *Daylight on Saturday: A Novel about an Aircraft Factory* (London: Heinemann, 1943).

91 The technique of the novel is analysed in Klein, *Priestley's Fiction*, pp. 132–49.

92 *Times Literary Supplement* (26 June 1943), p. 305.

93 Priestley, *Daylight*, pp. 305–6, 57–8.

94 'Complete analysis of the works of J. B. Priestley', Heinemann Archive, Rushden.

95 J. B. Priestley, *Three Men in New Suits* (London: Heinemann, 1945), p. 103.

96 Ibid., pp. 67–9.

97 Ibid., pp. 168–9.

98 Priestley, *Letter to a Returning Serviceman* (London: Home and Van Thal, 1945), p. 15.
99 Priestley, *Margin*, p. 221.
100 March 1941 – quoted in Nicholas, '"Sly demagogues"', p. 262.
101 Priestley, *Moments*, p. 213.
102 Steve Fielding, Peter Thompson and Nick Tiratsoo, *'England Arise!' The Labour Party and Popular Politics in 1940s Britain* (Manchester: Manchester University Press, 1995); N. Tiratsoo (ed.), *The Attlee Years* (London: Pinter, 1991); S. Fielding, 'What did the people want? The meaning of the 1945 General Election', *Historical Journal* 35 (1992), pp. 623–39; James Hinton, '1945 and the Apathy School', *History Workshop Journal* 43 (Spring 1997), pp. 266–73.
103 Barnett, *Audit*; Jim Fyrth, 'Days of hope: the meaning of 1945', in Fyrth (ed.), *Labour's Promised Land: Culture and Society in Labour Britain 1945–51* (London: Lawrence and Wishart, 1995).

6

'Now we must live up to ourselves': New Jerusalem and beyond

> In that magnificent summer of 1940, when I spent my days collecting infor-
> mation, and my nights broadcasting it to the world beyond the ring of steel
> around us, I think I felt better than ever before or since. We lived at last in
> a community with a noble common purpose, and the experience was not
> only novel but exhilarating. We had a glimpse then of what life might be if
> men and women freely dedicated themselves, not to their appetites and prej-
> udices, but to some great communal task, and not even the brute threat of
> war, the menace of the very skies, could remove from that glimpse the faint
> radiance of some far-off promised land.[1]

> One day in the late summer of '45, Revolutionary Young England was
> invited to 10 Downing Street, to be thanked for its election services, and was
> shot as it went upstairs. Who pulled the trigger, I don't know.[2]

Shortly before war broke out, Priestley had declared his despair at the
state of prewar Britain. 'What creative effort were we making now?
Where was the noble national idea?'[3] Surely, given some 'shining goal',
people would 'work day and night like madmen for next to nothing': but
no such goal was in sight.[4] In his VE Day broadcast, a whole world later,
he gave the answer. The year 1940 had brought out the best in the British
people, and its momentum might just carry them through to a new and
better world. So, at any rate, Priestley believed, and he was not alone. As
he said nearly twenty years later, when the world had indeed changed but
the New Jerusalem had not arrived and was no longer expected, 'there
was revolution in the air' in 1945 – a mild and 'very English' one, but
'bent on changing our society' even so.[5] Much of Priestley's postwar
social and political commentary was concerned with explaining why, in
his view, these high hopes had not been realised.

This narrative of 1940–45 – from the People's War to the People's
Peace – provided the dominant mythology of postwar Britain, which

Angus Calder has labelled 'the myth of the Blitz'.[6] From the 1940 *Postscripts* onwards, Priestley had been one of its main proponents. Labour's landslide election victory in 1945, and the reforms which followed, would extend the story into peacetime. The foundation of the NHS, and the establishment of a mixed, managed economy with a commitment to full employment, laid the foundations of a postwar settlement which would endure through the boom years of the 1950s and 1960s, some of its key elements surviving even the Thatcher era. The fact that Thatcherites even in the 1990s were still defining themselves in opposition to supposed wartime 'New Jerusalemists' indicates the continued power of this narrative.

Predictably, Priestley's response to postwar developments did not follow the orthodoxies of either left or right. As in all his political writings from *English Journey* onwards, the two central issues were England, and community. The war had created – or rather revived – a radical understanding of national character and identity, rooted in the people, and based on social cohesion and common purpose. Priestley saw this as an opportunity which must be seized: we had done great things, he told the readers of *Picture Post* just before VE Day, and 'now we must live up to ourselves'.[7] From the outset, however, he suspected that the opportunity was being let slip. With the coming of the Cold War, the idealistic internationalism of the early 1940s was in retreat. The postwar boom of the 1950s accelerated the cultural process of Americanisation, while leaving intact the structures of power in British society. The global culture of 'Admass' seemed to overwhelm both the social ideals of 1945 and the sense of national identity which the war had created. By the late 1950s, Priestley complained, 'we no longer appeared to know who we were'.[8] As in 1940, he did not shirk the task of reminding us.

To portray Priestley after 1945 as a disappointed and disillusioned figure, his hour of glory come and gone, his hopes and dreams unrealised, would be tempting but wrong. When the war ended, he was only fifty, and barely half-way through his career as a writer, with three energetic and productive decades ahead of him. Throughout the 1950s and 1960s, he remained in the public eye as a novelist, playwright, broadcaster, and prolific journalist, producing some sixteen novels and as many plays in the years after 1945, and writing regularly for left of centre popular newspapers such as *The Sunday Pictorial*, *The News Chronicle*, *The Daily Herald* and *Reynolds News*. He also became a regular contributor to the *New Statesman*, where much of his serious commentary on postwar society and politics appeared. Certainly, the different England that emerged after the war was increasingly not to his taste, but he was not a man who expected to be satisfied with what he saw around him, and he engaged with it with characteristic gusto, and across his usual broad canvas – novels and plays ranging from bitingly satirical to deeply symbolic to simply entertaining, autobiography, social and political analysis, journalism both serious and trivial, and occasional bouts of political activism. He developed a robust critique of the follies of the Cold War, and of the new social order he labelled 'Admass', while his long-standing interest in time, memory and history, and in Jungian psychology, deepened as he grew older. Towards the end of his life we can see his political, social and spiritual preoccupations flowing together in a way which almost, if not quite, makes him a figure of the 1960s countercul-ture. Throughout this period, though no longer at the centre of the historical stage as he had been in the early 1940s, he remained a notable public figure and a trenchant observer from the wings, feeling 'sometimes ... a depth of sadness; sometimes a new hope for England, the country I no longer much like yet still must love'.[9]

'We want a creative community and not an almshouse'[10]

An Inspector Calls, written during the winter of 1944–45 – and, like many of Priestley's best plays, at top speed – expressed both the idealism and the anxieties of its historical moment.[11] The play opened that summer in Moscow – at the time, of course, the capital of an allied power – and since then has been very widely performed all over the world. Today it is prob-ably the best known of Priestley's plays, partly because of its incorporation into the GCSE English Literature syllabus, partly because of Stephen Daldry's acclaimed revival at the National Theatre in 1992, itself intended partly as a riposte to Margaret Thatcher's attempted demolition of the 1945 legacy.[12] *An Inspector Calls* is set, significantly, in 1912. A mysterious Inspector arrives at the home of a well-heeled and complacent Edwardian family to question them about the murder of a young working-class girl. Family members are forced to face not only their own discreditable actions but the callousness of their attitude towards the dead girl and those like her. The Inspector's parting words resonate in 1945 as much as in 1912 – and, Stephen Daldry would no doubt argue, in 1992:

> But just remember this. One Eva Smith has gone – but there are millions and millions of Eva Smiths and John Smiths still left with us, with their lives, their hopes, their fears, their suffering, and chance of happiness, all inter-twined with our lives, with what we think and say and do. We don't live alone. We are members of one body. We are responsible for each other. And I tell you that the time will soon come when, if men will not learn that lesson, then they will be taught it in fire and blood and anguish.[13]

But, as Priestley's audience knew, 'fire and blood and anguish' had not made the lesson stick, and the result was the disaster of the 1930s. Now there was another chance to learn: but were the lessons of wartime to be forgotten, Priestley feared, the whole tragic history would be repeated – and he was writing before the unveiling of the atom bomb that same summer. To adapt a later distinction of Priestley's, the play is not a plea for an agenda – a set of political proposals – but for something deeper: an ambience – 'the total climate of values, ideas, opinions, fears and hopes, in which we live'.[14] The Inspector's parting message is a plea not for a National Health Service but for a whole new way of living, glimpsed, Priestley believed, in the experience of 1940.

Priestley was a strong but critical supporter of the 1945–51 Labour government. He campaigned energetically for Labour in 1945 and again in 1950, despite his reservations about much of what had happened in between.[15] In a party political broadcast in the 1950 campaign, he restated the idealism of 1945. The Labour government, he declared, still offered 'a noble example to the world': because 'the Labour Party is broadly based, has an ethic, and is not governed by cynical expediency; because it says what it means and does what it says it will do; because it has an outlook, a policy, a programme, that do justice to the whole nation'. But even in an election broadcast (and unthinkably in that context today), there crept in a hint of impatience with the government's style. 'There's still a lack of flexibility, too much routine Civil Service stuff, too much London School of Economics, too much of the old trade union outlook, too many cups of weak tea and not enough dash and devilment, fire and glory.'[16]

For Priestley, the welfare and social reforms which define the 1945–51 government – the NHS, full employment, a new state-guaranteed safety-net in place of the mass insecurity of the 1930s – were 'fine brave things', which he had spent the war arguing for. But there was something missing, and it had less to do with state machinery than with the human spirit. Looking back from the 1960s, not without a degree of hindsight, it seemed to him that for the young enthusiasts of 1945, 'Labour was being sent to Westminster not primarily to give the English security and welfare, but to transform our whole society. They wanted – as they said so many times – a different England'.[17] The great mistake the government made was to let the spirit of 1940, that exhilarating sense of a 'noble common purpose', which could have spurred the nation on to higher things, pass away, replaced with the rule of experts and bureaucrats. However necessary these may be, they could not replace the sense of collective purpose which had made people work night and day under impossible conditions to win the war. They would have done the same, or so Priestley felt, to build a new society after the war was won, but they were not being asked to. True social renewal could only come 'out of the people', but the people were not being mobilised. And so late 1940s Britain relapsed into a kind of sullen passive depression. 'And where there might have been drama, a gaiety of the spirit in taking on the odds, there is now a feeling of drabness and monotony, with dismal alternations of irritation and boredom.'[18]

As early as 1946 Priestley detected a souring of the postwar mood. People had grown selfish and cynical. 'They are trying to take as much as they can and give as little as possible in return. They are cutting themselves off from the welfare of the community. They are losing all pride and interest in the job. They are not behaving like good citizens ... They believe this to be a rotten world and they do not propose to do anything themselves to improve it.' To Priestley, the reasons were plain.

> For five years our people were made to feel that they were all engaged in one huge communal task, the defeat of the common enemy. The emotional drive was terrific. We all had parts in a national drama, played on a world stage. There, in a green spotlight, was the super-villain, and here were we, so many heroes and heroines. And then suddenly the curtain came down.

People had been told that a great national effort was now needed to restore things to normal. But what they should have been told was that 'the vast drama continues, with ourselves still the heroes and heroines of it'.[19] So 'all the nuisances and little hardships of the journey are there, but not the sustaining vision of the destination'. The left had become so preoccupied with means that they had lost sight of the end: 'a new creative Britain, hard-working but also full of fun, liveliness, colour and intelligence'. 'They fail to understand that political and economic changes are themselves only so much machinery that will help to create a finer quality of living. And it is this quality of living alone that really matters.'[20]

The government was criticised not just for losing the wartime sense of common purpose but for its cultural style: too dour, too solemn, lacking in 'colour, fun and glory'.[21] The austerity of the late 1940s is often portrayed as the necessary price of postwar reconstruction, to be succeeded by the frivolous pleasures of the boom years that followed. But for Priestley social reconstruction and popular pleasure should go hand in hand. 'We English have still a long hard pull in front of us, and, like carthorses on the old May Days, we need a few bells and ribbons on our harness.'[22] Visiting a Butlin's holiday camp, he wondered if Butlin knew better than Bevin what the people needed in their lives. But although touched by the enthusiasm of the holidaymakers, and ever reluctant to scorn the pleasures of the people, he eventually found them depressing. 'Too much noise and fuss on the surface, and too little going down into the depths, to nurture and comfort the hungry and bewildered soul of man. Everything so neat and clever, and everybody so lost.'[23] Dog-tracks, pubs, dance-halls and cinemas provided a much-needed escape from boredom, but in the end they merely revealed the emptiness of modern civilisation. At bottom, populist though he was, Priestley believed that only art, 'enduring and unforgettable', could really nurture the soul. But he was prepared to take a broad view of what 'art' was, and, careful to distance himself from any hint of elitism, he asserted that, given the opportunity, all were capable of actively appreciating and creating it, even if they did it badly. A socialist state should open those opportunities, 'turn a mass of people on to the arts', and then (in a faint echo of William Morris) 'we might find it possible to achieve a community in which every citizen felt himself to be something of an artist and every artist knew himself to be a citizen'.[24] But in the meantime, what was wrong with more frivolous ways of raising the spirits – a lick of paint, a few flowerpots, and little tables in the sun to brighten up Britain's dreary towns?[25]

Priestley's cultural politics overlapped with those of the Labour government, but differed in crucial respects. Labour's cultural policy regarded some activities as intrinsically better than others: the active was preferred to the passive, the communal to the individualistic. The government's mission was not simply to patronise the arts but to raise the tone of popular leisure by the creation of theatres, concert halls and art galleries, which it was hoped would eventually attract more takers than pubs, cinemas and dog-tracks. [26] So far, so good; but this approach was rooted in something Priestley found less attractive: the tradition of 'rational recreation' and the puritanism of the Labour movement, the belief that trivial entertainments diverted energy from really important things, a tradition which was still going strong in the postwar years. We remember the young Priestley in Bradford, open to all these 'serious' influences, but entranced by the popular arts of the day, and unable to contain his ebullience within the dour confines of chapel life and his father's standards of respectability. He would be the last man to agree with the old socialist John Burns that music-halls ought to become 'places of education and instruction', or feel the need, like another Edwardian socialist, to 'push football out of heads' in order to 'push Socialism in'.[27]

The cultural world of *Bright Day*, which embraced the music-hall as well as the symphony concert, and ends up in the cinema, was very different from that inhabited by the Bloomsbury 'highbrow' John Maynard Keynes, first chairman of the Arts Council. Priestley was all in favour of state patronage of the arts, but rather than 'high art' delivered from above he preferred zest and creative energy welling up from below, along the lines of the finale to *Let the People Sing*. In *The Arts Under Socialism* (1947) he proposed to end artists' 'exile from the broad community', and reconnect them with 'the great common movements of our time'. This was to be achieved not on the instructions of committees and commissars but by the free choice of artists re-established at the heart of communities, and nurtured by the wider dissemination of the means of artistic production and consumption – theatres, orchestras, bookshops, publishers, studios and galleries. Given this encouragement, Priestley argued, 'a fairly good average audience' would be built up for the arts, while a smaller number would become enthusiasts or even artists themselves. [28] This notion of artists nurtured within the community contrasts sharply with the increasing use of Arts Council funds to support a few national, metropolitan centres of excellence. It also conflicted with a tendency Priestley had long ago detected in the culture of the Labour movement itself - 'something narrow and grudging, puritanical and life-denying, never absent from one side of Labour ... ministers never saying *Do* but always *Don't* - which had held back the 'great positive acts, sudden glorious releases, a sense of living in a bigger and better country' which he felt ought to have accompanied the necessary austerities of the time.[29]

There was no separation between Priestley's desire to reawaken the creative spirit and his yearning for more zest and gusto in the pursuit of socialism: they flowed into each other, and both chimed in with his conception of the national character. As he reminded radio listeners during the economic crisis of 1947:

> We are an inventive, a creative people, with something like genius for improvisation. We do not find it as easy to plan and to organise in an almost brutal large-scale fashion as some other peoples do, if only because we have many individual twists and turns in our character, and are given to producing odd sports and freaks, rum and eccentric types, especially where the dim genteel tradition has least force ... They saved us in the war. And they alone can save us in this peace that is as menacing and challenging as a war.[30]

A national penchant for eccentricity and individualism did not chime in particularly well with the bureaucratic structures of the NHS, or the gospel of 'the man from Whitehall knows best' which the Labour government was suspected of believing in. For Priestley, the issue was about not just giving creative eccentrics their head but fostering the growth of community from the grass roots upwards. Some historians have argued that Labour's efforts to promote a sense of community fell on stony ground in a society still deeply divided along class, gender and regional lines.[31] Priestley agreed that people had become less community-minded than they had been in 1940, but for him this was because they had not been presented with a heroic challenge to bring out their 'courage and ingenuity and spirit'.[32]

This was Priestley on familiar territory, the need for community, which he had mapped out in *English Journey* a long decade and a half ago, developed in his novels and plays, returned to in the *Postscripts* and *Out of the People*, and addressed in *An Inspector Calls*. In the Slump, he had feared that the nation had ceased to be a community, caring for its own; in the War, he thought he saw that community reborn. In the late 1940s he welcomed what the government was doing, but feared that its rather cautious and bureaucratic approach would stifle the creative impulses of the people. By the end of the 1940s he had come to see the centralised state which had carried out most of Labour's reforms as a problem in itself, like other forms of overweening power. 'Contrary to much report, although I favour plenty of communal enterprise and control, I have never regarded the state with much favour', he explained to radio listeners after a visit to Coventry. 'The state is too large and unwieldy a mechanism, can easily become too powerful and clumsy, bruising the heart, crushing the spirit, by sheer size and weight.' Increasingly, he argued that it was the local society and culture, which he had found so alarmingly attenuated in his journey of 1934, which held the key: not 'far away, mysterious, but near at hand so that you can see the wheels going round and know who is pulling the levers'.[33] A democratic society, he declared, was one in which 'individual citizens are able to accept plenty of responsibility and play a constantly active part in deciding how they will live and how the life of their community will be shaped and coloured'. As ever, in seeking a better way Priestley looked back to Edwardian Bradford (or at any rate his own version of it) when, he asserted, 'at the age of nineteen I had more control over my life than I have now, thirty-five years later, as a middle-aged man'. This kind of democracy was, he feared, rapidly dying out: perhaps people didn't even want it any more. Too much power was passing to small groups: the rich Americans who controlled the media; commissars in Russia; and in Britain politicians and senior civil servants, who were 'beginning to decide how the rest of us shall live'. Even the NHS, the Labour government's flagship, was 'fundamentally undemocratic', whatever its virtues, because the personal relationship between doctor and patient had been turned into official business: 'you take your pills by permission of the Ministry of Health'. [34]

This last jibe was too much for Priestley's erstwhile allies. It provoked a front-page diatribe in the left-wing paper *Tribune* from its editor, Michael Foot, accusing Priestley of cynicism and defeatism, 'the nihilism of the intellectual who will not deign to join the strivings of the common people'.[35] This does seem unfair on Priestley, who, misguidedly or not, was in fact attempting to re-empower the 'common people' in a world which he felt was increasingly run by the few. He could have been more tactful about the NHS – which, as he admitted, he did not himself use – but he was not moving rightwards as Foot implied, rather reasserting a different, and older tradition of socialism from the centralised social democracy which had emerged from the Attlee years. This was to be an increasingly familiar theme in the years that followed.

It was hardly surprising that Priestley warmly welcomed one central government initiative, the Festival of Britain in 1951, combining as it did what was to be the last hurrah of postwar Labour collectivism with the spirit of popular pleasure. 'The best attempt at public gaiety in my time,' he later called it, 'which the Tory press attacked when it was there and has sneered at ever since.'[36] Priestley delivered an enthusiastic series of talks on BBC radio in which he reported on how the Festival was being celebrated in various places, including Bradford, which awoke childhood memories of the Bradford Exhibition of 1904.[37] His other contribution to the celebrations was his long comic novel *Festival at Farbridge*. This ebullient panorama of postwar English life, complete with caricatures of the upper classes, communists, Cambridge literary critics, and others from the contemporary cultural scene, reused the plot device of *The Good Companions* and *Let the People Sing* by bringing together a motley group of travelling strangers in a common enterprise – in this case, persuading the people and powers that be in a medium-sized Midlands town to join in the Festival celebrations. Like *Let the People Sing*, *Festival* is a call for national reawakening from the grass roots upwards. As Priestley's character Laura protests, 'what's wrong with us now is that we don't *feel* enough. There isn't enough richness and joy and glory in our lives. We're all living thin flat sort of existences ... Life ought to be wonderful, and now for most people it isn't.'[38] As so often with Priestley, *Festival*'s comic energy, satire and set-pieces belie this downbeat view of contemporary England.

A secret dream

> Then it was very quickly decided that we should make atomic bombs, a fateful decision as we know now, and one ... far removed from the spirit of 1945, and from the humanity and hopefulness of the old socialist pioneers ... Now was that glorious summer changed to the winter of our discontent.[39]

This was the other source of Priestley's postwar disillusionment. He had never taken much interest in international affairs, but the onset of the Cold War was to change that. In 1949, George Orwell – now virtually on his deathbed – revised and updated a long-standing list of 'crypto-Communists and fellow-travellers', and passed it on to his friend Celia Paget, who was employed by the Information Research Department, an anti-Soviet propaganda arm of the Foreign Office.[40] One of the 135 names on the list was Priestley's. The revelation in 1991 that Orwell had been involved in what, on the face of it, looked very much like early Cold War blacklisting caused some consternation, as in a smaller way did the appearance of Priestley's name on the list. Orwell, of course, was a long-standing left-wing anti-communist; but so too was Priestley, scorning the 1930s Marxists who uncritically idolised the Soviet Union after having 'discover[ed] "the proletariat" in late night talks in some tutor's rooms at Oxford', and putting his faith in an English socialism rather than any alien model.[41] What prompted Orwell to list this very English figure, politically so close to himself, as a Soviet sympathiser?

One reason might be *Russian Journey*, a book – or rather pamphlet – which Priestley wrote after a state-sponsored trip to the Soviet Union with his wife in the autumn of 1945.[42] With hindsight, some things in *Russian Journey* appear naive. Priestley asserts that 'we saw what we wanted to see', but it is clear from his account that they did not wander freely across the Soviet Union as they might in most other countries, but went where their hosts wanted them to go. [43] His claim that Russian writers, though not allowed to criticise the Party line, followed it 'instinctively', were free to promote 'challenging ideas of their own' and did not 'feel themselves to be fettered in any way' is unconvincing to say the least.[44]

But all this has to be seen in its historical context. Hindsight can easily obscure how fluid and unresolved the world situation was in 1945. The Soviet Union was at the height of its popularity in Britain and the West.[45] It was recognised that through great suffering and endurance its people had contributed more than anyone to the defeat of Hitler. Communist Party membership had been at an all-time high since Russia entered the war.[46] Priestley's articles on Russia were first published in Beaverbrook's *Sunday Express*, hardly known for its Stalinist sympathies. Winston Churchill, in the same speech in the United States in March 1945 in which he announced that an 'iron curtain' had descended over Europe, expressed the sentiments of the time:

> I have a strong admiration and regard for the valiant Russian people and for my wartime comrade, Marshal Stalin. There is deep sympathy and goodwill in Britain – and I doubt not here also – towards the peoples of all the Russias and a resolve to persevere through many differences and rebuffs in establishing lasting friendships.[47]

It is unfortunate that, in attempting to defend the notorious list, Orwell's biographer accuses Priestley of denying the existence of the Soviet secret police.[48] In fact, he spoke unambiguously of 'political police, sudden arrests, labour camps, and all the grim tactics of suppression', and had done so since the 1930s.[49] His sympathies did not lie with the Soviet regime but with the Russian people, whom he found 'warm-hearted, impulsive and expansive', uncorrupted by western commercialism, and eager for culture.[50] No doubt the regime was ruthless with dissenters, but, he argued, 'people cannot be bullied into long spells of sheer devotion and heroism' such as were witnessed during the siege of Leningrad: unlike Hitler's Germans 'they have to believe heart and soul in what they are defending'.[51] Beneath the regime, beneath Marxism, he found 'an intense feeling of fraternity, a conviction that men are brothers needing each other's help', and this leaning towards fraternity rather than liberty was an explanation, though not an excuse, for the 'startling severity' with which dissent was treated.[52] In the end, Priestley's view of Russia parallels his view of Britain. It was from the people, not from their rulers, that the true character of a nation arose; and as in wartime Britain he warmed to the prospect of a nation finally pulling together, so he found in the instinctive collectivism of the Russian people some hope for the future of humankind; and valuing that unity, he wanted the wartime alliance to remain in place after the war was over.

The following year, Priestley renewed this appeal in a pamphlet entitled *The Secret Dream*.[53] In a characteristic rhetorical flourish, he took the French Revolution ideals of liberty, equality and fraternity and applied them to the three wartime allies. The British had no time for equality, were only reluctant fraternalists and preferred individual freedom above all things, though they were currently at a loss as to what to do with it. America, despite its grossly unequal distribution of power and wealth, preferred the principle of equality: every man as good as every other, no one sticking their neck out above the crowd, even at the expense of the liberty to which they paid lip-service. Russia, as we have seen, was the homeland of fraternity, in which freedom was an indulgence, and some people more equal than others.[54] The conceit does not quite stand up (Priestley had, after all, hailed the Americans as natural collectivists in the 1930s), but it expresses an underlying idea, that all three nations, though in very different ways, had their roots in the principles of the Enlightenment and the ideals of the French Revolution. Each could learn from the others and thereby 'create a broad highway for a world civilisation' – as good a summary as any of the Enlightenment project – but this could happen only if the Soviet Union was brought in from the cold and made to feel secure and wanted. Averting the Cold – and possibly Hot – War in the name of underlying civilised values was Priestley's aim, but the possibility of any such reconciliation, if it ever existed, would very soon be gone, and his next foray into international relations would be in even less promising circumstances.

Admass: 'a huge, idle show'

If the moment of 1945 soon passed, it was not just because of the Cold War. The 1950s and 1960s saw a huge cultural change, with profound political implications, whose beginnings Priestley had observed in the 'new England' of 1934. The postwar economic boom, bringing full employment and rising real wages, convinced many that capitalism had been transformed from the failure it appeared to be in the 1930s, to a great engine of prosperity. This prosperity was now more widely shared than in its 1930s beginnings. With the help of expanding consumer credit, goods such as cars, refrigerators, washing machines and foreign holidays, previously the preserve of the middle class, became accessible to large numbers of working-class people. The structure of the labour force was also changing, with a shift away from unskilled manual work towards skilled and white-collar occupations, and the education system was expanding to meet this change. To many observers, these developments signalled the decline of class as the key reference-point in British society – and, by implication, the end of any socialist project that had depended on mobilising working-class consciousness.[55] Three successive Conservative election victories in the 1950s seemed to confirm this judgement: against all expectations, after the radical moment of 1940–45, the capitalist right appeared to have recaptured the spirit of the times, and the orthodox left was left wondering what to do about it.

As we have seen in Chapter 4, Priestley had spotted these changes early on, and his response to them was ambivalent. In *English Journey* he had been among the first to recognise the emergence in the 1930s suburbs of a new consumerist way of life, a 'new England' that was now coming to fruition. While he had regarded that way of life as in some respects cheap and tawdry, its inhabitants too passive and lacking in the essential 'gusto', he also, like a true radical, respected its democratic aspect: its classlessness, and its disdain for obsolete hierarchies. When everything costs sixpence, a duke is as good as a dustman.[56] Now, it seemed that the 'new England' had taken a turn for the worse. Travelling in America in 1954, Priestley coined a new word to describe the system which he saw coming into being both there and in England: 'Admass', which quickly entered the vocabulary of public discourse.

> This is my name for the whole system of an increasing productivity, plus inflation, plus a rising standard of material living, plus high-pressure advertising and salesmanship, plus mass communications, plus cultural democracy and the creation of the mass mind, the mass man ... It is better to live in *Admass* than have no job, no prospect of one ... but that is about all that can be said in favour of it. All the rest is a swindle. You think everything is opening out when it is narrowing and closing in on you.[57]

Intellectual criticism of consumerism and mass communication was, of course, nothing new in the postwar era, and came from both the left and the right of the political spectrum, both of them suspected of belittling ordinary people. The film director Lindsay Anderson wrote in 1957 of 'artists and intellectuals who despise the people, imagine themselves superior to them, and think it clever to talk about the "Ad-Mass"'.[58] The *Oxford English Dictionary* makes the same mistake, defining 'Admass' as 'that section of the community which is easily influenced by mass methods of publicity and entertainment', although none of its cited quotations support this definition.[59] But Admass for Priestley is not a body of people, but 'an economic-social-cultural system' within which people – and all of us, not just the 'masses' – increasingly have to live.[60] 'It is ... a dangerous mistake', he warned, 'to imagine that we ourselves are proof against the ... sorcery and spells'.[61] Under this deadening system of power, the people are unable to express the energy from below through which all historical progress should come. And this power is exercised through culture, through spectacle, through the way things are publicly represented, as 'in our new society everything is becoming part of a huge idle show'.[62]

In some ways, 'Admass' anticipated the debate on the left about postwar social change that would follow Labour's election defeats in 1955 and 1959.[63] But there were differences. To begin with, Priestley had never pinned his political hopes on the working class. He was more concerned about the impact of Admass on the old middle class, 'creative, enthusiastic, vigilant, and combative', with a sense of social responsibility and suspicion of power – as he had long argued, natural allies of the left but now seduced by Admass along with everybody else.[64] Nor did he regard Admass, as many did, as a process of 'Americanisation'. Shortly after Labour's 1955 election defeat, Hugh Gaitskell, soon to become leader of the party, spoke of 'a growing Americanisation of outlook' in British society that could have profound political effects. Priestley, already ahead of this particular game, and with *Journey Down a Rainbow* about to be published, was scathing. Gaitskell, he wrote, was 'years and years out of date': others, including Priestley himself, had been discussing this trend for a decade or more, but politicians had taken no notice – chiefly because they did not keep their ears to the ground, preferring to read the city columns of the *Times* rather than '*Mabel's Weekly* or *Filmfans Pictorial* ... the frivolities and trivialities, far below the level of a public man's attention', which told those prepared to listen which way the wind was blowing. But what Gaitskell had also not realised was 'the interdependence of things in this world', to which Priestley, an early observer of globalisation, had been drawing attention since the 1930s. [65] This new society had begun in America, true, but even in 1934 it had belonged 'more to the age itself' than to any particular country. 'The new society, which has no centre ... is now all around us ... it embraces almost all the earth.' It was a society 'much further removed from 1900 than 1900 was from 1850. We are always being told about invaders from some other planet. They have arrived, and may be found in the nearest street. They are the children of a new age.'[66]

But what was the proper political response to this new age? Here lies the main source of Priestley's impatience with Labour. Ever since 1940 he had been asking whether the party had 'any guiding vision of the kind of Britain they hoped to create when they came to power'.[67] Now, after a predictable election defeat, he knew they did not. As he was to put it later, they were driven by 'agenda-programme' rather than by 'ambience-atmosphere'. As the Tories had always known, 'if you can create the right atmosphere, then the programme can look after itself'. Labour had failed to keep alive the atmosphere that swept them to power in 1945, and now it was busy proscribing creative rebels like Michael Foot, leaving a vacuum on the left into which demagogues might move. 'It has now plenty of agenda men, ready to work overtime, but where are the ambience changers? In whose belly is the fire?'[68]

Interestingly, Priestley here comes close to saying that style matters more than substance: which indeed, under Admass, may well be true. For Admass is, above all, a culture of images and ambiences, rather than hard-nosed practicalities. What many postwar intellectuals (themselves long accustomed to material comforts) deplored about the 'live now, pay later' world of the postwar boom was its materialism. For Priestley this missed the point. 'The Americans, who created Admass ... are in fact less genuinely materialistic than most western Europeans.' The 'Blue Yonderism' of advertising appealed not to people's materialism but to their fantasies. 'It is dreamers of dreams, idealists on the wrong track, who spend more and more trying to reach the Happy Land. It is people still haunted by the vision of a good life whom the advertising agencies bamboozle.' And since our society no longer had any idealistic goals of its own, 'the *chimera* of that Happy Land is about all we have left'.[69]

Priestley argued this point through in wonderfully comic form in his longest novel, *The Image Men*, published in two volumes in 1968 and 1969, when he was seventy-four years old.[70] Two renegade academics, Owen Tuby and Cosmo Saltana, laying dubious claim to expertise in this business of dreams and images, set up an Institute of Social Imagistics, attached to a new university, from which they proffer advice on image creation and image change to a variety of clients. Social Imagistics is a kind of amalgam of sociology, psychology and what was to become known as cultural studies. The point about it is that it works: Tuby and Saltana are chancers on a heroic scale, but they are not frauds; the advice they give is soundly based in theoretical knowledge and common sense, and it produces results. The butt of the satire is not those who are taken in by the pair – they generally get what they want – but the culture in which happiness and success are achieved by a change of image rather than by what people actually do. At the end of *The Image Men* a general election is imminent and, in a final triumph of Social Imagistics, Tuby and Saltana rebuild the images of both the main party leaders – who have clearly heeded Priestley's advice that, in the politics of Admass, ambience is more important than agenda.

Analysing the visit to Britain of the American evangelist Billy Graham in 1955, Priestley compared his success to the failure of his 1920s prede-cessor Aimee Semple McPherson, which he attributed partly to the far more highly developed publicity and public relations methods of the 1950s. The main reason, though, was that 'what so many of us want now is a show, a show that has been written up in the press, a show that is linked to radio and TV ... Many of the postwar British now live from one show to the next ... Politics, to exist for them at all, must be a show. Patriotism is a show with an expensive regal cast. Sport is a show. The arts are a show on ice. And now ... religion is a show.'[71] Already the early precursors of 'reality TV' were amongst us, offering

> an elaborately contrived exhibition of other people under the stress of sudden emotion – a woman finds her house has gone, a man is brought face-to-face with an old sweetheart, and genuine bewilderment, grief, regret, deep embarrassment, are to be highlighted like juggling acts. We are almost within sight of the Roman Circus, with minds if not bodies being torn to amuse the mob.[72]

In other words, we were well into what Guy Debord would call the 'society of the spectacle', in which modern capitalism transforms itself into a consumer and entertainment society, social life 'presents itself as an immense accumulation of spectacles [and] all that was once directly lived has become mere representation', as individuals live in a world fabricated by others rather than making a life of their own – as Priestley would agree, not materialism but rampant idealism.[73]

Whether Priestley would have approved of the avant-garde aesthetic strategies employed by Debord's Situationists to try to disrupt the spectacle, we do not know, though he might have admired their gusto; but despite his pessimism he certainly thought resistance was possible: 'I still believe that what is wrong can be put right ... I refuse to accept the sleep-walking fatalism of our time.'[74] His supernatural thriller *The Magicians* (1954) depicted an evil magnate seeking to control the world through mass communications and narcotics, but foiled by an improbable consortium of white witches bent on saving humanity; while *The Shapes of Sleep* (1962) features a secret society called the Antiants, sworn to uphold individualism and work against the forces of Admass.[75] Admass, Priestley argued, created discontent, a sense of having been cheated by the 'new good life', especially amongst the young, who were 'restless, dissatisfied, longing for something they cannot find'.[76] Into the complacent world of 'You Never Had It So Good', 'the rebels arrived, and among them were almost all the young men and women gifted with any talent, insight and wit'.[77] It is to Priestley's relationship with these critical undercurrents of the 1950s and 1960s that we now turn.

The bomb

This 'whole new society' was not confined to the West. Russia did not have Admass, but it had Propmass, much the same thing but with official propaganda taking the place of advertising.[78] In parallel with his critique of both these systems, Priestley in 1954 began an onslaught on the nuclear arms race that was to culminate in the foundation of the Campaign for Nuclear Disarmament. 'That such societies should be piling up atom bombs should surprise nobody ... Soviet propaganda and American advertisements often seem to speak with almost the same voice: the management is different but the enterprise is broadly the same.' And although 'I would prefer writing TV advertisements for Cornflakes to lumbering on thin cabbage soup in Siberia', both sides in the Cold War were unbalanced in favour of Logos, the Yang, the masculine principle. 'We should really have formed a neutral block, wearing the colours of the Yin, under the banner of Eros.'[79]

A later article along similar but less Jungian lines, entitled 'Britain and the bombs', published on 2 November 1957, was the catalyst for the formation of the Campaign for Nuclear Disarmament, arguably the most long-lasting and coherent of postwar protest movements – and the occasion of Priestley's second and final incursion on to the national political stage.[80] The context of the article was the government's 1957 Defence White Paper, and Labour's support for the H-bomb, re-emphasised by Aneurin Bevan's Labour Party conference speech of that year, 'which seemed to many of us to slam a door in our faces'.[81] Those in charge seemed out of control, even out of their minds; the general public was left 'deafened or blinded by propaganda and giant headlines ... robbed of decision by fear or apathy'. H-bombs offered no defence to this country in a nuclear war, and merely made it more likely. Britain should renounce them forthwith, in the hope of at least marginally depolarising the world.[82]

The huge public response to Priestley's article prompted Kingsley Martin, the editor of the *New Statesman*, to call a small gathering of left-wing luminaries – including Priestley and his wife, the archaeologist Jacquetta Hawkes – which duly decided, in alliance with existing anti-nuclear groups, to form the CND, in much the same way as a similar gathering summoned by Edward Hulton, and including some of the same people, had formed the 1941 Committee. Priestley became its vice-president, addressed the hugely successful inaugural public meeting at Central Hall, Westminster in February 1958 – the first of many – wrote articles, and organised fund-raising events with the help of his theatrical contacts.[83] As if to emphasise the continuity with earlier radical movements, Peggy Duff, who had been the organiser of Common Wealth, became organising secretary of CND. But as with Common Wealth, the committee work and the internal wrangling proved too much for Priestley, and, when Bertrand Russell resigned as president in 1960 over the direct action issue, Priestley took the opportunity to bow out also. But he remained a supporter of CND, and Jacquetta Hawkes continued as an active member of its leadership.

CND was a broad front which contained within it many different political and ideological positions, ranging from the Marxist left to Christian pacifism, and most points in between. Within this spectrum, Priestley's position on nuclear weapons has been described as 'moralistic'.[84] This is true in the sense that he saw little point in the long political grind through the institutions of the Labour movement, the committee work, conference resolutions and election manifestos, which for many activists were what the campaign was all about. To him, as always, it was about changing ambience rather than agendas: a real change could only come from the people, and it was to them rather than to MPs and conference delegates that the message should be addressed. Nor, although still a man of the left, did he regard the anti-nuclear campaign as a stratagem for shifting the Labour Party, or British politics, leftwards: such sectional fixations narrowed its message and reduced its impact, just as much as would out-and-out pacifism. But this did not mean that his anti-nuclear stance was apolitical. In fact it was rooted in his critique of the postwar state and the power elite who controlled it, whom he later labelled 'Topside': 'the *VIP-Highest Priority-Top-Secret-Top-People Class*, men now so conditioned by this atmosphere of power politics, intrigue, secrecy, insane invention, that they are more than half-barmy'.[85] His stance was also pragmatic rather than moralistic. Nuclear weapons were an act of collective madness which threatened to destroy civilisation: a situation which Priestley had foreseen twenty years earlier in his pre-nuclear thriller *The Doomsday Men*.[86] The question was, what could Britain most effectively do to avert such an outcome? Since we were no longer an important player in stark geo-political terms, there might be some value in cashing in such prestige as we might still possess by setting an example in unilaterally renouncing nuclear weapons. This argument, which was the core of Priestley's original article, may have been mistaken, but it was, Priestley would have contended, more realistic than the strategies of those with conventional political agendas.

But it was the note on which the 1957 article concluded that was perhaps most significant for Priestley himself. Alone, the British people had defied Hitler: this, indeed, was the source of any moral authority they had left. But since then they had lost their way, 'hiding their decent, kind faces behind masks of sullen apathy or sour, cheap cynicism', waiting for 'something great and noble in its intention that would make them feel good again'.[87]

> We ended the war high in the world's regard. We could have taken over its moral leadership, spoken and acted for what remained of its conscience; but we chose to act otherwise – with obvious and melancholy consequences both abroad, where in power politics we cut a shabby figure, and at home, where we shrug it away or go to the theatre to applaud the latest jeers and sneers at Britannia.[88]

Perhaps this was the opportunity to reawaken the spirit of 1940.

Topside versus the gentle anarchists

CND was a single-issue campaign, but the wide range of people it gathered under its wing implied a critique of the status quo which was as much social or cultural as political. It was the only substantial organised expression of the strong undercurrent of intellectual discontent which ran beneath the affluent 1950s and early 1960s, from wartime radicalism and the spirit of 1945, through so-called 'Angry Young Men', the New Left, the early 1960s satire boom, the avalanche of Penguin Specials (another echo of wartime) anatomising power and inequality in British society, and even the modernising rhetoric of Harold Wilson in the general election of 1964, finally erupting in the political protests of the late 1960s and 1970s.[89]

Although Priestley was no longer young, he was angry enough to share the dissatisfactions of the younger 1950s malcontents. Like them, he planted himself firmly in the political wilderness, still radical in his views, but alienated by the sterility of conventional left politics, and increasingly suspicious of the state and those who ran it. But he had arrived there first. 'There is a wilderness atmosphere just now', he complained as early as 1953, 'with little that appears to be blossoming and fruitful.'[90] As in the 1930s and 1940s, he concentrated much of his fire on the British ruling class. In *Out of the People* he had depicted it as sterile and decaying, a greedy plutocracy concealed behind the tattered ermine of an aristocratic tradition.[91] Now, things were if anything even worse. The state was run no longer by a moneyed class in its own interests but by something even more sinister: 'Topside', the power system that 'stands for nothing except itself', and 'the idea that administration is the most important thing there is'.[92] Confident and impregnable, dominating communication and culture, and playing on the British genius for self-deception, Topside had brought stability and sterility to a nation which needed energy, originality and creativity, passion and belief. It was 'the reaction against a revolution that never happened', the lost revolution of 1945.[93] Most people, satisfied with their lives and no longer dreaming of anything better, went along with Topside, and the only opposition came from outsiders who believed in something: political extremists, 'rebellious radicals, saints, philosophers, crackpots', and the 'gentle anarchists' whom Priestley had recommended to radio listeners in 1954, who 'distrust and dislike the power systems, the immense machinery of authority, believing that men would do better to rely on mutual help and voluntary associations'.[94] 'I wonder sometimes', he said later, 'if a few economic charlatans, gaudy fellows over-addicted to women and champagne and always lunching well away from the Atheneum, might not save some of the English from being doomed to die by inches.'[95]

Topside clearly has some affinities with the idea of the 'Establishment' which carried all before it in the wave of social and political critique in the late 1950s and 1960s, even giving its name to a satirical nightclub. However, 'Establishment' conjures up the 'sleepy Tory Britain' of Church of England bishops and Harold Macmillan on the grouse-moor. Topside is something more sinister – not at all outdated but a new and dangerous form of power, a 'bowler-hat-and-umbrella-fascism' similar to the 'hard Corporate State Toryism' of which Priestley warned in 1945.[96] There are also affinities, and differences, with the polemics of younger writers in the late 1950s – the so-called 'Angry Young Men' - against what they saw as the stifling conformity and lack of creativity in English life.[97] Priestley, as he was wont to point out, had been denouncing this for over a decade, although this did not prevent John Osborne's Jimmy Porter in *Look Back in Anger* from dismissing him as a nostalgic Edwardian. Priestley responded by dismissing the 'Angry Young Men' in turn as 'imitation rebels', and chiding Osborne and Colin Wilson for their negativity and introversion, political quietism and lack of 'courage, faith, hope' – echoing his perennial complaints against modernist art ever since the 1920s.[98] In fact, their political views were not so distant from Priestley's. Reviewing *Declaration*, a key collection of 'angry, young' writings, Alan Pryce-Jones, the editor of the *Times Literary Supplement*, shrewdly observed that 'their indictments remind me of long-ago provincial Liberal meetings. They do not make the obvious terms of reference to Hegel, Marx and Lenin, but stick to the generalities of progressive thought forty years ago' – more like radicals of Priestley's generation, in fact, than the 1930s leftist writers who were Pryce-Jones's contemporaries.[99] But Osborne and the others tended to strike the modernist pose of alienated intellectuals rather than political activists: as Priestley complained, none of them had even joined CND, but left the job of rescuing the country from 'pitfalls and mantraps' to the 'old fuddy-duddies' of his own generation.[100] Priestley's own fictional treatment of Topside, however, eschewed the bitterness of his younger contemporaries and turned instead to fairly gentle satire. *Sir Michael and Sir George* (1964) features two rival senior civil servants, both arts administrators, and the disruptive impact on their bureaucratic manoeuvrings not only of disorderly poets, painters and musicians but of an 'unsound' civil servant, Tim Kemp – one of Priestley's 'gentle anarchists', who, by following his own nose and disobeying the rules, makes most things in the book happen.[101]

The creative anarchy of Tim Kemp represented, for Priestley, the deepest kind of Englishness, the one the Topsiders had trained themselves out of. In an essay published in the year of Suez, he put his money on 'the imaginative, creative, boldly inventive, original, and individual side of the national character', represented by the Unicorn, ageless and magical, as against the once manly and aggressive imperial Lion, now become tooth-less, blunt-clawed and mangy with age.[102] The Lion stood for the blustering 'Big England' of the imperial past, while the Unicorn repre-sented the 'poets and artists and scientific discoverers and passionate reformers and bold inventors and visionaries and madmen' whom the rest of the world so warmly admired about England.[103] This Englishness, with its familiar reliance on instinct and intuition, and its hazy boundary between the conscious and the unconscious mind, could never, Priestley argued, live at peace with Admass.[104] While true Englishness leaned towards the feminine, Admass, with its aggressive desire to conquer every-thing, its lack of concern for personal relationships and inner life, was dominated by the masculine principle, Logos rather than Eros, Yang rather than Yin.[105] In the 1950s heyday of Admass, we had almost lost our way. 'We no longer appeared to know who we were ... Suddenly we had lost face, no longer having any image of ourselves.' We were in danger of getting the worst of two worlds: 'America without social equal-ity, dash and energy, traditional England without responsibility and respect for herself, a show for the telly, the admen and the tourists'.[106] Yet despite Admass, traces of the Yin were still to be found in English life, 'in the flexibility of our official machinery, in our lingering respect for private life, in a traditional piety towards earth, in the wealth of our odd hobbies and pastimes, in the wide network of our voluntary associations'. [107] Englishness endured, despite everything, but its 'deep roots' needed nour-ishment.[108]

Englishness was under pressure because of an imbalance in the whole civilisation. What it needed was a shift towards the feminine. By this, Priestley did not just mean that women's status, opportunities and pres-tige should be enhanced – although as a self-declared feminist he believed they should – but that the feminine principle should be properly honoured. Without this, he feared that women would simply move 'out of the typists' pool into the boardroom', abandoning fundamental feminine values in order to exercise power in what remained a male-dominated world, and thus failing to challenge the masculine principle. What we needed was a different kind of society, not a masculine society run by women.[109]

Conventionally, for this kind of renewal one looks to the young. But in 1956, Priestley despaired at their 'air of conformity', their alternating blandness and sullen acquiescence, their lack of 'revolutionary ardour on behalf of any possible kind of changed England'.[110] Hindsight shows that youth culture in 1956 was on the cusp of a change. By 1963, things were looking up: 'the very best of the young English are out of this official England, spiritually and mentally ... they "want out"'.[111] By 1965 youth was in revolt, and there was 'chaos in the arts ... vandalism and violence in the streets'.[112] Priestley was unconvinced of the value of most postwar popular culture, but as his 1955 comments about Hugh Gaitskell's failure to consult *Filmfans Pictorial* show, like Orwell he kept a weather eye on it. Popular song, however repulsive, was prophetic, as it had been when he encountered ragtime in 1910:

> Out of the depths it suddenly reveals, great and terrible events will come: politicians and historians do not keep their ears open in the right places. (They should listen now [1962], however nauseating they find them, to the pop songs of the teenagers, so full of self-pity, so wandering and rootless and far removed from all public and national life, clinging so desperately to a sexual relationship, all expressing disinherited youth growing up with the Bomb.)[113]

With the 1960s pop culture just about to burst upon the scene, Priestley had seen nothing yet. But when it did, he was sadly less inclined to analyse its meaning, and reverted to stock older-generation grumbles about 'shaggy young men playing electric guitars and belting out one idiotic phrase over and over again'.[114]

The 1960s phenomenon which did attract Priestley's sympathetic interest was the counterculture of the hippy movement, in which he saw not only a rejection of Admass and its 'gimcrack values' but 'an attempt to escape from the dominance of the masculine principle, to re-establish the feminine principle, to confront the Yang with the Yin'.[115] As such, it should be welcomed by all who sought a re-balancing of the two. But he had interesting and perceptive reservations about it. The movement may lean towards the feminine, but it lacked 'some of Woman's most admirable qualities' – patience, practicality, social responsibility, love (as opposed to sex). These things were absent because the hippy movement had been created not by women but by young men. Girls had joined in, but 'they might be said to be more or less "tagging along"' – a view with which later feminist critics would concur.[116] They did not represent the feminine principle, so much as 'the woman hidden in the darkness of a man ... a poor creature, almost a caricature of femininity, when dragged out into daylight ... What is missing in this movement is the emergence of Woman herself, of the true and invaluable feminine principle, as distinct from a tawdry version of it arriving from the masculine unconscious' – a reference to Jung's 'shadow', the dangerous form in which repressed personality traits (in this case femininity) re-emerge from the unconscious. Priestley also complained about the counterculture's devotion to popular music – which, he felt, was more an example of successful commercialism and managerial manipulation than of a 'new free life'. On this last point, the eye for contradiction and ambivalence that he had formerly turned upon popular culture lets him down.

Time, memory, history

It may seem surprising that a man in his seventies whose public image was that of a down-to-earth, no-nonsense Yorkshireman should have philosophical and spiritual interests which brought him close to the youthful counterculture. On reflection, though, taking into account his views on the human condition, throughout his life but especially towards the end, the undercurrent of spirituality in his critical thought is hardly a surprise.[117] His social and political vision was, as we have seen throughout this book, founded on a deep sense of history, especially the history he had lived through. Beneath this ran a deeper, more philosophical, almost mystical fascination, beginning in the 1930s, with time, influenced by the writings of J. W. Dunne and the Russian philosopher P. D. Ouspensky, and with the human personality, inspired by Carl Gustav Jung.[118]

Priestley began reading Jung in 1936, and after the war met him several times, corresponded with him and delivered a BBC talk about him, which Jung heartily approved.[119] The influence of Jung's theories of archetypes and the human personality, and the relation between conscious and unconscious minds, are evident throughout Priestley's critique of postwar society, and especially in his view of Englishness, and as we have seen he increasingly framed his critique of modern culture in Jungian terms. It was also in 1936 when travelling in California that he picked up a copy of Ouspensky's *A New Model of the Universe*, which he read while staying in Death Valley.[120] Thereafter, Ouspensky's theories of time and its relation to the human personality were never far from Priestley's mind, and influenced several of his 'time plays', notably *I Have Been Here Before* (1937), but also *An Inspector Calls*.

Ouspensky argued that our conception of time as linear and one-directional is determined by the way it appears to our consciousness. To our limited perception it seems that past moments are gone for ever (surviving only in memory), while future ones are merely hypothetical possibilities, and only the fleeting present moment is real. But if we could perceive things properly, life could be grasped as a four-dimensional whole, not as an irreversible flow from one moment to the next. Perhaps (and here we enter the realm of science fiction) those who attain this level of consciousness can even change past events: the theme of Priestley's play *I Have Been Here Before*. J. W. Dunne, whose *Experiment With Time* Priestley had reviewed in 1927, cited precognitive dreams as evidence that the mind could move backwards and forwards along the time dimension of human life.

These theories were more a way of thinking than a set of clear-cut beliefs, but they were an important part of Priestley's world-view, so imbued with a sense of recent history and of the individual life-story

which parallels and intertwines with it. There is a sense in which any
novel, any narrative, seeks to escape the headlong rush of consciousness
through time – and therefore cheat death itself – by creating a world in
which we can *know how it ends*, something we can never know in the
open-ended world we actually live through: and Priestley, as his detrac-
tors would point out, had a non-modernist penchant for endings,
preferably 'happy' ones. Two of his strongest postwar novels, *Bright Day*
and *Lost Empires*, as well as the first part of his memoir *Margin Released*,
deal with the recapturing in memory and imagination of a particular
moment, immediately before the Great War, and the doom-laden shadow
which that event casts back over what precedes it: as if the present can,
intuitively, know the future, as his own teenaged self in *Margin Released*
unconsciously intuited the coming war.[121]

Priestley's writing is often imbued with a sense of historic loss, the
dropped threads of a history gone wrong: the promise of 1910 lost in the
trenches; that of 1940 in the follies of Admass; the whole human species
forever selling itself short, not realising what could be. But this is coun-
terbalanced by an insuppressible optimism, and the gusto comes back :
maybe those threads are, somehow, still there, waiting to be picked up:

> And if the universe is not simply an idiotic machine, grinding out nothing-
> ness, then in some queer but cosy dimension of it, my Aunt Hilda is still
> trotting round to the Miss Singletons to secure the last brown loaf and the
> remaining six Eccles cakes.[122]

Perhaps, as Priestley predicted in 1941, the people will at last awaken,
'freely functioning, zestful, unencumbered, thoroughly alive'. And
perhaps there is, after all, a happy ending, in which we make 'the life of
the community the true expression of our real inner life'.[123] But for this to
happen, as he argued twenty years later in the conclusion to *Literature
and Western Man*, the split between inner and outer worlds signalled by
the introversion of modernism on the one hand and the 'dehumanizing
collectives' of modernity on the other would need to be healed, and this
could not be achieved by conscious effort, but only at the symbolic level
of the unconscious. But a literature which no longer reflected the whole
person could not carry the symbolic load; nor could religion, whose
symbols had lost their power in a profoundly irreligious society. All
humankind could do was to wait. 'Even if we believe that the time of our
civilisation is running out fast, like sugar spilled from a torn bag, we must
wait.' But all is not lost: if we try to establish justice, order and real
community in the outer world, and, accepting the great mystery of existence, openly acknowledge the deepest needs of the inner world, we may
yet find the right symbolic tools to restore our wholeness.[124] If we were to
pick one theme which draws together Priestley's sprawling, many-faceted
life-work, it would be this: restoring our wholeness.

Notes

1 J. B. Priestley, 'Journey into daylight', *Listener* (17 May 1945), p. 543.
2 J. B. Priestley, *Topside, or The Future of England: A Dialogue* (London: Heinemann, 1958), p. 15.
3 Priestley, *Rain*, p. 215.
4 Ibid., p. 256.
5 J. B. Priestley, 'Fifty years of the English', *Moments*, p. 213. Originally published in *New Statesman* (19 April 1963).
6 Calder, *Myth of the Blitz*. An early statement of this view of the war can be found in Richard Titmuss, *Problems of Social Policy* (London: HMSO, 1950), p. 507.
7 J. B. Priestley, 'Tribute to Britain', *Picture Post* (28 April 1945), p. 17.
8 Priestley, 'Fifty years', p. 215.
9 Ibid., p. 218.
10 J. B. Priestley, *The Secret Dream* (London: Turnstile Press, 1946), p. 13.
11 Priestley, *The Plays of J. B. Priestley*, vol. 3 (London: Heinemann, 1950), Introduction, p. xii.
12 'Stephen Daldry interviewed by Giles Croft', Royal National Theatre, *Platform Papers 3: Directors* (London: Royal National Theatre, n.d.) pp. 5–6.
13 J. B. Priestley, *An Inspector Calls*, Act III, in *Plays*, vol. 3, p. 311.
14 J. B. Priestley, 'Ambience or agenda?', *The Moments*, p. 7. Originally published in the *New Statesman* (2 February 1962).
15 Ibid., p. 213.
16 J. B. Priestley, 'The Labour plan works', *Listener* (19 January 1950), p. 112.
17 Priestley, 'Fifty years', p. 213.
18 J. B. Priestley, 'The challenge of change', *Listener* (23 October 1947), p. 711.
19 J. B. Priestley, 'The mood of the people: 1 Bad behaviour', *Daily Herald* (23 September 1946), p. 2.
20 Priestley, 'The mood of the people: 3 Britain remade', *Daily Herald* (25 September 1946), p. 2.
21 J. B. Priestley, 'We need more than economics', *Daily Herald* (10 November 1947), p. 2.
22 J. B. Priestley, 'Tables in the sun', *Listener* (4 July 1946), p. 12.
23 J. B. Priestley, 'Crisis journey: 1 Does Butlin know better than Bevin?', *Daily Herald* (15 September 1947), p. 2.
24 J. B. Priestley, *The Arts Under Socialism* (London: Turnstile Press, 1947), pp. 18, 22. See also 'When work is over', *Picture Post* (4 January 1941), pp. 39–40.
25 Priestley, 'Tables', p. 11.
26 Fielding et al. *'England Arise!'*, chapter 6. Chris Waters, *British Socialists and the Politics of Popular Culture 1884–1914* (Manchester: Manchester University Press, 1990).
27 Waters, *British Socialists*, pp. 31, 35.
28 Priestley, *Arts*, pp. 20–1, 9, 18.
29 Priestley, 'Fifty years', p. 214.
30 J. B. Priestley, 'Here are our chances', *Listener* (30 October 1947), p. 31.
31 Fielding et al., *England Arise*, p. 128, and chapter 5 *passim*.

32 Priestley, 'Challenge', p. 711.

33 J. B. Priestley, 'So we went to Coventry', *Listener* (1 December 1949), pp. 933–4.

34 J. B. Priestley, 'The truth about democracy', *Sunday Pictorial* (23 January 1949), p. 5.

35 Michael Foot, 'The futility of Mr Priestley', *Tribune* (28 January 1949), p. 1; J. B. Priestley, 'J. B. Priestley replies to his critics', *Sunday Pictorial* (6 February 1949), p. 6.

36 J. B. Priestley, 'Gay with the arts?', *Moments*, p. 111, originally published *New Statesman* (27 April 1965). Becky E. Conekin, *'The Autobiography of a Nation': The 1951 Festival of Britain* (Manchester: Manchester University Press, 2003).

37 Weekly series in *The Listener*, from 10 May to 14 June.

38 Priestley, *Festival at Farbridge*, p. 25.

39 Priestley, 'Fifty years', p. 214.

40 This account is based on Taylor, *Orwell*, pp. 408–10.

41 Priestley, *Rain*, pp. 253–4.

42 J. B. Priestley, *Russian Journey* (London: Writers Group of the Society for Cultural Relations with the USSR, 1946).

43 Ibid., p. 4.

44 Ibid., pp. 39, 29, 37.

45 See, for example, Andrew Downing, *Passovotchka: Moscow Dynamo in Britain, 1945* (London: Bloomsbury, 1999), for an account of one poignant moment before the onset of the Cold War.

46 Andrew Thorpe, 'The membership of the Communist Party of Great Britain, 1920–1945', *Historical Journal* 43:3 (2000), p. 781.

47 David Cannadine (ed.), *The Speeches of Winston Churchill* (London: Penguin Books, 1990), p. 303.

48 Taylor, *Orwell*, p. 409.

49 Priestley, *Russian Journey*, p. 39.

50 Ibid., p. 38.

51 Ibid., p. 29.

52 Ibid., p. 39.

53 Priestley, *The Secret Dream*.

54 See Priestley's comments on the inequity of the Soviet rationing system as compared to the British, *Russian Journey*, p. 5.

55 Stuart Laing, *Representations of Working-Class Life 1957–1964* (London: Macmillan, 1986), pp. 13–22. Laing identifies George Orwell's 'England your England' (1941) as the precursor of these debates, although Orwell's account is very similar to Priestley's in *English Journey* seven years earlier.

56 Priestley, *Journey*, pp. 401–6. See above, Chapter 4.

57 Priestley and Hawkes, *Journey Down a Rainbow*, p. 50.

58 Tom Maschler (ed.), *Declaration* (London: Macgibbon and Kee, 1957), p. 172.

59 *The Oxford English Dictionary*, 2nd ed. (Oxford University Press 1989). *OED Online*. <http://dictionary.oed.com.lcproxy.shu.ac.uk/cgi/entry/50002810>, accessed 20 January 2006.

60 Priestley, *Wilderness*, p. 148.

61 Priestley, *Moments*, p. 51.

62 Ibid., p. 139.

63 See Nick Tiratsoo, 'Popular politics, affluence, and the Labour Party in the 1950s', in Anthony Gorst et al. (eds), *Contemporary British History 1931–1961: Politics and the Limits of Policy* (London: Pinter, 1991); Laing, *Representations of Working Class Life*; and Jim McGuigan, *Cultural Populism* (London: Routledge, 1992), esp. chapter 2, as well as contemporary accounts such as Richard Hoggart, *The Uses of Literacy* (London: Chatto and Windus, 1957); C. A. R. Crosland, *The Future of Socialism* (London: Jonathan Cape, 1956); Mark Abrams, Richard Rose and Rita Hinden, *Must Labour Lose?* (Harmondsworth: Penguin, 1960); F. Zweig, *The Worker in an Affluent Society* (London: Heinemann, 1961); and Jeremy Seabrook, *What Went Wrong?* (London: Gollancz, 1978).

64 Priestley, *Wilderness*, pp. 123–4.

65 J. B. Priestley, 'Our new society', *Wilderness*, pp. 120–1. Originally published *New Statesman* (16 July 1955).

66 Priestley, *Journey*, p. 401; 'Our new society', pp. 124–6.

67 Ibid., p. 125.

68 Priestley, 'Ambience or agenda?'.

69 J. B. Priestley, 'Blue yonder boys', in *The Moments*, p. 51. Originally published *New Statesman* (13 September 1963).

70 J. B. Priestley, *The Image Men,* vol. I: *Out of Town* (London: Heinemann, 1968); vol. II: *London End* (London: Heinemann, 1969).

71 J. B. Priestley, 'A note on Billy Graham', *Wilderness*, pp. 113–19. Originally published *New Statesman* (23 April 1955).

72 Priestley, *Wilderness*, p. 139.

73 Guy Debord, *The Society of the Spectacle* (New York: Zone Books, 1994). Originally published 1967.

74 Priestley, *Wilderness*, p. 138.

75 J. B. Priestley, *The Magicians* (London: Heinemann, 1954); J. B. Priestley, *The Shapes of Sleep* (London: Heinemann, 1962).

76 Priestley, *Moments*, pp. 50, 131.

77 Ibid., p. 216.

78 Priestley, *Rainbow*, p. 50.

79 J. B. Priestley, 'Eros and Logos', *Wilderness*, p. 38. Originally published *New Statesman* (30 January 1954).

80 J. B. Priestley, 'Britain and the nuclear bombs', in David Bolton (ed.), *Voices from the Crowd Against the H-Bomb* (London: Peter Owen, 1964). Originally published *New Statesman* (2 November 1957).

81 Priestley, 'Nuclear bombs', p. 38.

82 Ibid., pp. 40–1.

83 The formation and early history of CND are dealt with in detail by Richard Taylor, *Against the Bomb: The British Peace Movement 1958–1965* (Oxford: Clarendon Press, 1988). See also Diana Collins, *Time and the Priestleys: The Story of a Friendship* (Stroud: Alan Sutton Publishing, 1994), chapters 2 and 3.

84 Taylor, *Against the Bomb*, pp. 42–8.

85 Priestley, 'Nuclear bombs', p. 44.

86 J. B. Priestley, *The Doomsday Men* (London: Heinemann, 1938).

87 Priestley, 'Nuclear bombs', p. 45.

88 Ibid., p. 41.

89 See, among many others, Maschler, *Declaration*; E. P. Thompson (ed.), *Out of Apathy* (London: New Left Books, 1960); Hugh Thomas (ed.), *The Establishment* (Anthony Blond, 1959); Harold Wilson, *The New Britain: Labour's Plan Outlined: Selected Speeches 1964* (Harmondsworth: Penguin, 1964).

90 J. B. Priestley, 'Thoughts in the wilderness', *New Statesman* (5 September 1953).

91 Priestley, *Out of the People*, pp. 24–6.

92 Priestley, *Topside*, pp. 20, 30.

93 Ibid., p. 14.

94 Ibid., pp. 24, 17. J. B. Priestley, 'The gentle anarchists', *Listener* (25 November 1954), pp. 897–8.

95 Priestley, 'Fifty years', p. 210.

96 Priestley, *The Moments* p. 12; *Letter to a Returning Serviceman*, p. 15.

97 See, for example, Maschler (ed.), *Declaration*, especially John Osborne, 'They call it cricket'; and Lindsay Anderson, 'Get out and push!'. Robert Hewison, *In Anger: Culture in the Cold War 1945–60* (London: Weidenfeld and Nicolson, 1981), esp. chapter 5.

98 J. B. Priestley, 'The outsider', in *Wilderness*. Originally published *New Statesman* (7 July 1956).

99 Alan Pryce-Jones, 'The messiahs of the milk bars?', *The Listener* (7 November 1957), p. 735.

100 J. B. Priestley, 'Young rebels' anger is misplaced', *Reynolds News* (1 June 1958), p. 6.

101 J. B. Priestley, *Sir Michael and Sir George: A Tale of COMSA and DISCUS and the New Elizabethans* (London: Heinemann, 1964).

102 J. B. Priestley, 'The unicorn', *Wilderness*, pp. 162–8. Originally published *New Statesman* (31 March 1956). See also Orwell, 'The lion and the unicorn' – or rather, the title: having hit upon the metaphor, Orwell did not make much use of it.

103 Ibid., p. 167.

104 Priestley, *The English*, pp. 240–8.

105 J. B. Priestley, *Over the Long High Wall: Some Reflections and Speculations on Life, Death and Time* (London: Heinemann, 1972), p. 7. Priestley, 'Eros and Logos'.

106 Priestley, 'Fifty years', p. 215.

107 Priestley, 'Eros and Logos', p. 39.

108 Priestley, *The English*, pp. 247–8.

109 Priestley, *Over the Long High Wall*, pp. 7–11.

110 J. B. Priestley, 'The writer in a changing society' (lecture delivered 1956), *Thoughts in the Wilderness*, p. 225.

111 Priestley, 'Fifty years', p. 218.

112 J. B. Priestley, 'Doubt about dynamism', *The Moments*, p. 131. Originally published *New Statesman* (29 October 1965).

113 Priestley, *Margin*, pp. 66–7.

114 Priestley, *Outcries and Asides*, p. 94.

115 Priestley, *Over*, pp. 10–11.
116 See, for example, Sheila Jeffreys, *Anticlimax: A Feminist Perspective on the Sexual Revolution* (London: Women's Press, 1989).
117 See the Conclusion to *Literature and Western Man* (1960) for his strongest statement on the relationship between religion, literature and the human predicament.
118 P. D. Ouspensky, *A New Model of the Universe* (London: Kegan Paul, 1931); J. W. Dunne, *An Experiment with Time* (London: Black, 1927).
119 Brome, *Priestley*, pp. 182–4; William Schoenl, *C. G. Jung: His Friendships with Mary Mellon and J. B. Priestley* (Wilmett, IL: Chiron Publications, 1998).
120 Priestley, *Midnight*, p. 243ff. Chapter XIII of *Midnight* is Priestley's most cogent statement of his views on time, but see also *Man and Time* (London: Heinemann, 1964) and *Over the Long High Wall* (1972). See also Cooper, *Priestley*, pp. 219–29, and John Atkins, *J. B. Priestley: The Last of the Sages* (London: John Calder, 1981), pp. 79–94.
121 Priestley, *Margin*, pp. 78–9.
122 Priestley, *Bright Day*, p. 19.
123 Ibid., pp. 123–4.
124 Priestley, *Literature and Western Man*, pp. 454–7.

Bibliography

Newspapers and magazines

Bookseller
Clarion
Daily Herald
Daily Mirror
Daily News
Era
Evening Standard
John O'London's Weekly
Listener
London Mercury
News Chronicle
New Statesman
Picture Post
Radio Times
Reynolds News
Scrutiny
Spectator
Star
Sunday Chronicle
Sunday Dispatch
Sunday Graphic
Sunday Pictorial
Times Literary Supplement
Tribune

Books, pamphlets and articles

Abrams, Mark, Richard Rose and Rita Hinden, *Must Labour Lose?* (Harmondsworth: Penguin, 1960)

Addison, Paul, *The Road to 1945: British Politics and the Second World War* (London: Jonathan Cape, 1975)

Aldgate, Tony, 'Comedy, class and containment: the British domestic cinema of the 1930s', in J. Curran and V. Porter (eds), *British Cinema History* (London: Weidenfeld & Nicolson, 1983)

Allan, John, *England Without End* (London: Methuen & Co., 1940)

Anderson, Benedict, *Imagined Communities: Reflections on the Origin and Spread of Nationalism* (London: Verso, 1983)

Anderson, Perry, 'Origins of the present crisis', *New Left Review* 23 (1964), reprinted in Anderson, *English Questions* (London: Verso, 1994)

Atkins, John, *J. B. Priestley: The Last of the Sages* (London: John Calder, 1981)

Bailey, Peter (ed.), *Music Hall: The Business of Pleasure* (Milton Keynes: Open University Press, 1986)

Bainbridge, Beryl, *English Journey, or The Road to Milton Keynes* (London: Duckworth, 1984)

Baldwin, Stanley, 'England', in *On England and Other Addresses* (London: Philip Allan, 1926)

Baldwin, Stanley, *Our Inheritance* (London: Hodder and Stoughton, 1928)

Baldwin, Stanley, 'The Englishman', in British Council, *British Life and Thought: An Illustrated Survey* (London: Longman, 1940)

Barnett, Correlli, *The Audit of War: The Illusion and Reality of a Great Nation* (London: Macmillan, 1986)

Barnouw, Erik, *A History of Broadcasting in the United States Volume 1: A Tower in Babel* (Oxford: Oxford University Press, 1966)

Bartholomew, Michael, *In Search of H. V. Morton* (London: Methuen, 2004)

Baxendale, John, 'Anti-industrialism and British national culture: A case-study in the communication and exchange of social values', in A. Cashdan and M. Jordin (eds), *Case Studies in Communication* (Oxford: Blackwell, 1987)

Baxendale, John, '"... into another kind of life in which anything might happen ...": Popular music and late modernity, 1910–1930', *Popular Music* 14: 2 (1995)

Baxendale, John, '"You and I – all of us ordinary people": renegotiating "Britishness" in wartime', in Nick Hayes and Jeff Hill (eds), *Millions Like Us? British Culture in the Second World War* (Liverpool: Liverpool University Press, 1999)

Baxendale, John, '"I had seen a lot of Englands": J. B. Priestley, Englishness and the people', *History Workshop Journal* 51 (2001)

Baxendale, John, 'Re-narrating the Thirties: *English Journey* revisited', *Working Papers on the Web* (June 2003) (www.shu.ac.uk/wpw /thirties)

Baxendale, John and Christopher Pawling, *Narrating the Thirties: A Decade in the Making* (London: Macmillan, 1996)

Bell, Anne Olivier (ed.), *The Diary of Virginia Woolf*, vol. 3: 1925–1930 (London: Hogarth Press, 1980)

Bennett, Tony, Susan Boyd-Bowman, Colin Mercer and Janet Wollacott (eds), *Popular Television and Film: A Reader* (London: BFI/Open University Press, 1981)

Bloch, Ernst, George Lukács, Bertholt Brecht, Walter Benjamin and Theodor Aforno, *Aesthetics and Politics* (London: New Left Books, 1977)

Bolton, David (ed.), *Voices from the Crowd Against the H-Bomb* (London: Peter Owen, 1964)

Bourdieu, Pierre, *Distinction: A Social Critique of the Judgement of Taste* (London: Routledge & Kegan Paul, 1984)

Bourdieu, Pierre, *The Field of Cultural Production*, ed. Randal Johnson (Cambridge: Cambridge University Press, 1993)

Bracco, Rosa Maria, *'Betwixt and Between': Middlebrow Fiction and English Society in the Twenties and Thirties* (Melbourne: University of Melbourne, 1990)

Bradbury, Malcolm, *The Social Context of Modern English Literature* (Oxford: Oxford University Press, 1971)

Bradbury, Malcolm and James McFarlane (eds), *Modernism: A Guide to European Literature 1890–1930* (London: Penguin, 1976)

Braine, John, *J. B. Priestley* (London: Weidenfeld and Nicolson, 1978)

Briggs, Asa, *The History of Broadcasting in the United Kingdom*, vol. 1: *The Birth of Broadcasting* (Oxford: Oxford University Press, 1961)

Briggs, Asa, *The History of Broadcasting in the United Kingdom*, vol. 2: *The Golden Age of Wireless* (Oxford: Oxford University Press, 1965)

Briggs, Asa, *The History of Broadcasting in the United Kingdom*, vol. 3: *The War of Words* (Oxford: Oxford University Press, 1970)

Brome, Vincent, *J. B. Priestley* (London: Hamish Hamilton, 1988)

Bromley, Roger, *Lost Narratives: Popular Fictions, Politics and Recent History* (London: Routledge, 1988)

Bryant, Arthur, *The National Character* (London: Longman's, Green and Co., 1934)

Bryant, Arthur, *English Saga 1840–1940* (London: Collins, 1940)

Calder, Angus, *The Myth of the Blitz* (London: Cape, 1991)

Camporesi, Valeria, 'The BBC and American broadcasting, 1922–55', *Media, Culture and Society* 16 (1994)

Cannadine, David (ed.), *The Speeches of Winston Churchill* (London: Penguin Books, 1990)

Carey, John, *The Intellectuals and the Masses: Pride and Prejudice among the Literary Intelligentsia, 1880–1939* (London: Faber and Faber, 1992)

'Cato' [Michael Foot, Frank Owen and Peter Howard], *Guilty Men* (London: Gollancz, 1940)

Chambers, Iain, *Border Dialogues: Journeys in Postmodernity* (London: Routledge, 1990)

Churchill, W. S., *Complete Speeches*, ed. Robert Rhodes James (New York: Chelsea House, 1974)

Colley, Linda, *Britons: Forging the Nation 1707–1837* (New Haven: Yale University Press, 1992)

Collini, Stefan, *Public Moralists: Political Thought and Intellectual Life in Victorian Britain* (Oxford: Oxford University Press, 1993)

Collins, Bruce and Keith Robbins (eds), *British Culture and Economic Decline* (London: Weidenfeld and Nicolson, 1990)

Collins, Diana, *Time and the Priestleys: The Story of a Friendship* (Stroud: Alan Sutton Publishing, 1994)

Colls, Robert and Philip Dodd (eds), *Englishness: Politics and Culture 1880–1920* (London: Croom Helm, 1986)

Conekin, Becky E.,'*The Autobiography of a Nation': The 1951 Festival of Britain* (Manchester: Manchester University Press, 2003)

Connolly, Cyril, *Enemies of Promise* (1938) (Harmondsworth: Penguin Books, 1961)

Cook, Judith, *Priestley* (London: Bloomsbury, 1997)

Cooper, Susan, 'That's J. B. Priestley for you', *Sunday Times Magazine* (7 September 1969)

Cronin, A. J., *The Citadel* (London: Gollancz, 1937)

Crosland, C. A. R., *The Future of Socialism* (London: Jonathan Cape, 1956)

Cross, Andrew, *An English Journey* (London: Film and Video Umbrella, 2004)

Crossick, Geoffrey (ed.), *The Lower Middle Class in Britain 1870–1914* (London: Croom Helm, 1977).

Cuddy Keane, Melba, *Virginia Woolf, the Intellectual, and the Public Sphere* (Cambridge: Cambridge University Press, 2003)

Cunningham, Valentine, *British Writers of the Thirties* (Oxford: Oxford University Press, 1988)

Dawson, Graham, *Soldier Heroes: British Adventure, Empire, and the Imagining of Masculinities* (London: Routledge, 1994)

Day, Alan, *J. B. Priestley: An Annotated Bibliography* (London: Garland, 1980)

Dean, Basil, *Mind's Eye* (London: Hutchinson, 1973)

Debord, Guy, *The Society of the Spectacle* (New York: Zone Books, 1994)

Deeping, Warwick, *Sorrell and Son* (London: Cassell & Co., 1925)

Dodd, Philip, 'The views of travellers: travel writing in the 1930s', in Dodd (ed.), *The Art of Travel: Essays on Travel Writing* (London:

Frank Cass, 1982)

Dodd, Philip, *The Battle Over Britain* (London: Demos, 1995)

Downing, Andrew, *Passovotchka: Moscow Dynamo in Britain, 1945* (London: Bloomsbury, 1999)

Dunne, J. W., *An Experiment with Time* (London: Black, 1927)

Dyer, Richard, 'Entertainment and utopia', in *Only Entertainment* (London: Routledge, 1992)

Ellman, Richard, *James Joyce* (Oxford: Oxford University Press, 1959)

Featherstone, Mike, *Consumer Culture and Postmodernism* (London: Sage, 1991)

Fielding, Steve, 'What did the people want? The meaning of the 1945 General Election', *Historical Journal* 35 (1992)

Fielding, Steve, Peter Thompson and Nick Tiratsoo, *'England Arise!' The Labour Party and Popular Politics in 1940s Britain* (Manchester: Manchester University Press, 1995)

Freedland, Jonathan, *Bring Home the Revolution: The Case for a British Republic* (London: Fourth Estate, 1999)

Fyfe, Hamilton, *The Illusion of National Character* (London: Watts & Co, 1940)

Fyrth, Jim, 'Days of hope: the meaning of 1945', in Fyrth (ed.), *Labour's Promised Land: Culture and Society in Labour Britain 1945–51* (London: Lawrence and Wishart, 1995)

Gaskell, Martin, 'Housing and the lower middle class, 1870–1914', in Geoffrey Crossick (ed.), *The Lower Middle Class in Britain 1870–1914* (London: Croom Helm, 1977)

Gibbs, Philip, *European Journey: Being the Narrative of a Journey in France, Switzerland, Italy, Austria, Hungary, Germany, and the Saar in the Spring and Summer of 1934* (London: Heinemann, 1934)

Gibbs, Philip, *England Speaks* (London: Heinemann, 1935)

Gibbs, Philip, *Ordeal in England (England Speaks Again)* (London: Heinemann, 1937)

Giles, Judy and Tim Middleton (eds), *Writing Englishness 1900–1950: An Introductory Sourcebook on National Identity* (London: Routledge, 1995)

Girouard, Mark, *The Return to Camelot: Chivalry and the English Gentleman* (New Haven: Yale University Press, 1981)

Greenberg, Clement, 'Modern and postmodern', in Robert C. Morgan (ed.), *Clement Greenberg Late Writings* (Minneapolis: University of Minnesota Press, 2003).

Grossmith, George and Weedon, *The Diary of a Nobody* (1892) (London: Penguin, 1999)

Grover, Mary, 'The authenticity of the middlebrow: Warwick Deeping and cultural legitimacy, 1903–1940', unpublished PhD thesis, School of Cultural Studies, Sheffield Hallam University, 2002

Hall, Stuart, Dorothy Hobson and Andrew Lowe (eds), *Culture, Media, Language: Working Papers in Cultural Studies* (London: Hutchinson, 1980)

Hammerton, J. A. (ed.), *Mr Punch and the Arts* (London, n.d. [c.1930s])

Harrisson, Tom, 'Social research and the film', *Documentary Newsletter* 1: 11 (November 1940)

Hennessy, Peter, *Never Again: Britain 1945–51* (London: Jonathan Cape, 1991)

Hewison, Robert, *In Anger: Culture in the Cold War 1945–60* (London: Weidenfeld and Nicolson, 1981)

Hewison, Robert, *The Heritage Industry: Britain in a Climate of Decline* (London: Methuen, 1987)

Higson, Andrew, '"Britain's outstanding contribution to the film": The documentary-realist tradition', in Charles Barr (ed.), *All Our Yesterdays: 90 Years of British Cinema* (London: British Film Institute, 1986)

Higson, Andrew, *Waving the Flag: Constructing a National Cinema in Britain* (Oxford: Oxford University Press, 1995)

Hill, Howard, *Freedom to Roam: The Struggle for Access to Britain's Moors and Mountains* (Ashbourne: Moorland, 1980)

Hinton, James, '1945 and the Apathy School', *History Workshop Journal* 43 (Spring 1997)

Hobsbawm, Eric, *Industry and Empire* (Harmondsworth: Penguin, 1968),

Hoggart, Richard, *The Uses of Literacy* (London: Chatto and Windus, 1957)

Holdsworth, Peter, *The Rebel Tyke: Bradford and J. B. Priestley* (Bradford: Bradford Libraries, 1994)

Horne, Donald, *God Is an Englishman* (Harmondsworth: Penguin Books, 1969)

Howell, David, *British Workers and the Independent Labour Party 1886–1906* (Manchester: Manchester University Press, 1983)

Humble, Nicola, *The Feminine Middlebrow Novel* (Oxford: Oxford University Press, 2001)

Hussey, Mark, 'Mrs Thatcher and Mrs Woolf', *Modern Fiction Studies* 50: 1 (Spring 2004)

Hynes, Samuel, *A War Imagined: The First World War and English Culture* (London: Pimlico, 1990)

Inkless, Alex (ed.), *National Character: A Psycho-Social Perspective* (New Brunswick: Transaction Publishers, 1997)

Jeffreys, Sheila, *Anticlimax: A Feminist Perspective on the Sexual Revolution* (London: Women's Press, 1989)

Joad, C. E. M., 'The people's claim', in Clough Williams-Ellis (ed.), *Britain and the Beast* (London: J. M. Dent and Sons, 1937)

Joicey, N., 'A paperback guide to progress: Penguin Books, 1935–c.1951', *Twentieth Century British History*, 4: 1 (1993)

Joyce, Patrick, *Visions of the People: Industrial England and the Question of Class* (Cambridge: Cambridge University Press, 1991)

Keating, Peter, *The Haunted Study: A Social History of the English Novel 1875–1914* (London: Fontana, 1991)

Klein, Holger, *J. B. Priestley's Fiction* (Frankfurt: Peter Lang, 2002)

Kumar, Krishnan, *The Making of English National Identity* (Cambridge: Cambridge University Press, 2003)

Laing, Stuart, *Representations of Working-Class Life 1957–1964* (London: Macmillan, 1986)

Lears, Jackson, *Luck in America* (New York: Viking Penguin, 2003)

Leavis, F. R., *Mass Civilisation and Minority Culture* (Cambridge: Minority Press, 1930)

Leavis, F. R., 'What's wrong with criticism?', *Scrutiny* 1: 2 (September 1932)

Leavis, F. R., *The Great Tradition* (London: Chatto and Windus, 1948)

Leavis, Q. D., *Fiction and the Reading Public* (London: Chatto and Windus, 1965)

Lee, Martyn J. (ed.), *The Consumer Society Reader* (Oxford: Blackwell, 2000)

Lehmann, John (ed.), *Coming to London* (London: Phoenix House, 1957)

LeMahieu, D. L., *A Culture for Democracy: Mass Culture and the Cultivated Mind in Britain between the Wars* (Oxford: Oxford University Press, 1988)

Leonard, Mark, *BritainTM* (London: Demos, 1997)

Leybourne, Keith, '"The defence of the bottom dog": the Independent Labour Party in local politics', in D. G. Wright and J. A. Jowitt (eds), *Victorian Bradford: Essays in Honour of Jack Reynolds* (Bradford: City of Bradford Metropolitan Council, 1982)

Light, Alison, *Forever England: Femininity, Conservatism and Literature Between the Wars* (London: Routledge, 1981)

Lindsay, Jack, *England My England* (London: Fore Publications, n.d. [1939])

Lowerson, John, 'The battle for the countryside', in Frank Gloversmith (ed.), *Class, Culture and Social Change: A New View of the Thirties* (Brighton: Harvester Press, 1980)

Lynn, Vera, *Vocal Refrain: An Autobiography* (London: W. H. Allen, 1975)

McAleer, Joseph, *Popular Reading and Publishing in Britain, 1914–1950* (Oxford: Oxford University Press, 1992)

MacDonald, Peter D., *British Literary Culture and Publishing Practice, 1880–1914* (Cambridge: Cambridge University Press, 1997)

McGuigan, Jim, *Cultural Populism* (London: Routledge, 1992)

MacKenzie, J. M., 'The imperial pioneer and the British masculine stereo-type in late Victorian and Edwardian Britain', in J. A. Mangan and J. Walvin (eds), *Manliness and Morality* (Manchester: Manchester University Press, 1987)

McKibbin, Ross, 'Class and conventional wisdom: The Conservative Party and the "public" in inter-war Britain', in *The Ideologies of Class: Social Relations in Britain 1880–1950* (Oxford: Clarendon Press, 1990)

McKibbin, Ross, *Classes and Cultures in England 1918–1951* (Oxford: Oxford University Press, 1998)

McLaine, Iain, *Ministry of Morale: Home Front Morale and the Ministry of Information in World War Two* (London: George Allen & Unwin, 1979)

McMillan, Margaret, *The Life of Rachel McMillan* (London: J. M. Dent, 1927)

Macmurray, John, *Creative Society: A Study of the Relation of Christianity to Communism* (London: SCM Press, 1935)

Mandler, Peter, 'Against "Englishness": English culture and the limits to rural nostalgia, 1850–1940', *Transactions of the Royal Historical Society*, 6th ser. 7 (1997)

Mandler, Peter, 'The consciousness of modernity? Liberalism and the English "national character", 1870–1940 in M. Daunton and B. Rieger (eds), *Meanings of Modernity* (Oxford: Berg, 2001)

Mangan, J. A., '"Muscular, militaristic and manly": The British middle-class hero as moral messenger', *International Journal for the History of Sport*, 13: 1 (March 1996)

Marwick, Arthur, 'Middle opinion in the Thirties', *English Historical Review* 79 (April 1964)

Maschler, Tom (ed.), *Declaration* (London: Macgibbon and Kee, 1957)

Masterman, C. F. G., *The Condition of England* (1909) (London: Methuen, 1960)

Matless, David, *Landscape and Englishness* (London: Reaktion Books, 1998)

Mills, W. Haslam, *Grey Pastures* (London: Chatto and Windus, 1924)

Morgan, David and Mary Evans, *The Battle for Britain: Citizenship and Ideology in the Second World War* (London: Routledge, 1993)

Morton, H. V., *In Search of England* (London: Methuen, 1927)

Morton, H. V., *The Call of England* (London: Methuen, 1928)

Morton, H. V., *What I Saw in the Slums* (London: The Labour Party, 1933)

Morton, H. V., *I Saw Two Englands* (London: Methuen, 1942)

Mowat, C. L., *Britain Between the Wars 1918–1940* (London: Methuen, 1956)

National Trust, *Snowshill Manor* (London: National Trust, 1995)

Nicholas, Sian, '"Sly demagogues" and wartime radio: J. B. Priestley and the BBC', *Twentieth Century British History* 6: 3 (1995)

Nicholas, Sian, 'The construction of a national identity: Stanley Baldwin, "Englishness" and the mass media in inter-war Britain', in Martin Francis and Ina Zweiniger-Bargielowski (eds), *The Conservatives and British Society, 1880–1990* (Cardiff: University of Wales Press, 1996)

Nicholas, Sian, *The Echo of War: Homefront Propaganda and the Wartime BBC* (Manchester: Manchester University Press, 1996)

Nicholas, Sian, 'From John Bull to John Citizen: images of national identity and citizenship on the wartime BBC', in Richard Weight and Abigail Beach (eds), *The Right to Belong: Citizenship and National Identity in Britain, 1930–1960* (London: I. B. Tauris, 1998)

Nicolson, Nigel (ed.), *The Sickle Side of the Moon: The Letters of Virginia Woolf Volume 5 1932–1935* (London: Hogarth Press, 1979)

Nicolson, Nigel (ed.), *Leave the Letters Till We're Dead: The Letters of Virginia Woolf, 1936–41* (London: Chatto and Windus, 1980)

Orwell, George, *The Road to Wigan Pier* (London: Gollancz, 1937),

Orwell, George, *Coming up for Air* (London: Gollancz, 1939)

Orwell, George, *Collected Essays, Journalism and Letters*, 3 vols, eds Sonia Orwell and Ian Angus (London: Penguin Books, 1970)

Ouspensky, P. D., *A New Model of the Universe* (London: Kegan Paul, 1931)

Paris, Michael, *Warrior Nation: Images of War in British Popular Culture 1850–2000* (London: Reaktion Books, 2000)

Pelling, Henry, *The Social Geography of British Elections 1885–1910* (London: Macmillan, 1967)

Potter, David, 'The quest for the national character' (1962), in Don E. Fehrenbacher (ed.), *History and American Society: Essays of D. Potter* (London: Oxford University Press, 1975)

Potts, Alex, '"Constable Country" between the wars', in Raphael Samuel (ed.), *Patriotism*, vol. 3: *National Fictions* (London: Routledge, 1989)

Priestley, J. B., *The English Comic Characters* (London: John Lane The Bodley Head, 1925)

Priestley, J. B., *George Meredith* (London: Macmillan and Co., 1926)

Priestley, J. B., *Adam in Moonshine* (London: Heinemann, 1927)

Priestley, J. B., *The English Novel* (London: Ernest Benn, 1927)

Priestley, J. B., *Open House* (London: Heinemann, 1927)

Priestley, J. B., *Thomas Love Peacock* (London: Macmillan, 1927)

Priestley, J. B., *Benighted* (London: Heinemann, 1927)

Priestley, J. B., *Apes and Angels* (London: Methuen, 1928)

Priestley, J. B., *The Balconinny* (London: Methuen, 1929)

Priestley, J. B., *English Humour* (London: Longman, 1929)

Priestley, J. B., *The Good Companions* (London: Heinemann, 1929)

Priestley, J. B., *Angel Pavement* (London: Heinemann, 1930)

Priestley, J. B., 'Introduction' to *The Good Companions* (London: Heinemann, 1931 edition)

Priestley, J. B., 'Introduction' to *Adam in Moonshine/Benighted* (London: Heinemann, 1932 edition)

Priestley, J. B., *Self-Selected Essays* (London: Heinemann, 1932)

Priestley, J. B., *Wonder Hero* (London: Heinemann, 1933)

Priestley, J. B., *English Journey* (London: Heinemann, 1934)

Priestley, J. B., 'The beauty of Britain', introduction to Charles Bradley Ford (ed.), *The Beauty of Britain: A Pictorial Survey* (London: Batsford, 1935)

Priestley, J. B., 'Foreword' to Ivor Brown, *The Heart of England* (London: Batsford, 1935)

Priestley, J. B., *Midnight on the Desert: A Chapter of Autobiography* (London: Heinemann, 1937)

Priestley, J. B., *Open House* (London: Heinemann, 1937)

Priestley, J. B., *The Doomsday Men* (London: Heinemann, 1938)

Priestley, J. B., *Let the People Sing*, (London: Heinemann, 1939)

Priestley, J. B. (ed.), *Our Nation's Heritage* (London: J. M. Dent and Son, 1939)

Priestley, J. B., *Rain Upon Godshill* (London: Heinemann, 1939)

Priestley, J. B., *Britain Speaks* (New York: Harper & Brothers, 1940)

Priestley, J. B., *Postscripts* (London: Heinemann, 1940)

Priestley, J. B., *Out of the People* (London: Collins/Heinemann, 1941)

Priestley, J. B., *Blackout in Gretley: A Story of – and for – Wartime* (London: Heinemann, 1942)

Priestley, J. B., 'This land of ours', in Anthony Weymouth (ed.), *The English Spirit* (London: Allen and Unwin, 1942)

Priestley, J. B., *Daylight on Saturday: A Novel about an Aircraft Factory* (London: Heinemann, 1943)

Priestley, J. B., *Here Are Your Answers* (London: Common Wealth, 1943)

Priestley, J. B., *Letter to a Returning Serviceman* (London: Home and Van Thal, 1945)

Priestley, J. B., *Three Men in New Suits* (London: Heinemann, 1945)

Priestley, J. B., *Bright Day* (London: Heinemann, 1946)

Priestley, J. B., 'Preface' to Fenner Brockway, *Socialism Over Sixty Years: The Life of Jowett of Bradford (1864–1944)* (London: George Allen and Unwin, 1946)

Priestley, J. B., *Russian Journey* (London: Writers Group of the Society for Cultural Relations with the USSR, 1946)

Priestley, J. B., *The Secret Dream: An Essay on Britain, America and Russia* (London: Turnstile Press, 1946)

Priestley, J. B., *The Arts Under Socialism* (London: Turnstile Press, 1947)

Priestley, J. B., *Delight* (London: Heinemann, 1949)

Priestley, J. B., *The Plays of J. B. Priestley*, 3 vols (London: Heinemann, 1949–50)

Priestley, J. B., *Festival at Farbridge* (London: Heinemann, 1951)

Priestley, J. B., *The Magicians* (London: Heinemann, 1954)

Priestley, J. B., *Thoughts in the Wilderness* (London: Heinemann, 1957)

Priestley, J. B., *Topside, or The Future of England: A Dialogue* (London: Heinemann, 1958)

Priestley, J. B., *Literature and Western Man* (originally published 1960) (Harmondsworth: Penguin, 1969)

Priestley, J. B., *The Shapes of Sleep* (London: Heinemann, 1962)

Priestley, J. B., *Margin Released: A Writer's Reminiscences and Reflections* (London: Heinemann, 1962)

Priestley, J. B., *Man and Time* (London: Heinemann), 1964)

Priestley, J. B., *Sir Michael and Sir George: A Tale of COMSA and DISCUS and the New Elizabethans* (London: Heinemann, 1964)

Priestley, J. B., *Lost Empires* (London: Heinemann, 1965)

Priestley, J. B., *The Moments* (London: Heinemann, 1966)

Priestley, J. B., *The Image Men*, vol. I: *Out of Town* (London: Heinemann, 1968); vol. II: *London End* (London: Heinemann, 1969)

Priestley, J. B., *The Edwardians* (London: Heinemann, 1970)

Priestley, J. B., *Over the Long High Wall: Some Reflections and Speculations on Life, Death and Time* (London: Heinemann, 1972)

Priestley, J. B., *The English* (London: Heinemann, 1973)

Priestley, J. B., *Outcries and Asides* (London: Heinemann, 1974)

Priestley, J. B., *Particular Pleasures* (London: Heinemann, 1975)

Priestley, J. B. and Jacquetta Hawkes, *Journey Down a Rainbow* (London: Heinemann, 1955)

Priestley, J. B. and Hugh Walpole, *Farthing Hall* (London: Macmillan, 1929)

Radway, Janice A., *A Feeling for Books: The Book-of-the-Month Club, Literary Taste and Middle-Class Desire* (Chapel Hill: University of North Carolina Press, 1997)

Rich, Paul, 'Imperial decline and the resurgence of English national identity, 1918–1979', in T. Kushner and K. Lunn (eds), *Traditions of Intolerance* (Manchester: Manchester University Press, 1989)

Rich, Paul, *Prospero's Return? Historical Essays on Race, Culture and British Society* (London: Hanslib, 1994)

Richards, Jeffrey, *The Age of the Dream Palace* (London: Routledge, 1984)

Riesman, David, *The Lonely Crowd: A Study of the Changing American Character* (New Haven: Yale University Press, 1950)

Rose, Sonya A., *Which People's War? National Identity and Citizenship in Wartime Britain* (Oxford: Oxford University Press, 2003)

Rowse, A. L., *The English Spirit* (London: Macmillan, 1944)

Royal National Theatre, *Platform Papers 3: Directors* (London: Royal National Theatre, n.d.)

Rubin, Joan Shelley, *The Making of Middlebrow Culture* (Chapel Hill:

University of North Carolina Press, 1992)

Rubinstein, W. D., *Capitalism, Culture and Decline in Britain 1750–1990* (London: Routledge, 1993)

St John, John, *William Heinemann: A Century of Publishing 1890–1990* (London: Heinemann, 1990)

Samuel, Raphael (ed.), *Patriotism: The Making and Unmaking of British National Identity*, 3 vols (London: Routledge, 1989)

Schoenl, William, *C. G. Jung: His Friendships with Mary Mellon and J. B. Priestley* (Wilmett, IL: Chiron Publications, 1998)

Schwarz, Bill, 'The language of constitutionalism: Baldwinite Conservatism', in *Formations of Nation and People* (London: Routledge & Kegan Paul, 1984)

Seabrook, Jeremy, *What Went Wrong?* (London: Gollancz, 1978)

Sedgwick, John, 'Regional distinctions in the consumption of films and stars in mid-1930s Britain', www.history.ac.uk/projects/elec /sem18.html

Shaw, Marion, *The Clear Stream: A Life of Winifred Holtby* (London: Virago, 1999)

Shears, W. S., *This England: A Book of the Shires and Counties* (London: Hutchinson & Co., 1936)

Singer, Milton, 'A survey of culture and personality theory and research', in Bert Kaplan (ed.), *Studying Personality Cross-Culturally* (New York: Harper, Row, 1961)

Spring, Howard, *In the Meantime* (London: Constable, 1942)

Stedman Jones, Gareth, 'Working class culture and working class politics in Victorian London', in *Languages of Class: Studies in English Working Class History, 1832–1982* (Cambridge: Cambridge University Press, 1983)

Stevenson, John and Chris Cook, *The Slump: Politics and Society in the Depression* (London: Cape, 1977)

Stibbe, Matthew, *German Anglophobia and the Great War, 1914–1918* (Cambridge: Cambridge University Press, 2001)

Swingewood, Alan, *The Myth of Mass Culture* (London: Macmillan, 1977)

Taylor, A. J. P., *English History 1914–1945* (Oxford: Oxford University Press, 1965)

Taylor, D. J., *Orwell: The Life* (London: Vintage, 2004)

Taylor, John, *A Dream of England: Landscape, Photography and the Tourist's Imagination* (Manchester: Manchester University Press, 1994)

Taylor, Richard, *Against the Bomb: The British Peace Movement 1958–1965* (Oxford: Clarendon Press, 1988)

Taylor, Stephen, 'The suburban neurosis', in Judy Giles and Tim Middleton (eds), *Writing Englishness 1900–1950* (London: Routledge, 1995)

Thatcher, Margaret, *The Path to Power* (London: Harper-Collins, 1995)

Thomas, Hugh (ed.), *The Establishment* (Anthony Blond, 1959)

Thomas, Keith, *Man and the Natural World: Changing Attitudes in England, 1500–1800* (London: Allen Lane, 1983)

Thompson, Denys, 'Comments and reviews', *Scrutiny* 3: 1 (June 1934), pp. 68–9

Thompson, E. P. (ed.), *Out of Apathy* (London: New Left Books, 1960)

Thompson, F. M. L., *Gentrification and the Enterprise Culture: Britain 1780–1980* (Oxford: Oxford University Press, 2001)

Thorpe, Andrew, 'The Membership of the Communist Party of Great Britain, 1920–1945', *Historical Journal* 43: 3 (2000)

Tiratsoo, Nick, 'Popular politics, affluence, and the Labour Party in the 1950s', Anthony Gorst et al. (eds), *Contemporary British History 1931–1961: Politics and the Limits of Policy* (London: Pinter, 1991)

Tiratsoo, Nick (ed.), *The Attlee Years* (London: Pinter, 1991)

Titmuss, Richard, *Problems of Social Policy* (London: HMSO, 1950)

Vernon, James, 'Englishness: Narration of a nation', *Journal of British Studies* 36 (1997)

Ward, Paul, *Britishness since 1870* (London: Routledge, 2004)

Waters, Chris, *British Socialists and the Politics of Popular Culture 1884–1914* (Manchester: Manchester University Press, 1990)

Waters, Chris, 'J. B. Priestley: Englishness and the politics of nostalgia', in Peter Mandler and Susan Pedersen (eds), *After the Victorians: Private Conscience and Public Duty in Modern Britain* (London: Routledge, 1994)

Watt, Ian, *The Rise of the Novel* (Harmondsworth: Penguin, 1963)

West, Richard, *An English Journey* (London: Chatto and Windus, 1981)

Wiener, Martin J., *English Culture and the Decline of the Industrial Spirit 1850–1980* (Cambridge: Cambridge University Press, 1981)

Williams, Raymond, *Culture and Society 1780–1950* (London: Chatto & Windus, 1958)

Williams, Raymond, *Marxism and Literature* (Oxford: Oxford University Press, 1977)

Williams, Raymond, 'The Bloomsbury fraction', in *Problems in Materialism and Culture* (London: Verso, 1980).

Williams-Ellis, Clough, *England and the Octopus* (London: Geoffrey Bles, 1928)

Williams-Ellis, Clough (ed.), *Britain and the Beast* (London: J. M. Dent and Sons, 1937)

Williamson, Philip, 'The Doctrinal Politics of Stanley Baldwin', in Michael Bentley (ed.), *Public and Private Doctrine: Essays in British History Presented to Maurice Cowling* (Cambridge: Cambridge University Press, 1993)

Wilmott, Peter and Michael Young, *Family and Class in a London Suburb*

(London: New English Library, 1967)

Wilson, Harold, *The New Britain: Labour's Plan Outlined. Selected Speeches 1964* (Harmondsworth: Penguin, 1964)

Woolf, Virginia, 'Middlebrow', in *The Death of the Moth and Other Essays* (London: Hogarth Press, 1942)

Woolf, Virginia, 'Mr Bennett and Mrs Brown' (1924), in *Collected Essays* in vol. 1 (London: Hogarth Press, 1966)

Wright, Patrick, *On Living in an Old Country* (London: Verso, 1985)

Zweig, F., *The Worker in an Affluent Society* (London: Heinemann, 1961)

Index

Note: for Priestley's works see individual titles.

1941 Committee 154–5

Addison, Paul 141, 150
'Admass' 97, 114, 167–8, 176–80,
    185–6, 188
Adorno, Theodor W. 114, 121
Americanisation
    broadcasting 127–30
    consumerism 105, 113, 167,
        177–9
    democratic values and 120–2, 132
    English character and 98, 143
    popular culture and 117, 120–1,
        130–1
    see also United States
'Angry Young Men' 184
Anderson, Benedict 145
Anderson, Lindsay 177
Angel Pavement 22, 28, 50–2, 61,
    63, 68, 70, 132, 142, 159
An Inspector Calls 45, 168–9, 172,
    187
Arts Under Socialism, The 171–3
Auden, W. H. 106

Bailey, Peter 119
Baldwin, Stanley 78, 81, 86–7, 95
Barnett, Correlli 154, 161
BBC see British Broadcasting
    Corporation
Blackout in Gretley 157–8
Blackpool 112, 116–17, 119, 149
    Americanisation and 116–17,

    129–31
    Sing As We Go 66
Bloomsbury 12–14, 17–18, 24, 68,
    106, 171
    see also Woolf, Virginia
Book Society, The 20
Boulder Dam 133–4
Bourdieu, Pierre 6, 15–16
Bracco, Rosa Maria 48
Bradford
    beauty of 83–4
    cosmopolitanism 77
    classlessness 39–41, 133
    Edwardian 35–41, 171, 174
    interwar 55, 90, 94, 109, 111
    music-hall in 119
    Priestley's literary life in 7–11
    religious dissent in 38
    socialism in 37–8
Breugel, Pieter 60–1, 84
Bright Day 39–40, 42–3, 49, 51,
    112, 124, 131
British Broadcasting Corporation
    American radio and 128–9
    the 'battle of the brows' and 15,
        24–5
    cultural style of 92, 106, 126–9
    wartime
        Priestley's overseas broadcasts
        151–3
        Postscripts 148–51, 154–5, 161
        Vera Lynn 146
broadbrow 17–18, 24, 106

Bromley, Roger 78
Bryant, Arthur 78, 81, 94–5

Calder, Angus 78, 80, 141,167
Cambridge 10, 46
Campaign for Nuclear Disarmament
    181–3, 184
Carey, John 112, 117
Chambers, Iain 80
Churchill, W. S. 140–1, 146–8
cinema 59–63, 107, 114, 122–5,
    170–1
  British 59, 61, 65, 92, 124
  Hollywood 123–4, 134
  see also Sing As We Go
Cold War 174–6
  see also Soviet Union; Campaign
    for Nuclear Disarmament
Common Wealth 155, 181
communism 43, 142
  see also Soviet Union
community
  decline of 114, 171–3
  football and 118
  in Sing As We Go 67
  in The Good Companions 47
  in wartime 151, 153, 156–9, 167
Connolly, Cyril 28–9
Cook, Judith 45
Cooper, Duff 154
Cotswolds 82, 84, 89–90
Cronin, A. J. 28
  The Citadel 63
Cuddy-Keane, Melba 25, 26

Daylight on Saturday 158–60
Debord, Guy 180
Deeping, Warwick
  Sorrell and Son 48, 51
documentary movement 57–63,
    66–7, 124, 159
Dodd, Philip 80
Doomsday Men, The 182
Dunne, J. W.

Experiment with Time 187

Edwardian England 43–7
Eliot, T. S.
  Criterion, The 12
English Journey 36, 52–63, 65, 77,
    82–3, 89–90, 107–11, 116–17,
    131–2
English, The 91, 97–8
Englishness 76–104 passim
  Americanisation and 98, 132, 143
  Priestley's Englishness 76–8, 93
  rural images of 80–90
  tradition and 91–3
  in wartime 146, 148–9
  see also landscape; national
    character; monarchy

factories 54, 105, 108–10
Festival at Farbridge 17, 77, 174
Festival of Britain 173–4
Fields, Gracie 65–8
football 40, 67, 83, 117–18, 171
Foot, Michael 173

Gaitskell, Hugh 178
Galsworthy, John 83
gender
  feminine principle 185–6, 111
  masculinity 56, 111
  sexism and the counterculture 186
Gibbs, Philip 58
Gissing, George 7
globalisation 46, 77, 178
Gollancz, Victor 57–8
Good Companions, The 21–3, 40,
    47–50, 77, 83–4, 117–18
Gosse, Edmund 7, 20
Great War 10, 39, 44–6, 48, 94–5,
    188
Greenberg, Clement 15–16
Grierson, John 59
Grossmith, George and Weedon
  Diary of a Nobody 48

Hawkes, Jacquetta 181
Heinemann, William Ltd 19, 58
Hinton, James 161
hippies 186
Hobsbawm, Eric 37
Hoggart, Richard 5
Holtby, Winifred 28
Horne, Donald 79
Hussey, Mark 26

I Have Been Here Before 187
Image Men, The 179
imperialism: Priestley's views on 77,
    95, 98
Independent Labour Party 36–7
Jameson, Storm, 59
Joad, Dr C. E. M. 88
John O'London's Weekly 11, 26
Journey Down a Rainbow 177–8
Jowett, Fred 42
Joyce, Patrick 41, 46
Jung, C. G. 39, 96–7, 111, 168,
    181, 185–7

Labour Party 28, 65,
    in Bradford 36–8
    cultural policy 171–2
    and the H-Bomb 181–2
    in opposition 178–9
    1945 General Election 161, 167
    1945–51 government 167,
        169–70, 172–3
    Priestley campaigns for 161, 169
landscape 58, 79–81, 82–6, 89, 149
    and national character 96
Lane, John 11
Leavis, F. R. 17, 18–19, 20, 106
Leavis, Q D 13, 22
LeMahieu, D. L. 128
Letter to a Returning Serviceman
    160
Let the People Sing 69, 96–7,
    120–2, 140, 142–3
Light, Alison 76, 97

Literature and Western Man 26–7,
    188
Little Tich 119
London Mercury 11–12
Lost Empires 45–6, 77
Lynd, Robert 11–12, 25
Lynn, Vera 146

MacDonald, Ramsay 28, 65
Mackereth, James A. 9
Magicians, The 180
Mandler, Peter 81, 94–5
Margin Released 7–11, 39–41, 65,
    130–1, 134, 188
Mass Observation 58, 146
Masterman, Charles 48–9
Matless, David 81
middlebrow 5, 13, 15–16, 18–26,
    52, 63, 67, 115
Ministry of Information (MoI) 143,
    145
modernism 13–16, 21, 24, 26–7
    Englishness and 77
modernity
    America and 133–4
    the countryside and 81, 84, 89–90
    industry and 108–10
    Nazi Germany and 150
    popular culture and 130–1
    suburbia and 76, 105–6, 111–16
    writers and 14–15, 28, 48
monarchy 93–4
Morton, H. V. 58, 86–7, 145
music-hall 45, 98, 106, 118–21,
    122, 129–31, 171

national character 93–8, 172, 185
National Health Service 169, 172–3
newspapers 6, 10–11, 19–20, 56–7,
    64–5, 92–3, 125–6
New Statesman 167, 181
Nicholas, Sian 154
Nicolson, Harold 24–5

Orwell, George 61, 77–8, 95
  blacklists Priestley 174–5
  Road to Wigan Pier, The 54, 61–3
Osborne, John 184
Ouspensky, P. D.
  A New Model of the Universe 187
Out of the People 155–7, 183

Picture Post 58, 140, 154–5, 167
popular culture 113–32
  cultural democracy 113–14
  in the 1960s 185–6
  mass culture 113–14, 116–17
  see also cinema; football; music-
    hall; press; radio
popular music 130–1, 185–6
  see also music-hall
Postscripts 26, 140, 148–55, 161,
    167, 172
Potts, Alex 81
Priestley, Jonathan 37–8, 56–7
Pryce-Jones, Alan 184

radicalism 38, 41, 43, 56, 147
radio 92, 113–15, 126–9, 156, 179
  British versus American 128–9
  see also British Broadcasting
    Corporation
ragtime 130–1
Rain Upon Godshill 69, 92–3, 141
realism 13–15, 60–1
Reith, John 106, 127–8
Rich, Paul 80–1
Russell, George 8
Russian Journey 175

Second World War 140–65 *passim*
  Dunkirk 148–9
  'People's War' 147
  Priestley's overseas broadcasts
    151–3
  see also Churchill, W. S.; *Daylight
    on Saturday*; *Let the People
    Sing*; *Out of the People*;

Postscripts; *Three Men in
    New Suits*
Secret Dream, The 176
Shapes of Sleep, The 180
Sing As We Go 65–8, 77, 116
Sir Michael and Sir George 184–5
socialism 37–8, 41–3, 156–7
Southampton 107
Soviet Union 43, 133, 156, 174–6,
    180–1
Spring, Howard 8, 19, 28, 53
Squire, Sir John 11, 22–3, 25
Stedman Jones, Gareth 119
suburbia 13, 76, 105, 111–15
  Bradford 35–6, 112
  criticisms of 89, 113–15
  'middlebrow' culture and 20
Sutcliffe, Herbert 118

Taylor, Dr Stephen 115
Thatcher, Margaret 26, 78–9, 167–8
They Came to a City 158
They Walk in the City 45–6, 47,
    68–9, 84, 110, 120, 121, 123
Thompson, Denys 57
Three Men in New Suits 160
time
  Priestley's views on 187–8
  see also Dunne, J. W.; Ouspensky,
    P. D.
Topside 182–4

United States
  Arizona 83, 85, 133
  cultural democracy and 132–4,
    176
  mass culture and 124–5, 127–30
  New York City 133
  wartime broadcasts to 151–3
  see also Americanisation; cinema

Vernon, James 80

Walpole, Hugh 11, 26, 63

Waters, Chris 78, 80
Wells, H. G. 10, 14–15, 27–8, 37
When We Are Married 45
Whitman, Walt 41, 134, 141
Wiener, Martin J. 78–80, 91
Williams, Raymond
    The Country and the City 82

wireless *see* radio; British
    Broadcasting Corporation
Wonder Hero 40, 64–5, 124, 125–6,
    131
Woolf, Virginia 12–14, 22–6
Wright, Patrick 81